# EATING TOGETHER

## *BEING TOGETHER*

# EATING TOGETHER

# *BEING TOGETHER*

Recipes, Activities, AND Advice
FROM A Chef Dad AND Psychologist Mom

JULIAN C. E. CLAUSS-EHLERS
CAROLINE S. CLAUSS-EHLERS, PhD, ABPP

ILLUSTRATIONS BY DANIELLE GOLINSKI

PRINCETON ARCHITECTURAL PRESS ★ NEW YORK

**PUBLISHED BY**
Princeton Architectural Press
70 West 36th Street
New York, NY 10018
www.papress.com

Editor: Jennifer Thompson
Designer: Benjamin English
Illustrator: Danielle Golinski

**LIBRARY OF CONGRESS CATALOGING-
IN-PUBLICATION DATA**
**NAMES:** Clauss-Ehlers, Julian C. E.,
author. | Clauss-Ehlers, Caroline S., author.
**TITLE:** Eating together, being together :
recipes, activities, and advice from a chef dad and
psychologist mom / Julian C. E. Clauss-Ehlers,
Caroline S. Clauss-Ehlers, PhD, ABPP.
**DESCRIPTION:** New York: Princeton Architectural
Press, 2022. | Includes bibliographical
references and index. | Summary: "Recipes,
essays, tips, and activities exploring how
cooking and sharing meals helps to build healthy
relationships among family and with food"
—Provided by publisher. **IDENTIFIERS:**
LCCN 2022013114 | ISBN 9781648961137
(hardcover) **SUBJECTS:** LCSH:
Cooking. | Eating (Philosophy) | LCGFT:
Cookbooks. **CLASSIFICATION:** LCC TX714 .C563
2022 | DDC 641.5—dc23/eng/20220321
**LC RECORD AVAILABLE AT**
https://lccn.loc.gov/2022013114

The advice, tips, and suggestions in this book
are not a substitute for medical or mental health
advice; see your physician/pediatrician and/or
a mental health professional if you have health
and/or mental health related questions.

Please note that, where applicable, people in
real-life examples have been de-identified.

To our kids, Olliver, Sabrina, and Izzy,
who led us on this great adventure.

♥

To my dear Mum, a struggling cook who always
encouraged me to follow my culinary dreams.

*Julian*

♥

To Dad, whose unconditional love was a constant
source of strength. If he thought I could accomplish
something, it must be true.

*CC*

# CONTENTS

# Eating Mindfulness

## Having an Honest Food Conversation

The idea for *Eating Together, Being Together* was developed long before our COVID-19 world made its appearance. It came out of our areas of expertise as a chef (Julian) and a psychologist (CC), but mostly from the experience of raising our three kids. Over the years, we saw how much we engage with one another when we share a meal as a family, and we learned from the time our kids were young that magical things happen for people around food: kids open up while they measure flour or mix batter; adults tell stories of their childhood while they eat a favorite family recipe; bad feelings are mitigated; memories are made.

In our respective workplaces, we have seen that it's not always like this. When Julian volunteered with a program focused on teaching schoolkids about healthy foods, he saw that many of the students didn't know how to eat mindfully and weren't familiar with the concept of healthy eating. In my work as a psychologist, I've seen how parents, guardians, caregivers, and family members struggle to meet time demands, which often interfere with sitting down and having a meal together. Being married to a chef who works long hours, and being really unskilled at cooking myself, I can entirely relate to this reality.

Kids and parents are often busy and rush through meals, and older children may have their own schedules. Olliver, who is now six years old, would often have dinner with just me or the babysitter at 5 p.m. and be in bed by 7 p.m. Then his sisters and I would sit together and have dinner at 7:30 p.m. Julian would get home from work at 10 p.m. and have dinner by himself. Multiple lives, multiple meals, and multiple separations. But when we experienced quarantine, we were suddenly together for breakfast, lunch, and dinner. From one day to the next, we were literally having meals together all the time. This experience left us with a greater awareness of the value and benefits of family mealtime, and we know we are not alone.

We wrote *Eating Together, Being Together* because we wanted to share our unique insights as chef, psychologist, and parents. Trained in France, where healthy eating is part of the culture, Julian (British by birth) was surprised to learn that the culture of eating was very different in the United States. He saw that overly processed foods were often a go-to option for overworked, tired families (ours included) and aims to change this culture by instilling healthy eating habits in childhood that will continue throughout one's life. He wants to empower parents to support their kids in this journey.

For many years I've worked as a psychologist with families that face multiple stressors in their daily lives. Through my own family life and clinical work, I've seen the benefits of family members spending time cooking together and eating together. Mealtime is a way our families can connect to talk about the stress they face and brainstorm solutions. Families that have routines are more resilient, and sharing even one mealtime a day helps build that resilience.[1] Also, as my daughters have moved into the teen years, I'm grateful that they want to prepare delicious meals, helping me find a balance between work and other responsibilities. Did I mention I love food but am not good at cooking it?

The pandemic that began in 2020 raised unexpected challenges for family life. For working parents, the challenge was how to take care of children who were suddenly at home during the weekday, either in quarantine or attending school remotely, while simultaneously addressing work obligations. For parents with young children, this also meant finding a balance without the support of childcare or outside schooling. For parents of preteens or teens, this often meant watching the painful process of their adolescent's anxiety unfold as they lost the option to be with friends, explore identity through peer connections, struggle with online learning, and try to manage concerns about the future. Many parents across the globe lost their jobs (Julian was unemployed for about eleven months), and quarantine stress was magnified by economic insecurity and uncertainty around when or if family members would be employed again. The overlay to this sharp disruption, and sense of loss, was the anxiety about COVID-19 itself and fears about who would get sick and who we might lose.

Our son, Olliver, who was four at the time, said, "We all have to be human together." Being "human together" involved adjusting to this massive, overnight change in how we lived our lives and engaged in new and different ways with our community. We learned some revelatory things about being parents. Olliver was absolutely delighted to have us around. He started to talk so much that he graduated from speech therapy during the quarantine. Our daughters, Sabrina and Izzy, then fourteen and sixteen years old, talked about the dilemma so many teens were facing that involved the pros and cons of being at home versus losing time at school and with their peers.

And we liked being together with our kids and sharing daily meals. With a chef's schedule—twelve-hour days, six days a week—we had never experienced that kind of togetherness during the course of our marriage. The entire family got involved with meal planning at various stages: from shopping, to prepping, to cooking, to setting the table, to finally sitting down to share the same meal at the same time. The tips and tools that follow in *Eating Together, Being Together* provide ways families can enjoy a meal that has been prepared by everyone for everyone and helps to make people appreciate the effort of cooking and the fun of cooking together. Family members can also feel proud about eating a meal that has been contributed to by many. All of this builds positive relationships for families while also encouraging healthy eating.

The imprint of 2020 will undoubtedly have an impact on our lives ahead. It is hard to believe that our daughters are now seventeen and nineteen. As we move forward, many questions raised have to do with adjustment to a return to what was once viewed as normal life. Kids who have been going to school online may have understandable anxiety about being back in the classroom with their peers. Adults who have managed to find a balance with taking care of kids and working from home now have to adjust to resuming a commute and figuring out scheduling. And we ask the constant question about whether our loved ones will still get sick or whether there will be another shutdown. We are living in a state of uncertainty amid a virus with no closure. These adjustments can make shopping, cooking, and eating together less of a priority, when in fact, it remains of the utmost importance.

*Eating Together, Being Together* is designed to help you create or hold on to family time. It uniquely explores how cooking and sharing meals helps to build healthy family relationships as well as healthy relationships to food. Our own parenting philosophy is to be up front and interact with our kids in ways that help them make good choices that will carry over into their adult lives. *Eating Together, Being Together* is not a book about parents making healthy meals for their kids. *Eating Together, Being Together* is a book about enjoying food as a family, whether you are eight years old or eighty. Mealtime is not only nutritious for the body but also nutritious for the soul.

## OUR APPROACH:
## HAVING THE HONEST FOOD CONVERSATION

While many cookbooks focus on getting kids to eat healthy meals, some also promote sneaking nutritious ingredients into food by hiding it or disguising it, as a way to sidestep food aversions. These books tell parents this is a simple solution to getting their kids to consume recommended nutrients. But this approach comes with an underlying message—that kids don't need to know what they're eating, and if they do, they'll be turned off by healthy food.

We're perplexed by this messaging. We think it raises questions like: How do our kids become healthy eaters if they don't know what they're eating? How do our kids learn to make good eating choices if they aren't aware of the decision-making process? The deception approach assumes that kids aren't able to make the right choice—and that parents are too stressed or simply unable to help them to do so. The deception approach might argue that this is a strategy to use with young children. Our feeling is that this is exactly when our kids need to start learning about eating mindfully. We want kids to begin to be aware of what they're eating and make healthy food choices from an early age.

*Eating Together, Being Together* takes an eating mindfulness approach throughout. In doing so, it encourages parents to engage in an ongoing conversation with their kids about healthy food choices. We understand the appeal of hiding healthy foods; for toddlers, it can help avoid a drawn-out battle of wills or even a tantrum. But what seems like the easier choice at the moment can actually lead to more complex issues down the road. At some point, kids find out that you hid vegetables in their mac 'n' cheese (and it won't be pretty).

We say, "Get rid of deception. Don't avoid—be honest and transparent." Introduce children to a variety of foods from an early age—the good, the bad, the delicious, the horrible. Make food choice a regular part of their lives. Make them partners in getting groceries (even when shopping online), cooking, and eating food at home. Talk about the choices that are being made. Listen to what your child is saying about why they are choosing one thing instead of something else. Share with your child the reason why he can't just eat chicken nuggets his entire life. And guess what? In doing this, you and your child are having a conversation. You're thinking through decisions, considering outcomes, and, perhaps most important, listening to one another.

Keep in mind that there will always be foods that our toddlers, preteens, or teens simply don't like, just as we as parents have foods we won't go near. There will be foods our kids simply won't want to try. That's true for all of us. There may be foods that your child once liked but that now carry a bad association. This is all part of learning what we like and don't like to eat. Our relationships with each family member grow stronger by figuring this out together: we become aware of and are better able to understand each other's culinary preferences.

There's a developmental value to this as well. Research shows that obesity has a greater connection to early childhood eating patterns than previously imagined.[2] This reality points to learning about how good food choices early on can influence a child's weight and health later in life. To make these good choices, kids need to be aware of what they're eating instead of being fooled into consuming a healthy option without knowing it. Developing self-awareness about food choices and involving children in food preparation early on equips kids to be thoughtful eaters who make healthy choices.

Eating well gives our kids energy, stimulates brain function, and influences mood. When we think about the benefits that result from healthy eating, we have to ask: Why would we not engage in this process? *Eating Together, Being Together* supports parents by sharing the skills necessary to encourage kids to be open to a variety of foods, and as a result, to learn to choose well. These aren't "health food" recipes. They are designed to present you and your kids with a range of balanced food options. Our Halloween Cheesecake (page 206) isn't unhealthy per se; it's only unhealthy if that's the only thing your family eats. And treats aren't necessarily a bad choice as a reward; they're tricky if they're the only type of food you eat.

Shopping, prepping, cooking, and eating together are ways to raise an eater who learns to make thoughtful food choices; but these activities also provide a great way to bond and develop relationships with each other. Meaningful conversations with our kids tend to take place when we least expect them. How much is shared when we ask our kids to tell us about their day? I would guess that most of us would respond with an emphatic, "Not much!" Partnering together around food provides a myriad of opportunities to talk with one another.

For toddlers, prepping food is a magical way to spend time with a parent/guardian/caregiver (also known in *Eating Together* as the grown-up helper), mixing ingredients and observing how they turn out. The other day, Olliver made pita bread with us. He loved kneading the dough with his hands, rolling it out with a rolling pin, watching it rise in the oven, and sharing it with us at dinnertime. Olliver said seeing something change form like that was magical. And Olliver loves magic.

For preteens and teens, cooking together provides a natural forum for relaxing, making it easier to open up and talk about their day. Conversations are more organic and more likely to develop amid a workflow of food preparation than if you stop by your kid's room to "check in" when they're in the middle of something else. I recall making lunch with Izzy, who talked about concerns with college placement tests and feeling uncertain about how optional they really would be given the new landscape of restrictions related to COVID-19. While we didn't reach any conclusions—or have any solid answers (an all too familiar dynamic, especially during the pandemic)—we both felt comforted to be in the same space where we could share what we were experiencing with each other. In these moments, we are able to live and function more as a unit than as a collection of disparate people and concerns.

Preteens and teens might not necessarily come to us with their problems. Cooking creates a shared space and time to talk about things not related to food. It provides a different platform and neutral territory. If you ask your kid, "How was school today?"—chances are they'll say, "Fine." If you see your preteen or teen crying and ask, "What's wrong?"—they might say, "Nothing! I don't want to talk about it."

Developmentally this makes sense. Becoming an adolescent means moving away from us as parents. As a result, our teens might not feel comfortable speaking with us for a myriad of reasons—it's not cool, it's too embarrassing, we're too old to understand—and they may have forgotten how to talk to us in the ways that they did in their younger years. The key, and what cooking as a shared activity can do for our relationships, is to create a space where there are opportunities for conversations to emerge. By spending time together cooking, our kids have a relaxed setting from which to talk about the problems in their lives with us—when they're ready.

Cooking in the kitchen builds time together where we don't have to ask how our child is doing—we just have to listen for the moment when our child shares something with us and lets us into their experience.

With younger children, the dynamic is different. Young children often want to talk with us, and they're curious about how foods go together. For preschool children, conversations while cooking together support developing language and conversational skills as well as an ability to sustain focus on an activity. This is important, given the new levels of socialization our school-aged children are beginning to experience with other adults, like teachers. Making cooking a shared activity early on in our children's lives builds this environment in preparation for the teenage years, when there are shifts in who initiates the conversation.

Sometimes there may not be a conversation while you cook together, and that's okay, too. There can be comfort in doing something together even in shared silence. Keep in mind that sometimes kids don't want to talk—but they still want the comfort of doing something with someone who they know cares about them.

*Eating Together, Being Together* is not just about cooking together; it's also about the process of sitting down, talking with one another without screen-time distractions, and enjoying a shared meal. It's a time to share a common activity and see how everyone is doing. Our kids can let us know what's going on with them. And we can let our kids know what's going on with us. Eating the meals you prepare together is an extension of that safe territory we create when we're cooking together. It also brings the shared activity of cooking together to the larger family group, truly bringing everyone to the table.

## HOW TO USE THIS BOOK

*E*ating Together, Being Together reflects two voices. Julian's voice comes out in the recipes and cooking instructions. CC's voice is expressed in parenting writings and activities that tie in to cooking. Both of us thought a lot about parenting as we wrote these chapters. Our experiences as parents are shared as a joint voice, given that we experienced them together. Because our three kids range in age from six to nineteen (ages that were four to sixteen when we started to write this book), these experiences truly reflect our lives as parents raising kids with a wide range of ages and different developmental stages, all at the same time. Our hope is that by presenting both perspectives, cooking and parenting, we can empower parents to embrace ways to develop connection in the kitchen for children from toddlerhood to the teen years.

Each chapter of *Eating Together, Being Together* is full of Top Tips and Fun Facts about recipe ingredients and how they're cooked. Read them over with your helper as you learn about them together. It's fun, for example, to see that it's best to add seasonings to a sauce when it's still simmering so that the flavor is incorporated throughout your dish. Or who knew that pasta shouldn't be rinsed with water after it's cooked because that will reduce its flavor? Engage in this discovery of food and taste together.

Each chapter presents activities that helpers of all ages can consider when making these recipes. Perhaps you're a grown-up helper who wants more time with your preteen or teenage helpers. The activity with the Warm Apple Cider recipe (page 224) invites you to make a connection between nature and your kitchen by taking a trip to an apple orchard with your helpers. Activities are broken down into age groups, suggesting ways that young, preteen and teen, and grown-up helpers can participate. The last activity for each chapter captures the larger life theme that stems from the chapter's food-focused theme. Such life themes show that organizing our kitchens relates to organizing our lives (Chapter One), or that quenching our thirst is a parallel for quenching our lives (Chapter Eleven). We encourage you to make these connections as you read through the pages that follow.

# CHAPTER 1

# Before We Start

*Organizing Our Kitchens, Organizing Our Lives*

This is a different kind of book. It's a book about cooking and a book about parenting. It's a book about developing parenting skills and developing cooking skills. The chapters that follow encourage us as parents to think about ways that we can build connections with our kids as they grow. By cooking together, we're able to be intentional in spending time with those who are the most important to us—our kids and our other family members. This book encourages us to be transparent with our kids about what they're eating when we prepare meals for them. This is contrary to a deception approach, which doesn't let kids explore whether certain ingredients taste good or bad to them. And there are no guarantees—even dishes with disguised foods might be disliked. Kids may be eating healthy hidden ingredients but lack awareness or skill about how to make those healthy choices for themselves. In being intentional and open to these moments with our kids, we allow for a space to learn more about the choices they're making in their lives—whether these are life choices or food choices—from toddlerhood to the teen years. Let's get started with organizing our kitchens, and then we can think about how this translates to organizing our lives.

Many of us aren't even aware of what's in our kitchens. Doing a food inventory is a great way to orient ourselves to what we have and what we need. As a first step, take time to go through everything in the kitchen—even those areas at the back of a shelf that are hard to reach. This gives us a visual idea of everything we have—hopefully without too many unpleasant surprises. This process applies to the refrigerator and freezer as well. It might seem overwhelming at first, but it sets a great foundation for having fun when cooking as a family. This little bit of hard work now will save a lot of time going forward.

Before grocery shopping for one or more of our recipes, check the ingredients needed against what you have in your kitchen. This is a good habit to initiate so as to reduce waste by not over-purchasing. It's also important to check the use-by dates of ingredients that aren't used often, like baking powder or spices. If they aren't fresh, then compost or toss. Even things that we might not realize can go bad, like flour, can be out of date.

From creating a shopping list to helping put the groceries away, kids can get involved in the process. Grocery shopping can be fun for families, with the understanding that it can sometimes be stressful for us as parents. When taking your young child grocery shopping, for instance, you might need to focus on selecting things you actually need rather than things that look sugary.

We encourage families to create their shopping list together. For example, your teen might want to bake something during the week and can let you know what ingredients are needed. Your young child may share that there are certain snacks that work well during the school day. You can even leave the list on the fridge and collectively add to it over a couple of days. This makes for a team effort, whether you are going to the grocery store or ordering online.

Make sure you have your list when you get to the store. Not only does the list help you remember what you need, it can also help you set gentle limits about other items that family members may say they want. "Mama, can we please get these cookies?" "Sweetheart, it's not on the list we created."

There are all sorts of ways kids of all ages can be involved in grocery shopping. Teens might want to go to the store on their own with the list, or even a partial list of items they need for a particular recipe. Our daughter Izzy will often make a list on her phone of the ingredients she needs to make a dessert for her grandfather, and then run off to the store to get them. This helps reinforce ownership and awareness of the ingredients that go into the food we're eating.

With young children—and please allow more shopping time to do this—it can be fun for kids to search around the store for different ingredients, with you the parent/guardian/caregiver partner (aka grown-up helper) close behind. Just try to make sure your child isn't darting down the aisle—although if that's the case (and it may well be) then you'll get a workout trying to keep up. Similar to teens, young children develop a sense of ownership and excitement about grocery shopping when they can pick out foods and put them into the shopping cart themselves. For pre-readers, being able to identify a needed ingredient by recognizing its illustration or photo on a package is a fun way to encourage independence and focused attention. Early readers might just be starting to read the name of the food on the package and may be able to pair it with an illustration or photo of the item.

If you're a family with kids with a wide range in ages, like ours, you can mix and match your strategies. As a starter, divvy up the list so you're not all putting the same things into the cart; this has happened to us. It can be a bonding experience to have your teen go off with your younger child to find food items. Teens and preteens may also want to pick out items on their own, creating independence around the food shopping process. Either way, when you all come together at the checkout, each group or individual can show how they've contributed to the activity.

For kids (and grown-up helpers) of all ages, grocery shopping is a great way to practice math by comparing unit prices and figuring out how to shop for the best quality ingredients within a budget. For example, if avocados are available at a cost of $3.99 for four or $1.25 each, which is the better deal? If an individual four-ounce yogurt is $1.49 and a three-pack of three-ounce yogurts is $2.99, which price is more economical? Whether shopping in the store or online, everyone can learn about cost differences and how to make decisions based on value.

Now that you have your groceries, you're ready to organize your kitchen. Unpacking groceries presents a wonderful opportunity for kitchen organization.

In fact, how you organize your kitchen has an impact on the food choices you make and what you eat. If the kitchen is an inviting place without clutter, the desire to cook at home increases. Knowing where to find things in your kitchen provides easy access to ingredients and utensils when you're pressed for time. In the chef world, these are called "stations." Professional kitchens have appetizer, salad, fish, meat, sauce, and dessert stations. They're organized so that the chef can work quickly and efficiently to produce the meals that people order.

You, too, can organize stations in your kitchen. To whatever extent possible (given space constraints), divide your kitchen into sections for hot and cold food items. In one space, group hot food items like pasta, sauce, beans, and canned vegetables. For your cold station, group items like cereal, bread, rolls, granola bars, flour, and chocolate. Organize drink items in another section: teas, coffee, hot chocolate, and coffee filters. When you or your kids are thirsty, you'll know this is the area you need to visit.

If possible, place items that you use every day for cooking close to where you prepare food. These would be things like oil as well as salt, pepper, and other seasonings. In the fridge, place cooked and salad items on the top shelves. We recommend putting raw meat, poultry, and fish in a bottom drawer to prevent cross-contamination; you do not want droplets of liquid from the packaging to leak onto any other food items, especially fresh produce that you will be eating raw (e.g., salad ingredients). Not only is this yucky but it also can be dangerous if bacteria are present. The middle section of the refrigerator is an excellent place to store dairy products such as cheese, milk, and yogurt. Kid-friendly snacks like yogurt can be placed on the lower middle shelf for easy access. Raw vegetables can go right under the middle section and above the raw meat, poultry, and fish in the bottom drawer.

Another aspect of kitchen organization involves growing your own ingredients. Many of the recipes that we present here include herbs you can grow indoors throughout the year. Kids can be in charge of this process, tending windowsill planters of cilantro, oregano, chives, basil, thyme, bay leaf, mint, and parsley. It's yet another part of the food process in which our kids can feel connected and empowered.

Keep your counters clean and tidy so that you and your kids can work in an environment that's free of distractions. An organized kitchen not only helps family members eat better, it also helps families eat the variety of foods that they have in their kitchens.

We keep two glass fruit bowls on easy-to-reach shelves. When family members are rushing out the door and need to take a snack, they can quickly grab a piece of fruit to take with them. You can also put your kids in charge of packing their snacks. This gives them the chance to make choices about what they are going to eat while learning how to plan, prepare, and organize.

# Food Inventory

Go through your cabinets, shelves, fridge, and freezer to take stock of what you have and don't have at home. As you move through this process, check dates of food items to see if any have expired, discarding those that are out of date.

 **YOUNG HELPERS**

**GROUP AND COUNT YOUR FOOD ITEMS**
Group together similar types of food items and count them to see how much you have of each.

**GO ON AN EXPIRED FOOD ITEM SCAVENGER HUNT**
Find expired food items with your grown-up helper and throw them out or compost them.

 **PRETEEN + TEEN HELPERS**

**CHECK FOOD ITEMS AND LIST INGREDIENTS**
Check that you have staples like butter, eggs, pasta, sugar, pepper, salt, and things that you like to eat as a family.

Make a list of any ingredients you want to have on hand for your favorite recipes.

**GROWN-UP HELPERS**

**DEDICATE A DAY TO ORGANIZING YOUR KITCHEN**
Put time aside to go through your cabinets, shelves, fridge, and freezer to see what you have and what you need. Enlist your helpers in the process so that your inventory is organized in anticipation of cooking the recipes that follow.

# Grocery Shopping

Whether shopping online or in person, either in partnership with your grown-up or young helper or on your own, expand upon the list of inventory items that you started and add the groceries you need. Next, visit your grocery store, whether virtually or in person, to find, select, and purchase them.

**YOUNG HELPERS**

**CLICK ON YOUR GROCERIES**
For online shopping, click through the grocery store's website with your grown-up helper to identify the items you need.

**PARTICIPATE IN A GROCERY STORE SCAVENGER HUNT**
Find items from your shopping list with your grown-up helper.

**PRACTICE YOUR MATH**
When you see similar items from different brands, compare them to see which brand is cheaper. Does your grown-up helper agree with your calculations?

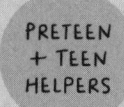
**PRETEEN + TEEN HELPERS**

**FIGURE OUT THE BEST DEALS**
Check prices to get the best deal.

**CROSS-OFF YOUR FOUND ITEMS**
Cross off the groceries on your list as they fill your shopping cart.

**GROWN-UP HELPERS**

**SCAN THE SALES**
See what sales and promotions are being offered at the store.

**CONFIRM YOUR ITEMS**
Read off the items and ask helpers of all ages to identify them in the shopping cart before checking out.

# Organizing Your Kitchen

HELPERS OF ALL AGES

You've completed your food inventory and done your grocery shopping. Either on your own or with your family, now it's time to organize your pantry and food closets. Food often gets lost or forgotten about in the fridge, freezer, or pantry, which can lead to waste. You can have better access to what you have with the right organization. We recommend the following system.

### ON YOUR SHELVES

Organize spices and seasonings, including salt and pepper, together.

Organize baking goods, placing items like flour, sugar, and baking powder together.

Organize your teas, hot chocolate, and coffee.

Organize your breakfast items, placing cereal, syrup, and pancake mix on one shelf.

Create a section for dessert items.

Make a space for snacks.

### IN YOUR FRIDGE

Place cooked and salad items on the top shelves.

Arrange dairy on the middle shelves.

Underneath dairy, place raw vegetables.

Lastly, place raw meat, poultry, and fish on the bottom shelves.

### IN YOUR FREEZER

Place freezer foods you are most likely to eat on upper shelves.

Place freezer foods you are least likely to eat on bottom shelves.

### ON YOUR COUNTERS

Clear off counter space to get ready to cook our yummy recipes.

Find new places to store the items that were on your counters.

Keep bowls of fruit on your counters.

# Prepping for a Recipe

With your kitchen inventoried and organized, the task of preparing for a recipe is going to be so much easier. After choosing your recipe, go through the list of ingredients, identifying those you already have at home and those you need to get on your next shopping outing. Once you have your ingredients, look through the recipe to see if there's anything you need to do in advance: Is there dough that needs to be chilled in the fridge for a couple days? Is there a mixture that has to be in the fridge for a few hours?

**FEAST YOUR EYES**
Draw a picture of the ingredients and supplies you need and put it on your fridge for all to see.

**ORGANIZE YOUR SCHEDULE**
Plan a time to do what needs to be done in advance to prepare for your recipe. Once prepared, you're ready to cook.

**PLAN YOUR DAY**
Set a time in your busy schedule to prepare what you need for the recipe.

**RELAX**
Once you have everything you need, it's time to relax and enjoy cooking with helpers of any age.

This variation of British flapjack bars presents interesting flavors and combinations of tart, sweet, chewy, salty, and spicy tastes and introduces a new treat. In the United States, a flapjack is a kind of pancake, but in the United Kingdom, everyone knows a flapjack to be a sweet oatmeal snack bar.

## INGREDIENTS

| | |
|---|---|
| ¾ cup | unsalted butter |
| 2 Tbsp | soft brown sugar |
| 2 Tbsp | jarred stem ginger in syrup, drained and chopped |
| 3 Tbsp | stem ginger syrup |
| | (Jarred stem ginger in syrup can be easily ordered online if you can't find it at your grocery store.) |
| ¼ cup | golden syrup (or pure corn syrup) |
| 2 cups | quick cooking oats |
| ⅓ cup | dried sour cherries or dried cranberries |
| 2 Tbsp | fresh lemon zest |
| 1 tsp | vanilla extract |
| 1 pinch | fine sea salt |
| 1 tsp | coarse sea salt for sprinkling |

**MAKES 16 BARS**

# LEMONY, GINGERY, FRUITY, BRITISH FLAPJACK BARS

Preheat the oven to 350°F and line an 8-inch baking pan with parchment paper.

In a medium saucepan, melt the butter, brown sugar, stem ginger syrup, and golden syrup over a low heat. Stir until the sugar has completely dissolved then remove from the heat. Add the oats, chopped stem ginger, dried fruit, lemon zest, vanilla, and fine sea salt, and stir until all the dry ingredients are coated with the wet ingredients. Transfer the mixture to the lined baking pan and spread it out evenly. Sprinkle the coarse sea salt on top.

Bake for 20 to 25 minutes, or until the top is golden brown. Remove the pan from the oven and place it on a wire rack to cool. After about 5 minutes, cut the flapjack into 4 squares and then cut each square into 4 quarters. Allow the flapjack to cool completely before you remove the bars from the baking pan.

### top tips!

Lemon zest gives these flapjacks a kick. Create your zest by using a grater to grate the skin of your lemon. You can use the fine holes or sharp grater teeth of a box grater. Catch the lemon peels in a bowl. Rotate the lemon so that you are grating the entire outside surface. Be sure to zest only the peel and not the bitter white pith.

# Taste Test

Part of figuring out what we like to eat involves exploring taste. Do you like sweet or sour, salty or bitter, or a combination of different tastes? Doing a taste test helps you and your helpers discover taste combinations and sensations that work for you and those that don't.

**YOUNG HELPERS**

### EXPLORE YOUR TASTE BUDS
Try each of the recipe ingredients and tell your grown-up helper if it's sweet, sour, salty, bitter, or a combination.

**PRETEEN + TEEN HELPERS**

### PLAY THE TASTE SENSATION GAME
Fill cups with different ingredients and ask your grown-up helper to sample each one. As your grown-up helper samples each ingredient, ask them to identify whether it has taste sensations of sweet, sour, salty, bitter, or a combination. Switch and ask your grown-up helper to give you the taste test.

**GROWN-UP HELPERS**

### GUESS THE INGREDIENT
As you complete each part of the recipe, conduct a taste test to identify different ingredients (you might need to do the prep alone to facilitate true guessing). Ask your helpers to close their eyes and taste the butter, sugar, stem ginger syrup, and golden syrup mixture (after it's cooled, of course). What ingredients are they tasting? Ask your helpers to close their eyes again, then add the oats, chopped stem ginger, dried fruit, lemon zest, vanilla, and fine sea salt and do a second taste test. Now what do they taste? Are there different tastes involved? Different combinations of taste sensations?

This dish is sophisticated and grown-up but also dramatic and so much fun.

Cooking in a bag is extremely healthy and delicious. It also explores the science of cooking with steam. You can see the bag expand as the liquid heats in the oven, creating steam that not only cooks the vegetables and fish but also transforms the bag into a sealed cooking vessel.

As with many recipes in this book, you can experiment with other ingredients using the same cooking method. Items like finely sliced chicken, shrimp, different fish, or vegetables and fresh herbs can all be used in this recipe.

## INGREDIENTS

| | |
|---|---|
| ½ cup | dried cannellini beans, soaked overnight in cold water |
| 1 sprig | thyme |
| 1 | bay leaf |
| 1 | small winter squash, peeled and cut into ¼-in squares |
| 4 Tbsp | extra-virgin olive oil |
| 8 Tbsp | unsalted butter, room temperature |
| 1 | medium leek, cut into ⅛-in thick rings, washed and dried |
| 1 | medium fennel bulb, cut into ⅛-in thick slices |
| 4 pieces | boneless red snapper fillet, 6–7 oz each, skin left on but scored with a sharp knife |
| 4 pinches | saffron pistils |
| 1 cup | white wine or vegetable stock |
| | fine sea salt and freshly ground black pepper |

**SERVES 4**

# BAKING IN A BAG: BALLOON BAKED RED SNAPPER

Preheat the oven to 375°F.

Place the cannellini beans in a saucepan and cover them with 2 inches of fresh cold water. Add the thyme and bay leaf. Bring everything to a boil. If you need to, skim the top of the water (see Fun Fact below). Next, reduce the heat to low and simmer everything for 20 to 30 minutes, or until the beans are soft but not mushy. After simmering, please do not strain the beans (doing so will dry them up)—just add 1 tablespoon of fine sea salt and place them to the side.

Toss the diced squash with 2 Tbsp of the olive oil. Season the squash with salt and pepper. Spread the squash out onto a nonstick baking sheet and bake for 10 to 15 minutes, or until just tender. Leave the oven on.

Now you are ready to make your cooking parcels: Fold four 24-×-12-inch sheets of aluminum in half and crease along the folded edges. Open up the sheets and spread 2 Tbsp of butter in the middle of each bottom square.

Toss the cooked squash with the leeks, fennel, and the remaining 2 Tbsp of olive oil. Season with a little salt and pepper. Arrange a quarter of the vegetables on top of the butter in each of the foil parcels.

Lightly season the fish fillets with salt and pepper and place them, skin-side up, on top of the vegetables.

## fun fact!

We have included white wine as a recipe ingredient. This may be a little shocking as this recipe is meant for grown-ups and kids. Interestingly, any alcohol evaporates during the cooking process. This leaves only the wine flavor with no alcohol in it. If an alternative feels more comfortable, vegetable stock works well, too.

When you cook dried beans, foam may rise up to the top of the boiling water. This happens because some of the additional protein and starch comes out of the beans when they're cooked.

Use a slotted spoon to remove the beans from the cooking water and place a quarter of them on top of each fish fillet. Lastly, sprinkle the fish, vegetables, and beans with a pinch of saffron.

Now it's time to close your cooking parcels: Fold the top sheets of aluminum foil over to cover the fish, vegetables, and beans. At one edge, start to crimp and seal the foil, being careful not to pierce it or create any holes. Work your way around the foil until you have about 1 inch left open. Lift up the opening slightly and add a ¼ cup of white wine or vegetable stock to each parcel. Close your cooking parcels by folding the aluminum over and sealing it tight.

Place the cooking parcels on a rimmed baking tray and bake for 15 minutes. Slide the parcels onto warm plates and serve immediately.

Guests of all ages will delight in opening their cooking parcels with a pair of scissors to reveal the delicately steamed fish, flavored with saffron and winter vegetables.

## Pack Your Bags

HELPERS
OF
ALL AGES

It is so often the case that our kitchens become a disposal area for all kinds of bags: plastic bags, mesh bags, bags from different stores, drawstring bags from different events. In keeping with this recipe's bag theme, work with your helpers to sort through and organize the bags in your kitchen. Can they be recycled? Used elsewhere in your house? Or washed and organized for easy access when you need them?

# Guessing Game

Chances are, you've never made a cooking parcel to prepare your food. Can you guess what will happen? Put your scientist hat on as you guess, or hypothesize, what comes next. Does the cooking bag inflate? Stay the same size? Does the food get fully cooked? Or not?

**YOUNG HELPERS**

### FEAST YOUR EYES
Draw a picture that shows how you think your food will look after being cooked in the cooking bag and place it on your fridge.

**PRETEEN + TEEN HELPERS**

### BRING SCIENCE TO YOUR KITCHEN
Transfer what you learn about science in school to science in the kitchen: What do you think is going on in the cooking parcel that makes it transform the way that it does? What property in science is at work in your cooking process?

**GROWN-UP HELPERS**

### ORGANIZE A GUESSING GAME WITH YOUR HELPERS
Ask your helpers to guess what they think will happen to the food parcel. Whoever makes the closest guess doesn't have to do the dishes.

# Organizing Our Lives

While this chapter is all about organizing our kitchens, it has a direct parallel to thinking about how we can organize our lives. As we take an inventory of our kitchens, we can also inventory our lives, thinking about what spaces are full, and those that might be empty or in need of replenishment. Just as we engage in grocery shopping to fill the inventory gaps in our kitchens, so too can we look to our own individual inventory as a foundation that inspires us to consider what we need to do to fill those gaps in our lives.

Personal inventories show up in different ways, depending upon where we're at in our lives. One way to develop a personal inventory is to listen to the internal voice that's whispering, or even shouting, to us about something we need: What is it I really want to be doing? What changes do I want make? It's fascinating to recognize what's identified when we take a moment to be intentional about our thoughts and feelings. Maybe we want to spend more time with an aging parent or grandparent. Perhaps we finally admit we want to go back to school. The possibilities are endless, but they begin and end with where we're at in our lives. Listening internally helps us get started. So, as we engage in the process of prepping for a recipe (although this may likely involve far less fear about outcomes), we are reminded of the preparation we need for upcoming life events and how to make them happen.

**YOUNG HELPERS**

### GET READY FOR SCHOOL
You might be getting used to going to school and learning lots of new things. With your grown-up helper, color coordinate folders with subjects. For instance, our son's school designated a green folder for science. Even though Olliver couldn't read yet, he knew he'd be able to pick the right folder for science class by recognizing the color green.

**PRETEEN + TEEN HELPERS**

### ENGAGE IN NEW WAYS
Is there a project you've wanted to do but haven't made the time to do it? Is there an event you want to participate in with your friends, but you haven't taken the time to find out about it? How can you make space to engage in some of the things you've been wanting to do?

**GROWN-UP HELPERS**

### DO THE PREP TO PREPARE
Are there upcoming events in your life that you need to prepare for? Or perhaps you're procrastinating—putting off preparation out of a fear of failure. What can you do to prepare for new experiences on your horizon?

In this chapter we've thought a lot about organizing our kitchens and the parallel process of organizing our lives. We've incorporated eating mindfully through opportunities for food-related decisions connected to how we organize our eating spaces. We've set the foundation, and now we're ready to turn the page to begin with breakfast, our first meal of the day.

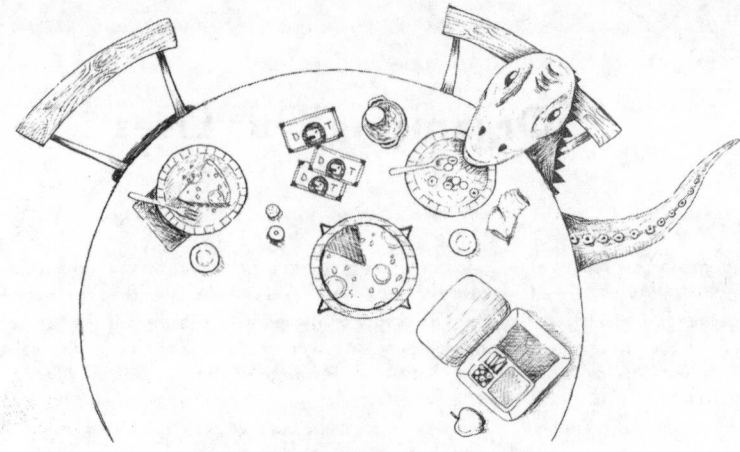

# CHAPTER 2

# Breakfast

*Our Relationship with Food, Our Relationship with Ourselves*

Of all the meals we eat, breakfast is the most overlooked. Grown-ups rush to get to work, kids hurry to get to school—it's no wonder that breakfast is often a meal eaten on the fly. And yet, we probably all have great memories of lounging around eating a delicious Sunday breakfast. These recipes encourage us to start our day in a new and different way, bringing breakfast back to the forefront.

This chapter invites us to think about our relationship with food. Perhaps food wasn't talked about in your household or community when you were young. Maybe it was assumed you would eat the food put before you and that was just the way it was. Maybe an experience of food insecurity shaped your relationship with food. What kind of access to food do you have now? Are there grocery stores that stock healthy foods in your neighborhood? Perhaps there isn't a grocery store nearby. When you go to work or school, is there a lack of time for healthy food options due to a long commute and the hustle of getting to where you need to be?

Knowingly or not, somewhere along the line, our relationships with food begin to develop at a young age. After all, we are not passive from the outset—we cry and scream for food as babies, which is exactly what we're supposed to do to survive. What were the food messages we received while growing up? Through writing this book, we learned that each of us received very different food messages in our childhoods. Julian's mum in England was a good enough cook, but he wanted to learn to cook for himself. He started to make simple things as a kid, like omelets and salads. When he was a young person, Julian found cooking to be all about independence and developing an independent identity.

The message was very different for me. Meals were something only my parents prepared. We came to the table at dinner time and were served foods we were expected to eat. I never really engaged in food preparation—although there was a kid's cookbook I treasured. While growing up in Venezuela, I was unable to get many of the ingredients required for the cookbook's recipes. I made a list of the recipes with ingredients I could find and taped it to the inside of the book. I still have it. My kids frequently reference it for recipe ideas—and to see the many recipes that weren't on that list.

Eating mindfulness encourages us to make healthy and balanced food choices. By "eating mindfulness" we mean building a relationship with food where we are aware of the food choices we're making, knowledgeable of the ingredients in those choices, reflective about trying different foods, and able to recognize how they make us feel.

While eating mindfulness sounds easy, it's actually quite challenging to achieve. Like any type of mindfulness, eating mindfulness requires intentionality and focus. It requires a commitment to being aware of and reflective about the food choices we make. Take portion size, for example. Unless we make the food ourselves, we usually don't have a choice about the amount of food we are served. A restaurant, cafeteria, grocery store, delivery service, or even a parent/guardian/caregiver usually makes the choice for us. The portion may be too big or too small, but it's often not a size that we choose for ourselves.

Part of eating mindfulness, and what we can model for our helpers, is the ability to recognize when we're hungry and when we feel full. An aspect of healthy eating is to know when to start and when to stop. Here eating mindfulness involves being able to acknowledge when we are full or still hungry, independent of how much food is still on our plates. This takes listening to how one feels and what one's body is communicating in the moment. When we are able to tune in to whether or not we really want more food, we can then choose how much we want to eat rather than simply eating the portion placed before us.

A strategy we've used to help our family members get a sense of when they feel full is to put the food we've made in bowls and serving plates, allowing everyone to serve themselves. By serving themselves, our helpers make choices about how much they want to eat. If you feel your helpers aren't eating enough or are overeating, one strategy is to be curious about this and to ask questions to try to understand what's going on.

Another strategy is to encourage your helpers to try different kinds of foods— foods that they may normally say they don't want to eat. When our girls were toddlers, we wanted them to like fruits and vegetables. Their pediatrician gave us a brilliant idea. She told us to put small pieces of different raw vegetables and fruits—cucumbers, carrots, broccoli, apples, and bananas—into separate bowls on the table. Our girls then got to choose what they wanted to eat from the different bowls. They made the choice, while also choosing from healthy options. This was a wonderfully developmentally sensitive idea for the toddler years, which are characterized by exploration, mastery, and having a sense of control.

Another area for eating mindfulness is to find that balance between sugar intake and healthy eating. We had to address this in our family because candy is our son's favorite thing. If he could, Olliver would eat candy all day, every day. To be completely honest, diet wasn't our main motivation to curb Olliver's sugar intake—it was about how hyper sugar made him. We realized this one day when Olliver snuck a pack of strawberry laces when we went to the grocery store. The change was instant. Olliver kept running around the store, up and down the aisles. This experience helped us realize the negative impact sugar has on Olliver.

We put a reward system in place as part of Olliver's eating mindfulness plan. Olliver loves dinosaurs. His room is decorated with them. He was a blow-up dinosaur for Halloween. His favorite color is green. We created Dino Tickets for Olliver. Each Dino Ticket is worth one point—which he can exchange for one treat at the end of the day (and by one treat we mean one piece of candy from a pack—not the whole pack). Olliver can earn a Dino Ticket for things like picking up the living room or making his bed. Each night, Olliver gets to trade in his Dino Tickets for candy from the candy jar. Three Dino Tickets equals three small pieces of candy. This strategy has given Olliver something to look forward to. It limits his requests for sugar throughout the day. It also motivates him to ask for ways to earn Dino Tickets rather than just ask if he can have candy.

I took Olliver to the dentist recently. As a toddler he had trouble with his teeth and some cavities. The dentist said how much better Olliver was doing. He had no cavities. When I told her about our Dino Ticket strategy, she said, "Couldn't it be that easy for all of us?!" While Dino Tickets (or Fairy Tickets, Unicorn Tickets, Basketball Tickets) are a strategy for young helpers, this type of reward system can be adapted for older helpers and grown-ups, too.

We can support our loved one's relationship with food by remembering that what one helper likes, another might not. It makes sense that not everyone is going to always like the same foods. Part of eating mindfulness is being aware of such preferences. If someone is eating something that another person doesn't like, we think it's important to set parameters so that the person gets to enjoy what they're eating without having their food choice criticized. We appreciate the saying "Don't yuck my yum."

In cooking, the success of your finished dish depends on the quality of the ingredients you use. French toast (*pain perdu*, as they call it in France) is no exception to this rule. There are just a few ingredients in this recipe, so it's important that they are of good quality. Every mouthful of this Classic French Toast is a treat for your senses.

**INGREDIENTS**

| 2 | large eggs |
| ½ cup | whole milk |
| 2 Tbsp | maple syrup |
| 1 Tbsp | granulated sugar |
| 1 tsp | vanilla extract |
| ½ tsp | ground cinnamon |
| 1 pinch | fine sea salt |
| 4 slices | stale brioche or challah bread, each about ¾-in thick |
| 4 Tbsp | unsalted butter |
| | confectioners' sugar (aka powdered sugar) for sprinkling |

**SERVES 4**

# CLASSIC FRENCH TOAST

In a medium bowl, whisk together the eggs, milk, maple syrup, sugar, vanilla, cinnamon, and salt. Submerge the brioche slices, one by one, in the egg mixture, making sure the bread is saturated all the way through. Pile the soaked bread on a plate while you get the skillet ready.

In 1 large or 2 small skillets, melt the butter over medium heat until it starts to bubble. Add the soaked bread and cook for 2 to 3 minutes, or until it starts to turn brown at the edges. Flip the bread and cook on the other side for 2 to 3 minutes, or until golden brown. Remove the French toast from the skillet and place on a cutting board. Cut each slice diagonally in half. Place 2 halves on each of 4 plates.

Give your finished dish that restaurant look by sprinkling a little confectioners' sugar on top. Bon appétit!

## fun facts!

Stale bread will absorb much more of the tasty custard than fresh bread, making for French toast that's moist and flavorful both on the outside and in the center.

# Decrease Food Waste

 **YOUNG HELPERS**

### GO ON A LEFTOVER TREASURE HUNT
Go on a treasure hunt for leftover and stray food items in your fridge. As you line them up and look them over, what can you make? A snack? Lunch? Dinner? Have fun combining stray items that might otherwise get thrown out into something delicious.

**PRETEEN + TEEN HELPERS**

### FREEZE YOUR STALE BREAD
Go through the bread in your pantry and take out the stale pieces to store in the freezer for future use. Bread can be frozen from 4 to 6 months. There's one exception here. Very crispy, crusty bread, like a French baguette, is not a good candidate for freezing. Once defrosted, this type of bread can become crumbly and dry.

 **GROWN-UP HELPERS**

### USE YOUR STALE BREAD
Use your stale bread. It can be incorporated into many dishes, such as our Rustic Tomato and Basil Soup recipe (page 92) and Classic Chicken Parmesan (page 133).

Here in the United States, we call porridge oatmeal, but I grew up in the United Kingdom, and we call oatmeal porridge and so do our kids.

For years, porridge was Sabrina's breakfast favorite and now our youngest, Olliver, loves it too. The first words from his mouth every morning are "Is my porridge ready yet?"

And why not? It's a filling, healthy, and yummy breakfast, as well as a versatile one. Our kids' preference has always been to have it with a little brown sugar, but sometimes they top it with honey, cinnamon, fresh berries, cocoa powder, chocolate chips, chopped bananas, or even sprinkle it with some Homemade Granola (page 41).

Porridge is also quick and easy. It only involves four basic ingredients and is ready in less than eight minutes. It's great for those hectic mornings before heading out to school or work.

### INGREDIENTS

| | |
|---|---|
| 4 cups | **whole milk** |
| 1 tsp | **fine sea salt** |
| 2 cups | **old-fashioned rolled oats** |
| 2 Tbsp | **soft brown sugar** |

**SERVES 4**

# OLD-FASHIONED PORRIDGE WITH BROWN SUGAR

In a medium saucepan, bring the milk to a simmer. Add the salt and stir with a wooden spoon, then add the oats. Continue simmering and gently stirring for about 5 minutes, or until the oats have absorbed the milk.

And that's it! Your breakfast is ready. Divide the oatmeal into bowls and finish with your favorite topping.

Blueberry muffins are an American breakfast staple, but the ones we buy ready-made from the store can be packed full of sugar, preservatives, additives, and hard-to-pronounce chemicals. Here's an option for homemade muffins. They are yummy and healthy and you control the ingredients: whole wheat flour, honey, Greek yogurt, and of course, fresh blueberries.

## INGREDIENTS

| | |
|---|---|
| 1 cup | whole wheat flour |
| ¼ cup | granulated sugar |
| 1 tsp | baking powder |
| ½ tsp | baking soda |
| ½ tsp | fine sea salt |
| ½ cup | Greek yogurt |
| ¼ cup | vegetable oil |
| ¼ cup | whole milk |
| ¼ cup | honey |
| 1 | large egg |
| ½ tsp | vanilla extract |
| 1 cup | fresh blueberries |

**MAKES 6 MUFFINS**

# GOOD MORNING BLUEBERRY MUFFINS

Preheat the oven to 375°F and line a muffin tin with 6 paper muffin cups.

In a medium bowl, whisk together the flour, sugar, baking powder, baking soda, and salt.

In a small bowl, whisk together the yogurt, vegetable oil, milk, honey, egg, and vanilla.

Pour the wet ingredients into the dry ingredients and gently mix with a rubber spatula. Add the blueberries and gently fold them in.

Divide the batter equally into the muffin cups and bake for 18 to 20 minutes. You can check that the muffins are cooked by sticking a wooden toothpick into the center of a muffin. If it comes out clean (there is no dough on it), your muffins are done. If it comes out with little crumbs sticking to a toothpick, your muffins need more time to bake.

Remove the pan from the oven and place it on a cooling rack. Allow the muffins to cool for 5 minutes then remove from the pan.

Eat your muffins warm or keep them in an airtight container to enjoy the next day. In addition to being a great breakfast, they make for a delicious snack as well.

## top tips!

When you add your blueberries to the batter, do not overmix or your muffins will be tough. This is due to gluten development: when flour is mixed with liquid ingredients, it releases proteins found in gluten. These proteins give your muffin its muffin shape; however, overmixing will lead to a tough or even chewy muffin.

## fun fact!

This recipe talks about folding in the blueberries. *Folding in* is a baking technique where you combine a lighter mixture or ingredient with one that is heavier, such as mixing blueberries into your batter.

# Know When Something Is Ready

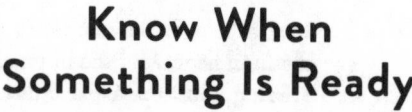

While we tend to focus on cooking as preparing food, it's also about knowing when the food we're making is done. For recipes baked in the oven, like Good Morning Blueberry Muffins (opposite) or Izzy's Banana Chocolate Bread (page 44), it may be challenging to know just when our creations are ready.

**YOUNG HELPERS**

**SET YOUR TIMER FOR TIMING**
Learn about two-digit numbers by setting your timer to 18 or 20 minutes when your grown-up helper puts the muffin pan in the oven.

**PRETEEN + TEEN HELPERS**

**CONDUCT A TOOTHPICK TEST**
Help test the muffins with a toothpick at 15 minutes, 18 minutes, and/or 20 minutes.

**GROWN-UP HELPERS**

**KNOW THAT TIMING IS EVERYTHING**
Make sure you don't get so caught up in doing something else that you forget to take the muffins out on time!

Vegetables are a really important part of our diets. Breakfast doesn't need to be a meal that excludes this food group. Making a frittata is a great way to start your day with veggies. It's also a useful way to incorporate vegetables in your fridge, here mushrooms and asparagus, before they go bad. A frittata is a perfect dish for breakfast, Sunday brunch, or even a light supper.

## INGREDIENTS

| | |
|---|---|
| 1 Tbsp | unsalted butter |
| 3 Tbsp | olive oil |
| ½ lb | asparagus, trimmed and cut into ½-in pieces |
| ½ lb | white mushrooms, sliced |
| 12 | large eggs |
| 2 Tbsp | half-and-half |
| 1 tsp | chopped fresh thyme |
| ½ Tbsp | fine sea salt |
| ¼ Tbsp | fresh ground black pepper |
| 3 Tbsp | freshly grated Parmesan cheese |
| ½ cup | shredded mozzarella cheese |

**SERVES 6**

# MUSHROOM & ASPARAGUS FRITTATA

Preheat the oven to 325°F.

In a large oven-safe nonstick skillet, melt the butter over medium heat. Add the olive oil and asparagus and cook, stirring, until the asparagus is tender, about 5 minutes. Add the mushrooms, and cook, stirring, until they're soft, about 5 minutes.

In a medium bowl, whisk together the eggs, half-and-half, thyme, salt, and pepper. Pour this mixture into the skillet and reduce the heat to low. Cover and cook for 5 minutes. Remove the cover and transfer the skillet to the oven. Bake for 10 to 15 minutes, or until the eggs are no longer runny. Remove the skillet from the oven and top with the Parmesan and mozzarella. Turn on the broiler and broil until the cheese is melted and lightly browned.

Now turn the frittata out onto a plate. To do this, put your serving plate upside down onto the skillet. Then put a kitchen towel on top of the plate (to prevent your hand from getting hot). Next, hold the handle of your skillet with your dominant hand and put your other hand on top of the towel that's holding the plate. Finally, carefully flip everything over, so the plate is on the bottom and the skillet is upside down on top. Your frittata will fall onto the plate and you can gently remove the skillet. You're now ready to cut the frittata into 6 wedges. Serve warm.

This recipe is inspired by our son Olliver's love of sour flavors. It also shows that it's quite easy and fun to make pancakes from scratch using fresh, healthy ingredients. And with many hands, measuring and mixing becomes a team effort. To make a mouse shaped pancake, combine one large circular pancake for the face with two smaller pancakes on top to make the ears. You will be everyone's hero when you present them with their very own mouse pancake. Serve with sour cream and a little maple syrup, or fresh berries.

## INGREDIENTS

| | |
|---|---|
| 1¾ cups | all-purpose flour |
| 3 Tbsp | granulated sugar |
| 3 tsp | baking powder |
| ½ tsp | fine sea salt |
| ¼ tsp | baking soda |
| 1 cup | whole milk |
| ⅔ cup | whole milk ricotta cheese |
| 3 | large eggs |
| 1 tsp | vanilla extract |
| 2 Tbsp | lemon zest |
| ⅓ cup | fresh lemon juice |
| 2 Tbsp | unsalted butter, for cooking |
| | sour cream (optional) |
| | maple syrup (optional) |
| | fresh berries (optional) |

**MAKES 8 PANCAKES**

# LEMON RICOTTA PANCAKES

In a large bowl, whisk together the flour, sugar, baking powder, salt, and baking soda for about 30 seconds.

In a small bowl, whisk together the milk and ricotta for 1 minute. Add the eggs and vanilla and whisk for another minute, or until everything is nicely incorporated. Finally, add the lemon zest and juice and whisk for about 30 seconds.

Pour the wet ingredients onto the dry ingredients and gently fold them together with a rubber spatula until your batter comes together. Do not overmix the batter, as this will cause the pancakes to become tough and not light and fluffy (see Top Tips, page 36).

Heat a nonstick pan over medium-high heat until it's quite hot. Add a little butter and then 1 or 2 spoonfuls of pancake batter, depending on the size of the pancakes you want. Add more batter to cook additional pancakes. Cook for 1 to 2 minutes, or until you see bubbles on the surface of the pancakes. Flip them over and continue cooking for 1 to 2 minutes, or until golden brown. Repeat to make more pancakes, adding more butter and adjusting the heat as needed.

Don't forget to make the mouse pancake!

# Whisk Just Right

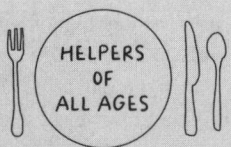

Whisks are great tools to have in your kitchen. When you're whisking, you're using movement to incorporate air into your creation (whether it be batter, eggs, or whipped cream). This gives whatever you're making a lighter, fluffier quality. Whisks are also multitaskers. Instead of mixing with one spoon, the many wire tines that make up a whisk are like mixing with many spoons, all at the same time.

Whisking is one of the more physical activities in the kitchen, so it can be a great way to release energy. It's also a good arm workout. Get out your frustrations while you whisk. Maybe you had a bad day or feel annoyed about something. Whisking might help you manage that anger. Every time you whisk, focus on identifying and letting go of something that's upsetting you. Just be sure not to over-whisk. Follow instructions regarding how long to whisk for the recipe you're making. For example, for Lemon Ricotta Pancakes (page 39), whisking occurs in 4 intervals of 30 seconds, 1 minute, 1 minute, and 30 seconds.

Granola is easy to find in the store. However, just a small bag of it can be quite expensive. Our recipe makes a lot of granola and costs much less. It's great for breakfast, lunch, and even as a snack.

## INGREDIENTS

| | |
|---|---|
| 4 cups | old-fashioned rolled oats |
| 1 cup | chopped almonds or pecans |
| 3 tsp | ground cinnamon |
| ½ tsp | fine sea salt |
| ¼ tsp | grated nutmeg |
| ½ cup | vegetable oil |
| ¼ cup | honey |
| ¼ cup | maple syrup |
| 2 tsp | vanilla extract |
| 1 cup | raisins (optional) |
| ½ cup | crushed dried bananas (optional) |
| ½ cup | chopped dried apricots (optional) |

**MAKES ABOUT 6 CUPS**

# HOMEMADE GRANOLA

Preheat the oven to 300°F.

Line a baking sheet with parchment paper.

In a large bowl, mix the oats, nuts, cinnamon, salt, and nutmeg.

In a small bowl, whisk together the vegetable oil, honey, maple syrup, and vanilla.

Add the wet ingredients to the dry ingredients and stir well.

Place the granola mixture on the lined baking sheet and spread it evenly to cover the entire baking sheet. Bake for about 15 minutes then remove the baking sheet from the oven and break up the granola with a wooden spoon. Return the baking sheet to the oven and bake for 5 to 10 more minutes, or until the granola is golden brown.

Remove your granola from the oven a second time and place the baking sheet on a cooling rack until the granola is cool. Break up the granola then mix in the bananas, apricots, and raisins, if using.

Store your granola in an airtight container for later use at breakfast time with some cold milk and fresh berries, as an on-the-go snack, or as a topping for ice cream or yogurt.

# Do Your Own Thing

Developing a sense of what tastes good to you—and what doesn't—is part of making food choices. While our Homemade Granola recipe (page 41) presents optional ingredients like dried bananas, dried apricots, and raisins, you may not like them and decide others make your granola taste better. The same is true for our Classic French Toast (page 33) and Mushroom and Asparagus Frittata (page 38). You and your helpers can make choices about what to serve on top of the French toast or what veggies to include in the frittata. This is all part of knowing what's in your food and, when preparing it, being intentional about the ingredients you want to add.

**YOUNG HELPERS**

### EXPERIMENT WITH WHAT TASTES GOOD TO YOU

Try the optional ingredients listed for the granola. If you don't like them, work with your grown-up helper to add other ingredients you find in your pantry like shredded coconut, dried cranberries, or chia seeds. See how it tastes: Is it sweeter? More chewy?

**PRETEEN + TEEN HELPERS**

### EXPLORE YOUR IDENTITY

The preteen and teen years are all about identity development. Exploring your interests, friendships, and the subjects you like and don't like are a part of this process. It's not so different for food as you explore what tastes right for you. Are there toppings you want to add? Fruits like blueberries, strawberries, and raspberries add a fresh element to granola. Or maybe you want to sprinkle it with some semi-sweet chocolate chips? There are no do's or don'ts. The right choice is what tastes right for you.

**GROWN-UP HELPERS**

### TAKE OWNERSHIP

Making your own granola—rather than buying it at the store—is an easy way to take ownership of your food. What kinds of granola do you prefer? While they're not ingredients included in this recipe, perhaps you want to add pistachios or other types of dried fruit. Pick your favorite ingredients to make this granola recipe all yours.

Coddled eggs are a fun and easy breakfast dish. You can also customize your eggs by adding your favorite savory breakfast ingredients like cooked chopped bacon, cooked chopped sausage, chopped ham, diced tomato, chives, sautéed onions, grated cheddar cheese, and cooked mushrooms…let your imagination run wild.

Coddled eggs are a little like poached eggs, but they're protected from the water by being cooked in a little porcelain pot. Original porcelain egg coddlers are easily available online, but if you can't wait for your coddlers to arrive, you can simply use ovenproof ramekins—the results will be almost the same (see Fun Fact below).

Depending on the size of your coddler or ramekin, you can use one egg or two. It's also important to select a yummy bread to make the toasted bread fingers to dunk into your creation.

## INGREDIENTS

| | |
|---|---|
| 8 | large eggs |
| 4 tsp | heavy cream |
| | your favorite savory ingredients, as required and desired |
| 4 tsp | sour cream |
| 4 slices | your favorite bread, toasted, lightly buttered, and cut into fingers |
| | fine sea salt and freshly ground black pepper |

**SERVES 4**

# CODDLED EGGS

Butter the inside of 4 egg coddlers or ovenproof ramekins, using your finger to evenly spread the butter on the bottom and sides.

Break 1 egg into each coddler or ramekin. Season each with a pinch of salt and a quarter turn of the pepper mill and top with 1 tsp of heavy cream. At this point in the cooking process, you can put your own unique spin on the recipe, adding 1 or more of the ingredients listed at the start of the recipe such as chopped ham, chives, or grated cheddar cheese. Next, break a second egg on top. Season each with a little salt and pepper and top with 1 tsp of sour cream and a little more of your special ingredients.

Screw on the lids of your coddlers or cover your ramekins with aluminum foil, sealing the edges tightly. Place the coddlers or ramekins in a pan that will hold them all at once and set on the stove. Do not turn on the heat. Boil some water in a separate kettle or pan and carefully pour enough water between the coddlers or ramekins to come three-fourths of the way up the side. Make sure the water doesn't get into the eggs!

Heat over medium heat and bring to a light simmer. Cook the eggs for about 8 minutes. Turn off the heat, and then carefully remove the coddlers or ramekins from the water. Allow the eggs to rest for a few minutes, then remove the lid or foil and serve immediately with the toast fingers.

## top tips!

This breakfast dish is great for dipping! Make toast fingers by toasting a piece of bread and cutting it into strips.

## fun fact!

The main difference between porcelain egg coddlers and ovenproof ramekins is that egg coddlers have a screw-on lid with a ring on top. This makes it easier to remove them from the water.

As someone who works with food professionally, it's difficult for me to throw food out. I find it wasteful and therefore costly. When buying bananas at the store or market, they are often still green or, hopefully, just right. We bring them home, life happens, and they're forgotten, until, oops… they're spotted or just plain brown and mushy and frankly, unappetizing or inedible.

Don't worry, for this recipe the bananas should be very ripe. Remove the skin, place the peeled banana in a freezer bag, and freeze it. When you have enough bananas and are ready to make banana bread, remove the frozen bananas from the freezer, place them in a strainer set over a bowl, and allow them to defrost at room temperature for a few hours. Voilà, the bananas have been rescued from ending up in the trash can!

## INGREDIENTS

| | |
|---|---|
| ½ cup | unsalted butter |
| 4 | large ripe bananas |
| ¼ cup | vegetable oil |
| 2 | large eggs |
| 1 tsp | vanilla extract |
| 2 cups | all-purpose or whole wheat flour |
| ½ cup | granulated sugar |
| ½ cup | packed soft brown sugar |
| ½ cup | semisweet chocolate chips |
| 1 tsp | baking soda |
| ½ tsp | ground cinnamon |
| ½ tsp | fine sea salt |
| ½ cup | toasted chopped almonds, walnuts, or pecans (optional) |

**MAKES 1 LOAF**

# IZZY'S BANANA CHOCOLATE BREAD

Preheat the oven to 350°F. Spray the inside of a 9-×-5-inch loaf pan with nonstick cooking spray or line it with parchment paper (either option works well).

In a small saucepan over low heat (or in the microwave), melt the butter.

In a medium bowl, mash together the bananas, melted butter, and vegetable oil. Add the eggs and vanilla and mix well.

In a large bowl, mix the flour, granulated sugar, brown sugar, chocolate chips, baking soda, cinnamon, salt, and nuts, if using.

Add the wet ingredients to the dry ingredients and mix with a rubber spatula until all your ingredients are just combined. Do not overmix, as this will make your bread chewy or tough (see Top Tips, page 36).

Pour the batter into the loaf pan and level off the top with your spatula. Bake for 45 to 55 minutes. You can test your bread by inserting a wooden toothpick into the center of your bread. If it comes out clean, it's ready.

Remove from the oven and allow the banana bread to cool and set for about 15 minutes. Then turn over the loaf pan onto a cutting board and gently shake the pan until the banana bread comes free. Remove the parchment paper if necessary.

Serve your banana bread warm or cold.

# Start a Home Food Recycling Program

HELPERS
OF
ALL AGES

Don't throw out those bananas! Food can be recycled. While we might traditionally think of composting as a way to recycle food, we define food recycling as using food in new and creative ways rather than throwing it out, as seen with Izzy's Banana Chocolate Bread (opposite). Starting a home food recycling program allows you and your helpers to consider creative ways to use extra foods in new dishes. You can also recycle food by freezing leftovers. This is a wonderful way to reduce waste while also having a meal or snack ready when you're short on time.

# The Start to Our Day

I'll be honest: starting the day is not my favorite thing. I shudder at the sound of the alarm clock. The task of getting up and getting everyone to where they need to be on time feels daunting, and I haven't even left my bed yet. But thinking about breakfast helps me take a different approach to starting the day.

**YOUNG HELPERS**

### GET OUT OF BED
It can be challenging to get up in the morning and get ready for school. This can be especially true on those cold winter mornings, when staying in your cozy bed is much more appealing. Make one of these breakfast treats with your grown-up helper the night before. Knowing you have something fun to enjoy for breakfast can help you get the day started.

**PRETEEN + TEEN HELPERS**

### GET OUT THE DOOR
What's the first thing you think about when you wake up in the morning? What gets in the way of getting out the door and to school on time? What would you do differently to improve your early morning routine?

**GROWN-UP HELPERS**

### GET ON TOP OF YOUR STRESS
Mornings are stressful. As parents/guardians/caregivers, we have the dual role of having to get both ourselves and our kids ready. It seems there's always something we've forgotten about that throws off our very best intentions. Save time in the morning by making breakfast the night before. Good Morning Blueberry Muffins (page 36), Homemade Granola (page 41), and Izzy's Banana Chocolate Bread (page 44) are all options. Pack what's left over in your helper's lunchbox for a tasty school snack.

I can't believe we were able to make this dressing! It tastes great!

# CHAPTER 3

# Salad

*It's Not Just about Lettuce (Choice versus Deception)*

We make a lot of assumptions about salad. We think it's for adults not kids, women not men, to be eaten in the summer and not in the fall or winter. We assume salad is just about lettuce and nothing else. We think our kids won't eat it and often give up way too early before we give them a chance. The salad recipes in this chapter fly in the face of these assumptions—they're colorful, full of all kinds of ingredients, and can be eaten by anyone, of any age, at any time of the year. And some of them don't even include lettuce.

A good mom friend once shared that salad scared her kids. Her sons, who loved ninjas and battleships, were literally terrified of greens.

Six-year-old Olliver is a self-proclaimed salad hater. While writing this chapter, I asked him why he didn't like it. "I just don't," he said. "I don't like it, it's yucky."

"But Olliver," I said, "you've never tried salad before. How do you know you don't like it if you've never tried it?"

"Well, I just know," was his assured response.

This got me thinking—was there an expectation in our house that Olliver wouldn't like salad? Were we somehow subtly saying that it was okay for him to not eat it? His sisters always ate salad from a young age—what was the difference?

Thinking about this reminded me of two other occasions when kids were confronted with eating salad. A few years ago, Julian was involved in a nonprofit group for which chefs donate their time to a local school to help kids learn about healthy eating. Julian chose a neighborhood grade school as a way to support our community. There were about thirty middle schoolers in the class. The plan was to make a salad and salad dressing after visiting a local farmers' market.

"How many of you have eaten salad before?" Julian asked. Only three kids raised their hands.

Nevertheless, they were an adventurous group and willing to try. As Julian walked the kids through the process of making a salad, he could feel their excitement growing—so much so that the teacher told the kids they had to wait to try their creations until everyone was served.

The suspense was building. "It smells great," said one child. "I can't wait to try it!" They loved the salad. They clapped for Julian and proclaimed they would make it at home that very weekend.

The second scenario was when one of my daughters was a preteen and a close friend came over for dinner. When the friend's dad dropped her off, he vehemently proclaimed that if we were having salad, his daughter wouldn't eat it. "Just to let you know, she's not going to eat salad. That's fine, she can just have the pizza."

"Okay," I said. "No worries."

I was curious. Sabrina, Izzy, and I love salad. Julian's homemade salad dressing is so delicious (see page 67). Salad is one of our favorite meals. The get-together was going well. Everyone was having fun. When it was time for dinner (pizza and salad), my daughter's friend watched as both my girls eagerly served themselves salad. "This salad dressing is so good," Izzy exclaimed. "You have to try it."

"Okay," her friend said reluctantly. She put a small piece of lettuce and dressing on her plate and poked it with her fork. Then she slowly, very slowly, tried the salad—just barely eating it. She stopped and chewed, turning to look at Sabrina and Izzy. "Wow," she said. "This is really good. I want some more."

Later that week my daughter's friend's dad called. He sounded so happy as he shared how much his daughter loved the salad and the dressing. "Can we have the recipe for the dressing?" he asked.

How can we understand this shift from absolutely not eating any salad to eating it, loving it, and owning it as an *eating mindfulness* choice?

Perhaps a couple of things are going on, things that can help us as grown-up helpers to encourage our kids to eat healthy foods. First, as a parent, I think it's important to recognize someone's concerns, or even fears, about a certain type of food. Olliver just knew he wasn't going to like salad. My friend's sons were scared of it. Recognizing feelings and emotions about food is an important starting point. In doing so, we are validating concerns, opinions, and fears.

After validation, modeling is a powerful tool to help reshape picky eating behaviors. With modeling, we show someone how something can be done.

We're giving someone access to something through our example. Modeling provides a pathway. It's like a road map, letting us know where we are and where we need to be going.

Unbeknownst to them, Sabrina and Izzy were modeling eating salad for their friend. Modeling makes people think if someone is doing something, they can do it, too, whether that something is getting good grades, playing an instrument, winning a sports game, getting into college, or yes, eating a salad.

You might be thinking to yourself, "Well, I eat salad but my kids still won't eat it." Identify friends of theirs who love salad and invite them over. There is something to be said for positive peer pressure. Just as negative peer pressure can get kids in a jam, positive influences can encourage kids to study more, participate more, socialize more, whatever that more is that you would like for them in their lives.

There's something else at play in these examples. Something that underscores the idea of encouraging kids to make healthy food choices rather than use deception. This something is about expectations. Take the example of academic success. We know from research that if parents communicate "positive expectations…and the encouragement of academic engagement" with regard to their children's academic progress, this expectation can in fact lead to improved academic outcomes that are "more effective in realizing parental expectations."[1]

It couldn't be that different for food. If we have the expectation that our kids will eat salad and we make it available to them because of that expectation, we are assuming there's no issue at all. It's normative, how we live and how we eat.

Perhaps our friend's daughter didn't eat salad because there was an expectation that she wouldn't—so much so that we were politely given a heads-up beforehand, when we were informed to not expect her to eat salad. The same was true when Julian collaborated with the school. Most of the kids had never eaten salad, but when given the expectation that they would create one and try it, they did. You can change your expectations in light of helpers who say they don't like salad.

Now, it may be that your child just really doesn't like lettuce. Your child might literally cringe at the thought of eating it. That's okay, too. As you will see from the recipes in this chapter, salad is not just about lettuce. There are so many different kinds of ingredients that can make up a salad. Lettuce is just one of them.

And notice that in all these examples, with kids of all ages, the kids knew exactly what they were eating, or not eating, or scared to eat. They were not deceived. Instead, they were given a decision to make about a food choice.

We will see what happens with Olliver.

This salad celebrates the end of winter with wonderful seasonal ingredients that start to emerge in the spring. It also introduces a very simple way to make your own salad dressing. A versatile dish, it can be enjoyed on its own or as a side.

## DRESSING

| ¼ cup | extra-virgin olive oil |
| 2 Tbsp | fresh lemon juice |
| ⅛ tsp | fine sea salt |
| | freshly ground black pepper, to taste |

## INGREDIENTS

| ½ cup | freshly grated Parmesan |
| ½ cup | sliced almonds |
| 1 bunch | green asparagus |
| 1 lb | fava beans in the pod |
| 1 bunch | green onions |
| 2 Tbsp | extra-virgin olive oil for cooking (approx.) |
| 8 oz | fresh ramps or the white part of a leek, sliced |
| 8 oz | organic spring salad mix (mesclun greens) |
| | salt and freshly ground black pepper, to taste |

SERVES 4

# SPRING SALAD

Preheat the oven to 300°F.

### TO MAKE THE DRESSING

In a large bowl, whisk together the extra-virgin olive oil, lemon juice, and salt. Add pepper until you feel the dressing has the right taste. Set aside.

### TO MAKE THE SALAD

Spread the Parmesan cheese in a thin even layer on a nonstick baking sheet. Bake for 5 to 8 minutes, or until it bubbles and starts to turn light brown. Remove the cheese from the oven, allow it to cool slightly, and then release it from the pan with a spatula. When the cheese has cooled completely, break it into small pieces and set aside. Leave the oven on.

Spread the sliced almonds on a baking sheet and bake for 5 to 8 minutes, or until they take on a golden-brown color. Watch the nuts carefully as they toast. Remove from the oven and let cool.

Bring a medium saucepan of salted water to a boil. Fill a bowl with ice water.

Cut off the last inch from the base of the asparagus. With a peeler, peel the last 2 inches of the asparagus skin from the stem. Finely slice the asparagus at an angle. Add the asparagus to the boiling water and cook for 2 minutes. Then remove the asparagus from the boiling water with a slotted spoon and place it into the ice water for a couple of minutes. Remove the cooled asparagus from the water and set it aside in a large mixing bowl. Keep the saucepan of hot water, return it to the stove, and bring it back to a boil. Add more ice to the bowl of water.

### top tips!

People often shy away from asparagus because they don't know how to cook it, but it's really easy to prepare. While it's used as a salad ingredient here, you can follow the same cooking method and serve it as a side dish with a squeeze of lemon or grated Parmesan cheese.

It's fun to open the fava bean pods and remove the beans. Pop out the inner bright beans from the outer shell. Then add the beans to the boiling water and cook for 2 minutes. Place the beans in the ice water to cool for 2 or 3 minutes. Remove the cooled beans from the water and combine with the asparagus in the bowl.

Trim and rinse the green onions in cold water. Cut them into ¼-inch pieces. Warm a medium-sized sauté pan over medium heat, then add a drizzle of olive oil. Sauté the green onions for 1 minute then season with a little salt and pepper. Put the green onions in the bowl with the beans and asparagus.

Wash the ramps or leeks in cold water. Warm the medium-sized sauté pan over medium heat, then add a drizzle of olive oil. Sauté the ramps or leeks for 2 or 3 minutes then season with a little salt and pepper. Put the ramps or leeks in the bowl with your other cooked ingredients.

In a separate large bowl, combine the lettuce, asparagus, fava beans, ramps or leeks, green onions, and dressing. Toss the salad to make sure all the ingredients have a little dressing on them.

Add the final touch by sprinkling the salad with the toasted almonds and broken pieces of Parmesan crisps.

# Pop the Beans

Push pop bubble toys and accessories are popular at the moment. These sensory toys and gadgets are described as helping with stress, anxiety, and fidgeting. Our spring salad recipe comes with its very own, all-natural push pop toy: fava beans! Check in with helpers of any age as they pop them out of the pod.

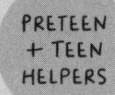

**YOUNG HELPERS**

**POP OUT THE FAVA BEANS**
Are some beans easier than others to pop out? Why?

**PRETEEN + TEEN HELPERS**

**IDENTIFY YOUR FEELINGS**
Think about how you feel as you pop out the beans. Where do your thoughts and feelings take you? Do you find the experience soothing or frustrating? Does it help you get out negative energy or think about what you're going through?

**GROWN-UP HELPERS**

**ASK YOUR HELPERS ABOUT THEIR DAY**
As your helpers pop out the beans, start a conversation by sharing a memory from your own childhood or asking your helper to share three things that describe their day. What's been going on for them? How are they doing? What comes to mind for them—and for you—as you both pop out the beans?

This salad has its origins in the Middle East and North Africa. Interestingly, even though it's called a salad, it has no traditional salad leaves. In this part of the world, the heat makes it difficult for salad leaves to grow, but tomatoes, peppers, olives, and cucumbers thrive.

Preserved lemon, also known as lemon pickle, is a lovely condiment to have around. Intensely lemony, it lasts a long time and can be used in many dishes with chicken, fish, or vegetables. It's used widely in North Africa and the Indian subcontinent, and surprisingly, is often found in eighteenth century English recipes. You can buy preserved lemon in stores or online or make it yourself with just two ingredients, lemons and salt.

## DRESSING

| | |
|---|---|
| ⅓ cup | vegetable oil |
| ¼ cup | extra-virgin olive oil |
| ¼ cup | fresh flat-leaf parsley leaves, packed |
| ¼ cup | fresh mint leaves, packed |
| 2 | preserved lemon halves, seeded and rinsed in water |
| 2 Tbsp | fresh lemon juice |
| 1 tsp | honey |
| | fine sea salt and freshly ground black pepper |
| 1 | Calabrian chile pepper in oil, seeded and chopped, or a good pinch of red pepper flakes (optional) |

# MEDITERRANEAN SUMMER SALAD WITH PRESERVED LEMON DRESSING & CHIA SEEDS

### TO MAKE THE DRESSING

In a blender, combine the vegetable oil, olive oil, parsley, mint, 1 preserved lemon half, the lemon juice, honey, and the chile pepper or pepper flakes, if using. Purée until smooth, then pour into a small bowl. Remove the flesh from the remaining preserved lemon half. Finely dice the preserved lemon skin and add it to the dressing. Mix with a spoon and season with salt and pepper. Set aside while you prepare your salad.

*fun fact!*

Chia seeds come from a flowering plant in the mint family. They contain antioxidants and can help manage blood pressure and lower cholesterol, among many other benefits.[2]

## INGREDIENTS

| | |
|---|---|
| 2 cups | ripe grape tomatoes, halved |
| 1 | small red onion, peeled and finely sliced |
| 1 | red bell pepper, stemmed, seeded, and finely sliced |
| 1 | yellow bell pepper, stemmed, seeded, and finely sliced |
| 1 | English cucumber, peeled, seeded, and sliced |
| ½ cup | French green beans |
| 4 oz | feta cheese, diced |
| ½ cup | pitted black Niçoise or Kalamata olives |
| ¼ cup | chia seeds |
| 10 | fresh basil leaves, torn by hand |
| | toasted pita (optional) |
| | grilled focaccia bread (optional) |

**SERVES 4 TO 6**

## TO MAKE THE SALAD

In a large bowl, combine the tomatoes, red onion, red and yellow bell peppers, and cucumber. Set aside.

Bring a medium saucepan of salted water to a boil.

Top and tail the green beans (see Top Tips below) and cut into 1-inch pieces. Add the green beans to the boiling water and cook for 3 minutes. Drain the green beans and place them into ice water to cool. When the green beans are cold, add them to the bowl of vegetables. Add the feta, olives, chia seeds, and torn basil, and toss to combine. Set aside.

Drizzle the dressing over your salad. Mix well and serve. This salad goes really well with toasted pita or grilled focaccia bread.

### top tips!

The French green bean has a stalk part at the top and a thinner part at the bottom. When directions say to "top and tail" something like French green beans, it just means to cut off the tips at each end.

When a recipe says that something is packed, like the ¼ cup fresh flat-leaf parsley leaves or the ¼ cup fresh mint leaves in this recipe, it simply means that you push down the ingredients in the measuring cup. Packing your ingredients into a measuring cup removes the spaces of air between them, which leads to more of your ingredient being in the cup. Keep in mind that a cup is a measurement of volume, while a scale is a measurement of weight.

# Make Your Very Own Preserved Lemons

The process of making preserved lemons was created in North Africa and the Mediterranean. It's hundreds of years old. To make your own, you will need 6 fresh medium lemons and 6 tsp of fine sea salt. You will also need a sterilized, pint-sized canning jar to store and preserve your lemon.

Wash your lemons and remove the ends of 5 of them with a sharp knife. Cut the lemons as if cutting them into quarters, but do not cut all the way to the bottom—stop cutting about three quarters of the way down so you have a lemon that has 4 quarters but is attached at 1 end.

Next, open 1 of the lemons and sprinkle the inside with a teaspoon of salt. Place the lemon in your jar then repeat this process until all 5 lemons are in the jar. Squeeze and push the 5 lemons in the jar, so their juice is released. Top the lemons with the remaining 1 teaspoon of salt and the juice of the remaining lemon.

Seal your jar with a tightly fitting lid and leave it out in your kitchen. Turn and shake the jar daily. After 3 to 4 days, place your jar in the refrigerator for 3 to 4 weeks, again turning and shaking the jar every 2 to 3 days.

Your patience will be rewarded with amazingly soft, zesty, tangy lemons, ready to give a zing to your taste buds.

**YOUNG HELPERS**

### HOST A COMPARISON TASTE TEST
Once your preserved lemons are ready, compare their taste to that of a slice of fresh lemon skin. Cut a piece of skin off a lemon and eat it. Now do the same with the skin from the preserved lemon. How do they taste different? What is the texture like? Which do you prefer? Which does your grown-up helper prefer?

**PRETEEN + TEEN HELPERS**

### CONDUCT AN EXPERIMENT
Make hypotheses about how you think the lemons might change over time. Will they change color? Will their texture look the same or different? Keep watching your lemons throughout the process to see what happens.

**GROWN-UP HELPERS**

### MODEL MINDFUL EATING
Making your own preserved lemons shows you and your helpers that you can create ingredients at home instead of buying them at the store.

# Add to Your Bowl

This Mediterranean Summer Salad recipe is fun because it's all about cooking in one bowl. One by one, you add your tomatoes, red onion, peppers, cucumbers, French green beans, feta cheese, olives, chia seeds, basil leaves, and your salad dressing. What does your bowl look like as you add each ingredient?

**YOUNG HELPERS**

**PLAY THE COLOR OF THE INGREDIENT NAMING GAME**
As you add each ingredient, practice saying the name of its color with your grown-up helper. If you're learning another language at school, practice saying the colors in that language.

**PRETEEN + TEEN HELPERS**

**PACK A SALAD FOR YOUR SCHOOL LUNCH**
Find another bowl—a portable one—and pack your salad in it. Whether you add salad dressing to the salad in your portable bowl, or put it in a separate container, this makes for a fresh and healthy school lunch!

**GROWN-UP HELPERS**

**CONSERVE YOUR CLEAN-UP TIME**
As you clean up the kitchen with your helper, notice how much easier it is when you conserve supplies and prepare all your ingredients in one bowl.

We are used to eating salad in the summer when the weather is warm and salad ingredients are in season. Here's a salad that's been especially created to be enjoyed in the fall or winter, using lettuces grown in a greenhouse, Brussels sprouts, and root vegetables. The salad greens are slightly bitter, so I've added grapes to create an interesting bittersweet contrast.

I also really like the combination of hot and cold. To give this salad another dimension, I've added warm vegetarian, root vegetable pancakes to put on top, making this a truly seasonal and delicious appetizer or light lunch.

### ROOT VEGETABLE PANCAKES

| | |
|---|---|
| 2 | parsnips, peeled and grated |
| 2 | carrots, peeled and grated |
| ½ | medium sweet potato, peeled and grated |
| 2 Tbsp | cornstarch |
| 1 Tbsp | extra-virgin olive oil |
| | fine sea salt and freshly ground black pepper |

### SALAD

| | |
|---|---|
| 1 | small head curly endive, chopped |
| 1 | medium head radicchio, shredded |
| 1 | Belgian endive, sliced lengthwise on an angle |
| ½ cup | shaved Brussels sprouts |
| 8 oz | baby arugula |
| ¾ cup | Concord grapes or any seasonal red table grape, halved and seeded |

# WINTER SALAD WITH SHAVED BRUSSELS SPROUTS, CONCORD GRAPES, & BAKED ROOT VEGETABLE PANCAKES

## TO MAKE THE ROOT VEGETABLE PANCAKES

Preheat the oven to 400°F. Spray a nonstick baking sheet with olive oil cooking spray.

In a large bowl, combine the grated parsnips, carrots, and sweet potatoes, along with the cornstarch and olive oil. Season with salt and pepper and mix well.

Divide the vegetable mixture into 16 equal parts and arrange on the prepared baking sheet. Gently pat the mixture out to make 16 vegetable "silver dollar" pancakes. Roast for 10 minutes then use a spatula to turn the pancakes over. Continue roasting for another 8 to 10 minutes, or until the pancakes are a combination of crisp and tender. Remove the pancakes from the oven but keep them on the baking sheet. Do not turn off the oven, as you will need to reheat them just before serving.

## TO MAKE THE SALAD

In a large bowl, toss together the curly endive, radicchio, Belgian endive, Brussels sprouts, baby arugula, and grapes.

### *fun fact!*

Concord grapes were cultivated in Concord, Massachusetts. They grow very well in the United States, particularly in the Northeast. They are often used in grape jelly and grape juice. Sometimes they are hard to find. If that's the case, you can use another sweet red grape for this recipe.

## DRESSING

| | |
|---|---|
| 2 | lemons, juiced and strained |
| ⅓ cup | extra-virgin olive oil |
| | fine sea salt and freshly ground black pepper |

**SERVES 4**

## TO MAKE THE DRESSING

In a small bowl, whisk together the lemon juice and olive oil. Season with a little salt and pepper. Drizzle the dressing over the salad and toss to coat. Check the seasoning and add salt and pepper if necessary.

Divide the dressed salad among four plates and top each with 4 warm vegetable pancakes.

A favorite salad of ours is, and I quote, "Salad with Bits," meaning a wonderfully crisp salad with a whole bunch of yummy morsels.

This Cobb salad is an entrée-sized salad with tasty treats. Your artist helper of any age can express creativity by carefully arranging the delectable ingredients on top of the richly dressed romaine leaves.

## GORGONZOLA DRESSING

| ½ cup | good-quality mayonnaise |
|---|---|
| ¼ cup | sour cream |
| ¼ cup | buttermilk |
| ½ tsp | Dijon mustard |
| ½ tsp | minced garlic |
| ½ cup | chilled and diced Gorgonzola dolce (young, mild Gorgonzola) |
| 3 tsp | fresh lemon juice |
| | fine sea salt and freshly ground black pepper |

## INGREDIENTS

| 8 oz | cooked turkey or chicken breast, thinly sliced |
|---|---|
| 8 oz | white fontina, mozzarella, Swiss, or other mild, white cheese, thinly sliced |
| 6 oz | salami or mortadella, or smoked bacon, thinly sliced |
| 4 | firm but ripe vine tomatoes |
| 4 | large eggs |
| 1 | ripe but not too soft large avocado |
| 2 | medium hearts romaine lettuce, cut into ½-in pieces |
| 1 bunch | watercress |

**SERVES 4**

# SALAD WITH BITS

## TO MAKE THE DRESSING

Find a good helper to whisk together the mayonnaise, sour cream, buttermilk, and mustard until smooth. Fold in the garlic and Gorgonzola (see Top Tips, page 197). Add the lemon juice, season with salt and pepper, and mix well. Refrigerate your dressing for at least 1 hour before using.

Now get all your salad "bits" together. Once prepared, keep each ingredient separate. Ask the person at your deli to slice the meat and cheese into slices that are ⅛-inch thick. When you're at home, cut the turkey or chicken first into ⅛-inch-wide strips and then cut it again in the opposite direction to create ⅛-inch cubes (professionally, we call this dicing). Cube the cheese in the same way, keeping it separate from the turkey or chicken. Cube the salami or mortadella in the same way, keeping it separate. If you want to use bacon, cook it in a 375°F oven for 10 minutes or until crispy. Strain the bacon and remove any excess fat with a paper towel. Allow the bacon to cool completely and then chop it finely with a sharp knife.

Cut the tomatoes into quarters and remove the seeds. Cut the flesh into ⅛-inch squares.

## HOW TO HARD-BOIL YOUR EGGS

Fill a medium saucepan half full of water and bring to a boil. This tip is very important: Do not add salt! Salt breaks up the egg whites, and when we're boiling an egg, we want to keep it as intact as possible. With a slotted spoon, carefully lower the eggs into

### top tips!

Have you ever had an overcooked hard-boiled egg? Yuck! To avoid overcooking, make sure that you take your hard-boiled egg out of the boiling water and run it under cold water from the sink. Don't put the hard-boiled egg in a bowl of cold water because it will warm up the water and start to cook again!

This recipe calls for 4 hard-boiled eggs. Since you're boiling eggs already, why not make 6 or 8? Refrigerate the extra eggs for a future snack. They will last in your fridge for about a week.

### fun fact!

There's a difference between a pit and a seed. The pit is the shell that contains many seeds. The seed is what actually produces the plant. For the Salad with Bits recipe, for instance, the tomatoes and cucumbers have seeds, while the avocado has a pit.

the boiling water, and reduce the heat to a simmer. Then set your timer for 10 minutes. When you hear the timer alarm, remove the saucepan from the heat, pour off the hot water, and run cold water over the eggs (you can stop the running water and put them in an ice bath that consists of some cold water and a lot of ice).

## HOW TO PEEL YOUR EGGS

Did you know that it's a good idea to peel an egg in water? It makes the shell come away from the egg easier. Have fun doing some underwater peeling.

Completely chill the eggs and then peel them. Once peeled, carefully cut around the yolk with a sharp knife to separate the white from the yolk. Chop the egg whites. Crumble the egg yolks.

Cut the avocado in half and remove the pit. Cut in half again to make 4 quarters. Carefully peel the skin off the avocado. Starting at the wide end of each quarter, cut lengthwise slices, two-thirds of the way toward the narrow end of each quarter. Gently push down on the slices to create avocado fans.

## NOW FOR THE REALLY FUN PART

Place the chopped romaine in a large bowl and add enough dressing to moisten the leaves. Toss your salad and divide it among 4 salad bowls.

Ask your eager helper of any age to arrange the bits around the salad and crown each salad with a small bunch of watercress. Salad with Bits is a visual and gastronomic treat, any time of year!

### top tips!

If you have extra dressing, use what you need for the salad and refrigerate the rest for another time. This dressing is great to use on different salads, a baked potato, or as a dip for raw vegetables. It's long lasting and will keep in the fridge for 2 to 3 weeks.

While avocados are a healthy people food, research has shown that they can be dangerous for certain pets. Avocados contains persin, which "according to studies is potentially toxic to dogs and cats, as well as other animal species such as mice, rats, birds, rabbits, horses, cattle and goats."[3] We mention this so that you and your family can take the necessary precautions to keep the beloved animal member of your family from getting sick.

# Grow Your Very Own Avocado Tree

Growing your own tree is an activity all family members can get excited about. This project combines food, health, science, and wonder. Save the avocado pit from the recipe. Wash off the pit, removing the slimy bits of avocado stuck to it. This can be a fun (or yucky) tactile experience. Once your avocado pit is washed off, find some toothpicks to poke into it. You want to arrange your toothpicks around the equator of the pit. Then fill a bowl with water and submerge the larger part of the pit in it. The toothpicks should be resting on the side of the bowl, serving to keep the larger part of the avocado pit under the water while the more narrow part remains above water. Please be careful here, as the avocado seed may still be slippery and you could stick yourself with a toothpick. Once the toothpicks are balancing on the sides of the bowl, find a place to put it. This can be an area that's sunny but does not have direct sunlight. Make sure to change the water often to keep it fresh. The roots of your plant should begin to sprout from the seed in 2 to 6 weeks. When the roots grow so much that they fill the bowl, transfer your plant to soil in a planter. While this makes a lovely indoor tree, it is unlikely that it will produce avocados. There's a range of indoor temperatures in which avocado plants can thrive. They like heat, but an indoor temperature can range from the 60s up to 85°F. This activity is bonding in and of itself because at the outset, your very young helper will be seeking you out every minute to see if anything has grown. In fact, I found myself checking the pit every day!

**YOUNG HELPERS**

### CREATE A SCIENCE CENTER AT HOME
With your grown-up helper, find a place at home to put the bowl with your avocado seed, somewhere with indirect sunlight. Find a space with room to add other experiments, making this your very own at-home science center.

**PRETEEN + TEEN HELPERS**

### WATCH FOR ROOTS
Wash off the avocado seed. Prepare a pot with soil to move the seed once it has roots.

**GROWN-UP HELPERS**

### FIND A BALANCE FOR YOUR BALANCING ACT
Poke toothpicks around the equator of the avocado pit—the pit is slippery, so be careful not to poke yourself—finding the spot around the center where the toothpicks need to go so that only the bottom of your avocado seed will be immersed in water.

During the summer months, when it's hot and humid, there's a real desire to eat light. This dish is a classic and there's good reason for its timelessness—it's simple, fresh, and delicious. It was created in a small resort village in the Gulf of Naples, the village and island being, of course, Capri. This salad pays homage to the colors of the Italian flag and highlights some of the best ingredients Italy has to offer.

There truly is beauty in simplicity—just a few perfect ingredients, eaten when they are in the prime of their season, and you have a caprese salad. I have introduced a little arugula to this dish to give it another intriguing dimension, which is a good example of our intention to bring new flavors to the family dining table. As we learn to eat and enjoy food, we can, by default, learn to be un-experimental with it. This can result in eating the same foods all the time, which can limit diet and nutrition opportunities. With eating mindfulness, it's important to be experimental, trying many different foods, textures, and flavors to have a varied and balanced diet that makes for a healthy life.

## INGREDIENTS

| | |
|---|---|
| 4 | large ripe vine tomatoes |
| 4 | egg-sized balls of fresh buffalo mozzarella (about 4 oz each) |
| 1 bunch | fresh basil, leaves torn into small pieces |
| 2 oz | baby arugula leaves |
| | extra-virgin olive oil, for drizzling |
| | kosher or coarse sea salt |
| | freshly ground black pepper |
| | aged balsamic vinegar, for drizzling (optional) |

**SERVES 4**

# THE SALAD OF CAPRI

Begin by slicing each tomato and ball of mozzarella into 6 roughly ¼-inch-thick slices. Arrange the slices, alternately the tomato and mozzarella, on 4 plates. Season the tomato and mozzarella with a sprinkle of salt and a couple turns of the pepper mill. Lightly drizzle the olive oil over the salad and add the torn fresh basil leaves.

Allow the salad to sit on your counter at room temperature for 5 to 10 minutes. This helps the flavors marry one another (see Activity: Flavor Experiment, opposite). Just before you serve your delectable creation, add a few leaves of baby arugula on top of the salad and drizzle it with a little aged balsamic vinegar, if using. Happy summer!

## top tips!

Enjoy the Salad of Capri either as a traditional appetizer or as a side for a main course. It will go well with Roast Chicken Legs with Potatoes, Vegetables, and Herbs (page 132) or Broiled Fillet of Chilean Sea Bass or Halibut (page 166).

## fun fact!

For balsamic vinegar, much of the water evaporates during the aging process, giving this traditional Italian vinegar a syrupy consistency and a complex flavor that is delicate and slightly sweet.

We recommend extra-virgin olive oil rather than plain olive oil because it has a deeper flavor profile and because it retains antioxidants and anti-inflammatories.

Did you know that flavor is really about smell and not taste? Do the Flavor Experiment (opposite) to see how cheese at room temperature tastes better. Why do you think this is? Because cheese at room temperature has a more potent smell, which intensifies the flavor.

# Flavor Experiment

The directions for our Salad of Capri include leaving it on your counter for 5 to 10 minutes. You might wonder why this is the case. Can't we just eat it right away? Letting things sit together gives flavors an opportunity to combine with one another. It evens out the tastes and smells so your dish will taste better. Some foods taste better at room temperature. If you take a piece of mozzarella from the fridge and eat it, will it taste different than a piece of mozzarella that's at room temperature? Which slice of mozzarella tastes better? Try below and see!

 **YOUNG HELPERS**

### CONDUCT A FLAVOR EXPERIMENT
Taste a piece of mozzarella cheese that's been in the fridge and taste a piece that's been out of the fridge for 10 minutes. Which tastes better?

**PRETEEN + TEEN HELPERS**

### PARTICIPATE IN A PATIENCE EXPERIMENT
Try a little bit of the salad before you let it sit for 5 to 10 minutes, then try it after. When does it taste best?

 **GROWN-UP HELPERS**

### SAVE YOUR LEFTOVERS
The Salad of Capri shows that letting ingredients sit together can actually improve their taste. The same is true for leftovers. The next time you have leftovers, put them in the fridge to serve at another time. How do they taste? This is a delicious and economical way to reduce food waste. Rustic Tomato and Basil Soup (page 92), Braised Short Rib Stew (page 145), and Meatballs: Fun Forming Food (page 143) are some dishes that taste best when they have time to sit.

This is a restaurant recipe that's really popular, but it's also one of Sabrina's and Izzy's favorites—they love the beet and goat cheese combination. It's architectural, colorful, and quite delicious and has loads of flavor, texture, and eye appeal. And don't forget: beets are a superfood, full of nutrients including magnesium, vitamin C, potassium, and dietary fiber. If you want, you can omit or change ingredients to make this recipe your own. Use feta or mozzarella instead of goat cheese; add pecans or almonds instead of pistachios; mixed greens or romaine can be substituted for arugula; you can use apples or nectarines instead of pears. Go ahead, mix it up!

## INGREDIENTS

| 3 large | red beets, peeled |
| 1 | orange, peeled and juiced (save the peels) |
| 1 | lemon, peeled and juiced (save the peels) |
| ¼ cup | extra-virgin olive oil, plus more for drizzling |
| ¼ cup | red wine vinegar |
| ½ cup | water |
| 1 sprig | fresh thyme, leaves removed |
| 1 | fennel bulb with fronds (see Activity: Reduce Food Waste, Use Your Fennel Fronds, opposite) |
| 1 | pear, ripe but firm |
| 3 oz | baby arugula |
| 8 oz | crumbled goat cheese, room temperature |
| ¼ cup | whole pistachio kernels, lightly roasted and chopped |
| | balsamic vinegar |
| | fine sea salt and freshly ground black pepper |

**SERVES 4**

# ROASTED BEET SALAD

Preheat the oven to 300°F.

Use a mandoline or knife to slice the raw beets. Just please be careful—both kitchen tools can be really sharp (see Fun Fact, opposite). Then lay your beet slices in a 6-x-10-inch baking dish. Mix the orange and lemon juice, olive oil, vinegar, and water, and season with salt. Pour your mixture over the beets. Next spread the orange and lemon peels and thyme on top. Cover the baking dish with aluminum foil and cook your beets in the oven at 300°F until they're soft. This will take between 1 to 2 hours. Test with a toothpick to see if the beets are soft and if so, remove them from the oven and allow them to cool.

Use the mandoline or a sharp knife to finely shave the fennel bulb. Most mandolines also have an additional blade attachment to make thin strips. Attach the additional blade and slice the pear, avoiding the core, to make fine pear strips. In a medium-sized bowl, add the arugula leaves, shaved fennel, half the goat cheese, half of the pistachios, and half of the pear strips. Lightly season them with salt, freshly ground black pepper, a drizzle of extra-virgin olive oil, and a splash of balsamic vinegar. Now lightly toss.

Divide the remaining goat cheese and place in the middle of four 10-inch plates. Cover each portion of goat cheese with three slices of beets. Divide the mixed salad and place on top. Then lay the remaining sliced beets around each portion of salad, so that it looks like a volcano.

Top your salad with the remaining pear strips and fennel fronds. Sprinkle the rest of the pistachios around the plate and drizzle the beets with a little olive oil.

## fun fact!

Cutting fruit and vegetables into very fine strips—a quarter of the width and depth of a matchstick—is called julienne. There are a number of ways to achieve a julienne. One is to cut by hand with a sharp knife. Another is to use a mandoline slicer (see Fun Fact on the next page). A third way is to use a julienne y-shaped peeler. This peeler has thin teeth attached. When you peel your slices, the teeth cut them into strips.

## fun fact!

A mandoline slicer is a vital piece of equipment in any professional kitchen, but it's also really useful in a home kitchen. A mandoline can be used for many things, like slicing vegetables and salad ingredients super thin, slicing hard cheeses like Parmesan into shavings, and even cutting fruit like apples into thin slices that you can slowly bake to make apple chips for a snack. There are many types available either in the store or online. They range in price from the most economical plastic kind to the more expensive professional stainless-steel versions. A note of caution: be careful, as this kitchen gadget is strictly for grown-ups. I have been nicked more than once by its super sharp blades.

# Reduce Food Waste: Use Your Fennel Fronds

Sometimes we unknowingly throw out parts of a food item that can be eaten. In the spirit of eating mindfulness, we can reduce food waste by knowing more about the makeup of the ingredients we're eating. With this recipe, we might have assumed that fennel fronds need to be thrown out—a fair assumption, as the fronds look like weeds on the top of the fennel bulb. However, this part of the fennel is edible. Fennel fronds add flavor, can decorate your creation, and can even be used to tickle someone!

 YOUNG HELPERS

### TICKLE
Tickle your grown-up helper with the fennel frond. What does a fennel frond taste like?

 PRETEEN + TEEN HELPERS

### DECORATE
Decorate your roasted beet salad with fennel fronds. What other dishes would benefit from them?

 GROWN-UP HELPERS

### IDENTIFY
Identify parts of foods that can be used to extend eating mindfulness. We may throw out parts of foods when, in fact, those discarded bits are usable. For instance, we might discard the peelings created from preparing carrots, onion, or garlic. These can actually be saved to make a vegetable stock (vegetables, water, seasoning, herbs) as a base for soup. Freeze your peelings and collect more as you cook. They'll last in your freezer for a month. When you have enough collected, defrost to make your vegetable stock.

This recipe invites everyone to explore making a different type of salad. The classic salad as we know it—with lettuce, tomatoes, and cucumbers—gets replaced with lentils, chickpeas, and figs. This may be one of those "yuck or yum" moments when you and your helper determine if this new kind of salad is appealing to the palate or not. Whatever the outcome, it's the exploration and trying of something new that's important!

## DRESSING

| ½ tsp | ground cumin |
| ½ tsp | Spanish paprika |
| ¼ cup | fresh lemon juice |
| ½ tsp | fine sea salt |
| ¼ tsp | freshly ground black pepper |
| ¼ cup | extra-virgin olive oil |
| | zest of 1 lemon |

## INGREDIENTS

| ½ cup | brown lentils, rinsed |
| 1 stick | cinnamon, broken into 2 pieces |
| 4 tsp | fine sea salt, divided |
| ¼ cup | dried chickpeas |
| ½ Tbsp | extra-virgin olive oil |
| 1 cup | peeled and diced carrots |
| 1 cup | peeled and diced red onion |
| 6 | dried figs, sliced |
| ⅓ cup | very thinly sliced fresh mint leaves |
| 3 Tbsp | chopped fresh cilantro leaves |

**SERVES 4**

# MOROCCAN-STYLE LENTIL, CHICKPEA, & VEGETABLE SALAD

## TO MAKE THE DRESSING

In a small pan over medium heat, warm the cumin and paprika, gently stirring, for a few minutes, or until very fragrant. Transfer the spices to a large bowl and add the lemon juice, salt, and pepper. Whisk in the olive oil and then stir in the lemon zest.

## TO MAKE THE SALAD

Place the lentils in a medium saucepan with enough water to cover them by 2 inches. Add half of the cinnamon stick and bring to a boil. Reduce the heat and simmer gently for 15 minutes. Stir in 2 tsp salt and continue simmering until the lentils are just tender but not at all mushy. This usually takes 5 to 10 minutes more. Drain well, remove the cinnamon stick, and set aside.

Repeat the same process for the chickpeas, using the remaining half of the cinnamon stick and the other 2 tsp salt. Simmer the chickpeas for 30 to 40 minutes in total, or until tender. Drain well, remove the cinnamon stick, and set aside.

Meanwhile, heat the olive oil in a large skillet over medium heat. Add the carrots and red onion and cook stirring occasionally, for 10 to 15 minutes, or until tender. Remove from the heat and set aside.

Add the lentils, chickpeas, carrots, red onion, and figs to the dressing and stir until well combined. Just before serving, add the finishing touch by mixing in the mint and cilantro. Taste and see what your palate tells you.

### top tips!

It's a balancing act to cook beans long enough to make sure they're cooked but not so long that they become mushy. To see if your beans are ready, remove one of them when you think they're almost cooked. Quickly run it under cold water and try it. The texture will tell you if you need to cook your beans more or if they're ready. If the bean is hard and crunchy, it's not cooked yet and needs more time.

This delicious salad dressing can be used on all types of salads and is so easy to make! It has a hearty maple flavor at its core and is delicious during any season.

## INGREDIENTS

| | |
|---|---|
| ½ cup | maple syrup |
| ¼ cup | red wine vinegar |
| ¼ cup | balsamic vinegar |
| ¼ cup | light soy sauce |
| 1 Tbsp | Dijon mustard |
| 1 Tbsp | minced shallot |
| 2 tsp | crushed garlic |
| 1 cup | extra-virgin olive oil |
| 1 cup | vegetable oil |
| | fine sea salt and freshly ground black pepper |

**YIELDS 3 CUPS**

# MAPLE SALAD DRESSING

In a blender, blend together the maple syrup, red wine vinegar, balsamic vinegar, soy sauce, mustard, shallot, and garlic. While blending, slowly drizzle in the olive oil and vegetable oil. This will create an emulsion (an oil suspended in a liquid). Season with salt and pepper. Keep your dressing in the refrigerator for up to a month and use as the perfect accompaniment with your favorite fresh salad.

## top tips!

To crush garlic, peel the garlic clove, put it onto a cutting board, lie the flat edge of a large kitchen knife against it, and then push down hard. Finish by chopping it.

Our Maple Salad Dressing is versatile and can be used on our Spring Salad (page 50) and Winter Salad with Shaved Brussels Sprouts, Concord Grapes, and Baked Root Vegetable Pancakes (page 57).

Remove your Maple Salad Dressing from the refrigerator at least an hour before using it. This is because olive oil solidifies at low temperatures and it needs to be in liquid form to use as a dressing.

# Taste as You Go

Tasting as you go is so important. It allows you to get to know what tastes good to you. It's easy to add a little more of an ingredient to make it just right, but it's really hard, and sometimes impossible, to take an ingredient out. So taste as you go, adding seasonings and ingredients to reach the right taste point for your palate.

**YOUNG HELPERS**

### ADD INGREDIENTS TO EXPLORE YOUR TASTE
After your grown-up helper blends the Maple Salad Dressing ingredients, slowly add the salt and pepper, trying the dressing as you go. With your grown-up helper, explore these questions: "What tastes good to me? Which combinations work? How do I know when to stop adding an ingredient?" (Hint: Because your creation tastes great as it is!)

**PRETEEN + TEEN HELPERS**

### APPRAISE YOUR TASTE
Experiment with adding the salt and pepper, determining how much is just enough for your taste buds.

**GROWN-UP HELPERS**

### CULTIVATE EATING MINDFULNESS BY DEVELOPING YOUR SENSE OF TASTE
Explore taste with your helpers, adding the seasonings to see how much of each one tastes right for them and for you. Taste the dressing before adding salt, before adding pepper. What happens after you add these seasonings?

# We Can Make Salad Dressing and Do Something We Never Thought We Could

I bet you've never made salad dressing before. We tend to rely on the many varieties available to us in the store, many of them quite tasty, some not so much. Why is it that we don't think about salad dressing as something we can actually make? Like pancakes or hamburgers? It's easy to get in a rut and think that things are out of reach, that they won't change, and will always stay the same. And yet, these salad dressing recipes show us we can do something we haven't done before—and it can be delicious, healthy, and fun, too.

**YOUNG HELPERS**

### DO SOMETHING YOU NEVER THOUGHT YOU COULD

Learning how to write can be really hard. There are uppercase letters and lowercase letters. How do you keep it all straight? One way to practice writing is to make a sight word box. Sight words are those words that appear a lot when we read—words like a, the, and of. One pre- and early reading strategy is to teach kids how to automatically recognize sight words. This allows them to immediately know those words when reading, which helps when trying to comprehend other words on the page that may appear less frequently. Get a large cardboard box (perhaps one that came in the mail with a delivery) and write a sight word on it each day. Not only does this help you practice writing sight words but also, when you're trying to write something out, you can look to your box for the correct spelling of the sight words you need to make your sentence.

**PRETEEN + TEEN HELPERS**

### REACH FOR SOMETHING DIFFERENT

Maybe you're bored and every day feels like the same old thing. Is there something you've been wanting to do but aren't sure how to achieve it? Something new like learning how to play basketball or being in the school play? Talk with your grown-up helper about your ideas. Together you can think about who to talk to, like a coach or drama teacher, to figure out next steps.

**GROWN-UP HELPERS**

### BE INTENTIONAL AS A PERSON AND A PARENT

As a grown-up helper, take time to listen to what your young helpers are telling you about their dreams and aspirations. As you listen, you might want to share an experience from your own life that relates to the challenge they're talking about. Just like a salad doesn't have to have lettuce, life doesn't have to be categorized or boxed in. As we listen and share, we can think about exploring outside of those boxes.

# CHAPTER 4

# Light Lunches

*Start the Conversation by Not Starting It*

Being honest and open about salad and its ingredients shows our kids that we're about choice, not deception. It says we're open to engaging in a conversation about healthy food choices. This involves listening to when our kids tell us they don't want to eat something and also hearing when they talk about the foods they do want to eat. It involves perspective-taking to try to be in their shoes and understand what's going on with them. All of this sounds like what we want to be doing in our family conversations: talking openly with our kids. Lunch provides a wonderful time to do this.

The deceptive approach hides healthy foods in recipes. But we wouldn't want to hide decisions about life situations, would we? The recent college admissions scandal showed the world this is just not a good idea. When we engage in honest conversation, we demonstrate our acceptance of the reality we're talking about. Honest conversations, like being open about the ingredients in our food, involve an element of mutual trust. As parents/guardians/caregivers, we trust that our kids will understand why it's important to let them know what they're eating. At the same time, we have to trust ourselves to take this route, knowing that our kids may say they actually don't like the ingredients we've just told them they're about to eat. Through this type of honest exchange, we commit to an open, transparent conversation to get a better sense of where everyone's at.

Lunch is not characterized by the rush of the morning. It doesn't come at the end of the day like dinner, when people are tired or have homework to do. Lunch on a weekend or holiday provides a wonderful opportunity to connect. This chapter is all about starting those conversations while making lunch together.

"So how do I do this?" we ask ourselves. Maybe your toddler doesn't say much about preschool or your school-age child suddenly seems too busy. Your teen might ignore you most of the day until asking for something. All of these scenarios leave us in a bind about how to start the conversation—so don't start it. Has any parent consistently sat down and said to their child, "Let's talk. What's going on?" and received a satisfying response?

I challenge us to do something different. Instead of trying to have a conversation, prepare lunch together. Engaging in an activity can be a catalyst for talking. Doing something together with our helpers may easily translate into learning more about bits and pieces of their lives. The conversation doesn't need to be lengthy, and it usually doesn't take long to connect.

"But is that deceptive? Am I tricking my child into talking to me?" Not at all. In fact, by being ready and watchful of our child's cues, we are letting them make the choice about when they want to share and what they want to talk about. We can even say to a helper of any age, "Hey, while we're making lunch, I'm here to listen if there's something you want to talk about." And then leave it at that. After all, you're just making grilled cheese.

For toddlers and young helpers, so much of what gets communicated happens through play. Play symbolizes what they are experiencing. It's their way of communicating. The recipes in this book are all about play. Make cooking with your young helper a game. Organize a scavenger hunt to find the recipe ingredients for Chicken Wraps. Have a race to see who can build their BLTE first. There are many ways to incorporate fun in the kitchen.

School-age children go through a lot. Each year they're adjusting to a new grade, new teachers, and new academic requirements. They're learning how to get used to the school day and develop skills like reading, writing, and math. Cooking together gives your helper a chance to decompress, to do nothing that's evaluated while enjoying the security and comforts of home. By not starting a direct conversation, we can learn about their day through questions that relate cooking to their life experiences. For instance, we can ask what preparing a certain dish reminds them of. "Did you do counting today in math like we're counting these Chicken Wraps?"

Olliver has always loved school. His description for preschool was "school party." When Olliver started kindergarten he liked the idea of being with big kids at school. The reality, however, was that he really struggled with the separation from home and family. The transition from his small neighborhood preschool to a big school housing kindergarten through eighth grade was drastic. Because of COVID-19, kindergartners had to be dropped off at the front entrance and make the long trek up the stairs to their classrooms on their own. The need for quick goodbyes to keep the line moving made the departure even more abrupt.

Preparing food together in the kitchen is a way that Olliver and I can reconnect after school. As we stir and chop and assemble, eventually Olliver will say something like, "I'm sad and I'm happy."

"What are you sad about and what are you happy about?" I'll ask.

"Which do you want to hear first?" he'll ask back with a smile.

"Tell me about what's sad first."

"I'm sad that I didn't see you the whole day. I missed you," he'll say.

"I missed you, too, sweetheart. It's really hard not seeing each other for so long."

"How many minutes was I gone?" he'll ask.

"Well, school is 6 hours and 20 minutes, so that means you've been gone 380 minutes."

"That's a lot of minutes."

"What are you happy about?"

"I'm happy that I'm home and you're with me."

"I'm happy about that, too."

And then just like that—he'll start to play with his toys that are in the kitchen or busy himself with our food preparations.

Not starting the conversation while preparing food together can help you meet your kids at their pace and when they're ready to speak with you.

Having this sense of control and decision-making about when to share is particularly important for preteens and teens as well. Consider the following situation that parents, guardians, caregivers, and family members of preteens and teens can relate to:

A day of celebration isn't turning out as hoped, and your teen is at home and feeling sad in spite of having made an elaborate plan to be elsewhere. It seems things changed at the last minute.

"Let's cook something together," you offer sheepishly. You know doing something with mom isn't going to cut it. It's a powerless feeling when you can't make everything better for your kids. Together you start to prepare something to eat in the kitchen. It feels like that's all the two of you can do—make something together in the midst of your child's sadness.

As your teen starts to mix the ingredients really quickly, you notice the tears. Your teen shares the sense that something was going on at school, something that all the kids seemed to be talking about. Your child takes pride in being a sleuth and decides to investigate what the deal is.

As much as we may want to know what's going on, finding out is really painful. Your teen's sleuthing leads to social media, where posts by kids in the class are found. They're together, at a classmate's house, celebrating. Your child is devastated. You are, too. You feel so bad and so angry that your child would be left out. The school has a rule that everyone must be invited to events—and, if that's not feasible, limit them to just a couple of classmates.

"Do you want me to talk with the school?" is the only thing you can think of to say.

"No," your child says through the tears. "That will make it worse."

"How are you going to deal with this?" you ask.

"I don't know. How I always do I guess, just business as usual."

In that moment, being in the kitchen together is like a safe haven, a cocoon where you can both heal the wounds before moving outward. Being there is the only thing you feel you can do in that moment.

The focus on providing a safe haven for our loved ones continues in the following chapter. As parents, we have had or will have many difficult conversations with our children. These conversations might address issues related to loss, illness, sadness, and anxiety. Chapter Five encourages us to extend ourselves to engage in these conversations, even though they can be difficult and painful. The hope is that in doing so, we model care and support in the face of sadness. This lets our kids know that they can come to us to talk about the hard stuff.

"What? A recipe for a grilled cheese sandwich?" I hear you cry. Does something so simple and quick deserve its own recipe? Yes, it does. Simple and quick it may be but do it well and it will be a light lunch you and your family go back to again and again.

There are a few things to keep in mind. Melting cheeses like cheddar and Swiss lend themselves perfectly to this sandwich because they have a strong flavor. For the best results, buy a whole block of cheese and grate it yourself. Use good bread, something artisanal, perhaps sourdough, whole wheat, or your family's favorite. And use unsalted butter—the flavor is so much nicer than oil. You can also perk up your grilled cheese by adding chopped scallions, sautéed peppers or onions, or finely chopped jalapeño, to name a few options.

### INGREDIENTS

| | |
|---|---|
| 8 slices | **good bread** |
| 8 Tbsp | **unsalted butter, room temperature** |
| 3 cups | **grated sharp cheddar cheese** |
| ⅔ cup | **washed and sliced scallions** |
| | **raw peeled baby carrots (as an optional side dish)** |

**SERVES 4**

# GRILLED CHEESE

Butter all 16 sides of your 8 slices of bread, each with ½ Tbsp of butter. Make 2 sandwiches at a time. Or, if you have 2 large nonstick pans, make all 4 sandwiches at the same time.

Warm a large nonstick pan over medium heat. Place 2 slices of bread in the pan and allow them to get just a little brown. Remove the slices and repeat with 2 more slices of bread. Flip the bread over in the pan and top each with ¾ cup of cheese, flattening it out into an even layer that covers the entire slice of bread. Sprinkle with scallions. Arrange 1 of the pre-toasted slices of bread, toasted side down, on top of each. Use a spatula to press your sandwiches down to help the bottom slices turn golden brown, about 2 to 3 minutes. Flip the sandwiches over and press this side down too. Cook this other side 2 to 3 minutes as well or until golden brown. Remove your grilled cheese sandwiches from the pan and cut them diagonally. Repeat to make 2 more sandwiches. Serve with raw baby carrots or our delicious Rustic Tomato and Basil Soup (page 92), which is great for dipping.

### *fun fact!*

We recommend buying a block of cheese to grate yourself for the best taste. Most pre-grated cheeses have an added coating to prevent clumping or sticking. Also, when cheese is exposed to air, which is more likely to happen with grated cheese, its flavor is reduced. Home grated cheese tastes more like cheese and has no additives.

# Have a Cozy
# Movie Afternoon

Grilled Cheese and Rustic Tomato and Basil Soup (page 92) are the perfect pair for a cozy movie afternoon. Enjoy dipping your grilled cheese into the tomato soup. It doesn't get better than that!

**YOUNG HELPERS**

**GET READY FOR SHOWTIME**
Pick a movie to watch with your grown-up helper. Get the bowls and plates ready and set up the place where you'll eat.

**PRETEEN + TEEN HELPERS**

**START THE CONVERSATION WITH A MOVIE**
Pick a movie that reflects something you're going through or that you've been thinking about. Sometimes it's hard to talk with grown-up helpers about experiences or feelings. A relatable movie can be a catalyst to start a conversation about what's been going on for you.

**GROWN-UP HELPERS**

**SET THE GROUNDWORK**
Pick a movie that reflects a theme you want to talk about with your helper. If you think your helper is going through something, but you aren't sure how to bring it up—or if you should even raise your concern—pick a movie that reflects what you think is going on. See if it sparks a conversation with your helper.

I have to thank our daughters for this recipe. Sabrina and Izzy love to make this quick and easy lunch and have made it their own with the addition of cherry tomatoes, red onion, and everything bagel seasoning.

For this dish to be its best, you need perfectly ripe avocados. If they are too hard or overripe it just won't be the same, so take the time to select the best avocados. When you hold them in your hand, lightly squeeze them. If they feel like a golf ball, they're not ripe. If they feel like a spongy ball, they're too ripe. But if they feel like a tennis ball, they should be just right!

## INGREDIENTS

| | |
|---|---|
| 2 | large ripe avocados |
| 2 | small limes, juiced |
| 4 | thick bread slices, toasted |
| 1 | small red onion, diced |
| 1 cup | sliced cherry tomatoes |
| 2 Tbsp | everything bagel seasoning |
| 2 Tbsp | extra-virgin olive oil |
| | fine sea salt and freshly ground black pepper |

**SERVES 4**

# AVOCADO TOAST

With a sharp knife, cut around the avocado, all the way to the pit. Hold the avocado in both hands and twist the halves to separate them. With a spoon, scoop out the avocado flesh and place it in a small bowl. Discard the pit and the skin. Season the avocado with the lime juice and a little salt and pepper, then mash it with a fork until smooth.

Spread the mashed avocado on your 4 slices of toast. Top each slice with red onion, cherry tomatoes, everything bagel seasoning, and a drizzle of olive oil.

Serve immediately with a knife, fork, and napkin!

### top tips!

If you can only find underripe avocados, take them home and put them on your countertop in a closed paper bag. They should ripen quickly and be ready to eat in a day or two.

# Watch for Ripeness

When food is ripe, it's ready to be eaten or picked as a crop, but in our modern farming system, produce is often harvested before it's ripe. This is done to offset transportation time and to increase shelf life at the store. Therefore, being aware of when something is ripe is an important skill for recipe prepping. With our avocado toast, we want to make sure the avocados are ripe enough to eat, otherwise the recipe won't taste good. We can use our senses to know if something is ripe. Our tactile sense helps us feel if the avocado is soft enough to eat, while our sight guides us once we have opened the avocado. With our eyes, we can see if the avocado is a solid, rich green color throughout. If, however, the avocado is brown or has dark veins, that's not ideal.

 **YOUNG HELPERS**

### TEST FOR RIPENESS
Feel the avocado to see if it's ripe. Is it soft? Hard? Remember, if it feels like a tennis ball, it's ripe and ready to eat!

**PRETEEN + TEEN HELPERS**

### REDUCE FOOD WASTE
Ripen your awareness to reduce food waste. So often we end up wasting fruits and vegetables because we forget about them, and they get so ripe that they begin to rot. Go through your shelves and fridge to locate your fruits and vegetables. Put the ripe and almost ripe items where you can see them to help you remember to use them before they go bad.

 **GROWN-UP HELPERS**

### PLAY THE RIPENESS GAME
Go through your pantry and refrigerator and take out your fruits and vegetables. With your helper, test out each one to see which are ripe. As you identify the ripe items, figure out a way to use them in your meal planning.

This lunch is a winner in so many ways. First, it's yummy. Second, it's easy to prepare. Third, it's versatile. Fourth, it's fun to make. And fifth, it's a great way to use up those bits and pieces in the fridge. There are really no hard and fast rules about what to wrap in your wrap, but the following recipe provides a guideline for many delicious lunchtimes to come.

The chicken you use for this recipe can be leftover roasted chicken with the skin removed and the meat shredded. You can also sprinkle three skinless chicken breasts with some chili powder or taco seasoning, cook over medium heat for five to six minutes per side, and shred with two forks.

Have a blast at constructing and rolling these wraps. Also check out the fridge to see what can be used up, like black beans, cooked rice, sweet corn kernels, avocado, cooked bacon, and lettuce.

**INGREDIENTS**

| | |
|---|---|
| 2 Tbsp | good-quality mayonnaise |
| 2 Tbsp | sour cream |
| 1 tsp | onion powder |
| 4 | flour tortillas |
| 3 cups | cooked and shredded chicken |
| 1 | tomato, chopped |
| 2 Tbsp | chopped fresh cilantro leaves |
| ⅓ cup | freshly grated cheddar cheese |
| ½ Tbsp | vegetable oil |

**SERVES 4**

# CHICKEN WRAPS

In a small bowl, mix the mayonnaise, sour cream, and onion powder. Set aside.

On a clean surface, lay out the tortillas. Arrange about a quarter of the chicken lengthwise in the center of each tortilla, leaving about 1½ inches on each side. Top the chicken with tomato, cilantro, the mayonnaise sauce, and cheese. Fold the sides over the chicken filling and then roll up each wrap into a huge almond shape.

Warm a large grill pan or sauté pan over medium heat. Brush the pan with a little vegetable oil and then add the wraps. Gently heat the wraps for a few minutes, then give them about a third of a turn. Heat for another couple of minutes and then give them another third of a turn to warm the rest.

Remove your wraps from the heat, cut them in half, and serve with The Best Guacamole Ever (page 109). Delicious!

# Host a Refrigerator Scavenger Hunt

**SEARCH AND ADD**
Look through your fridge to see what you can add to your chicken wrap.

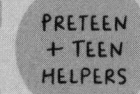

**LIST AND LOOK**
Make a list of potential chicken wrap fillings, then look through your fridge to find them. This is a way to use food that you might have otherwise forgotten about. It also allows you to recycle, rather than waste food.

**ORGANIZE A FRIDGE SCAVENGER HUNT**
Create a scavenger hunt in your fridge. Start by making a list of items that can go with your chicken wraps and are in your fridge. Read out your list to young helpers that can't read yet and ask them to go on a refrigerator scavenger hunt to find them. Give the list to your preteen/teen helpers to find the items. Your scavenger hunt prevents food waste as you and your helpers seek out the items in the fridge that can be used for your yummy creation.

Everyone knows what a BLT is, we've even heard of a BLTA (bacon, lettuce, tomato, and avocado) but what is a BLTE? Bacon, Lettuce, Tomato, and—Egg!

Scrambled eggs make a wonderful creamy addition to this classic sandwich. Scramble the eggs while you're cooking the bacon, and everything will come together perfectly at the same time. I have also used baby arugula in this recipe. This spicy, peppery leaf adds another terrific flavor dimension, as long as your young helper is game. If not, you can use the more traditional romaine or butter lettuce, but older and grown-up helpers might really enjoy this variation.

As for bread, this is such a personal choice. I prefer a hearty, nutty multigrain loaf, whereas the rest of my family leans toward more conventional white bread. I'll leave it up to you!

## INGREDIENTS

| | |
|---|---|
| 2 | ripe vine tomatoes, sliced |
| 8 strips | smoked bacon |
| 3 | large eggs |
| 1 Tbsp | unsalted butter |
| 2 Tbsp | sour cream |
| 4 Tbsp | good-quality mayonnaise |
| 4 | medium-thick bread slices, toasted |
| 2 oz | baby arugula |
| | fine sea salt and freshly ground black pepper |

**SERVES 2**

# BLTE

Season the tomato slices with a little salt and pepper. Set aside.

Cook the bacon in a large skillet over a medium heat for about 3 minutes per side, or until brown and crispy. Remove the bacon from the skillet and place on a paper towel to remove any excess fat.

Break the eggs into a small bowl and whisk them with a little salt and pepper. In a small nonstick skillet, melt the butter over low to medium heat. Add the eggs and cook, stirring occasionally with a wooden spoon or heat-resistant rubber spatula, until they are set but still loose. Remove them from the heat, add the sour cream, and gently mix.

See the Activity opposite to create your sandwich.

# Build Your Food

Sandwiches provide a wonderful way to express your creativity. When you build your food, you layer your favorite ingredients to make a tasty treat. For your BLTE, start by spreading 1 Tbsp of mayonnaise onto 1 side of each slice of toast. Next, layer 2 toast slices with 4 tomato slices, followed by 4 bacon strips, half the scrambled eggs, and half the arugula. Cover with another slice of toast, mayo-side down. Gently press down on the sandwiches, then use a serrated knife to cut them diagonally in half. Serve immediately. Our Spring Salad (page 50) makes for a great BLTE side dish.

**YOUNG HELPERS**

**STACK YOUR SANDWICH**
Stack your sandwich items on the bread. What order do you prefer?

**PRETEEN + TEEN HELPERS**

**CREATE A SANDWICH TOWER**
Stack your ingredients in different ways. Is one way easier to eat than another?

**GROWN-UP HELPERS**

**HAVE A BUILD-YOUR-FOOD RACE**
Who can arrange their BLTE ingredients to build their sandwich first? The winner doesn't have to clean up!

Whole wheat quesadillas are a great light lunch option, because they are delicious and can be made quickly. In addition to our list, you can use a wide variety of ingredients, odds and ends, and leftovers to fill them. Tortillas are a versatile staple to keep in the fridge and perfect for making easy lunches, snacks, and even dinners. You can also use any spare tortillas to make wraps for another light lunchtime.

## INGREDIENTS

| | |
|---|---|
| 1 Tbsp | vegetable oil |
| 1 | small white onion, finely diced |
| 4 oz | white mushrooms, sliced |
| 1 lb | ground beef |
| ½ tsp | chili powder |
| ½ tsp | ground cumin |
| 1 | lime, juiced |
| 8 | 7-in whole-wheat tortillas |
| 1½ cups | chopped or grated queso fresco |
| 2 Tbsp | chopped fresh cilantro leaves |
| 4 Tbsp | sour cream |
| | fine sea salt and freshly ground black pepper |
| 1 | jalapeño, chopped (optional) |

**SERVES 4**

# WHOLE WHEAT BEEF & VEGETABLE QUESADILLAS

Warm the vegetable oil in a large nonstick skillet over medium heat. Add the onion and cook for about 5 minutes, or until translucent (see Fun Fact below). Add the mushrooms and jalapeño, if using, and cook for 2 minutes more. Add the beef, chili powder, cumin, and a little salt and pepper and cook, stirring, for 6 to 8 minutes, or until the meat is no longer pink. Remove the skillet from the heat, pour off any excess fat, and place the meat mixture in a bowl. Mix in the lime juice.

Clean out the skillet and return it to medium heat. Add a tortilla and spread with a quarter of the beef mixture, a quarter of the cheese, and ½ Tbsp of the cilantro. Cover with a second tortilla and cook for about 3 minutes, or until the bottom tortilla is light brown. Remove from the heat and place a large plate over the skillet. Hold your hand on the plate and carefully invert the skillet so the quesadilla falls onto the plate. Slide the quesadilla back into the skillet and cook for 2 to 3 more minutes, or until the bottom is light brown. Remove your quesadilla from the skillet and keep warm. Repeat to make 3 more quesadillas.

Cut your quesadillas into wedges and serve with sour cream and The Best Guacamole Ever (page 109).

## *fun fact!*

Translucent means you can't fully see through something, but you can see light through it.

# Sweat Your Onions

Onions are at the heart of many dishes. They provide flavor, texture, and a wonderful aroma. But preparing onions can be tricky. Slicing them leads to tears. They also cook very quickly and can easily burn in your frying pan. Timing and the use of your senses are key to cooking onions just right. The first thing you'll see when you cook onions is that they begin to sweat. Onions are 89 percent water so when you heat them, they start to release their moisture, giving them a sweaty look. If you continue to cook your onions after they're sweaty, they will gradually become translucent. As you cook them further, they'll start to release their natural sugars, which will begin to caramelize, turning the onions brown.

YOUNG HELPERS

### LET YOUR NOSE GUIDE YOU
Use your nose to guess when the onions are cooked and ready. How long does it take?

PRETEEN + TEEN HELPERS

### GET YOUR TIMING JUST RIGHT
Watch as you stir your onions to make sure they are cooked enough but not overcooked. Let your senses guide you. You know your onions are ready when you see them become translucent. If you push them with a spoon, they'll be softer. They won't have the same resistance as a raw onion. Your onions will also smell sweet when they're ready. This differs from the acrid smell they'll have if they're burned.

GROWN-UP HELPERS

### SHARE AN ONION OBSERVATION
For this activity, you and your helper can explore the properties of the onion. See how it transforms into a multilayered vegetable as you slice it. Then start to cook the onion. Show your helper (be careful to not get too close to the stove) how it turns from a solid, dry ingredient into a moist, sweaty food and becomes translucent as you continue cooking it.

This delicious sandwich is healthy and easy to make. It also introduces a new skill: making chipotle mayonnaise. We hope you gain additional confidence in the kitchen by being able to make a special kind of sauce that makes your sandwich taste great.

## INGREDIENTS

| | |
|---|---|
| 3 Tbsp | extra-virgin olive oil |
| 1 | lime, juiced |
| ⅓ tsp | Cajun seasoning |
| 1 lb | boneless, skinless chicken breasts, trimmed of fat |
| 8 slices | artisan multigrain bread |
| 4 | large romaine leaves |
| 2 | beefsteak tomatoes, each cut into 4 slices |
| 4 slices | pepper jack cheese |
| 1 | avocado, sliced |

## CHIPOTLE MAYONNAISE

| | |
|---|---|
| 2 | chipotle chiles in adobo |
| ½ cup | good-quality mayonnaise |
| ¼ cup | sour cream |
| ¼ tsp | smoked paprika |

**SERVES 4**

# SEVEN GRAIN SANDWICH WITH CAJUN GRILLED CHICKEN, PEPPER JACK CHEESE, & CHIPOTLE MAYO

In a shallow bowl, whisk together the olive oil, lime juice, and Cajun seasoning. Set aside.

Have fun placing the chicken breasts between pieces of wax paper and lightly pounding them with a meat tenderizer or a rolling pin. Pounding the chicken breasts makes them a little thinner and gives a more consistent thickness so they'll cook evenly. Place the chicken breasts in the Cajun seasoning mixture and turn them to coat with the marinade. Cover and refrigerate for about 15 minutes.

While the chicken is marinating, chop your chipotle peppers finely. Put in a small bowl, add the mayonnaise, sour cream, and paprika and whisk well until fully combined. Cover and refrigerate.

Remove the chicken from the marinade and discard the excess marinade.

Heat your grill to high then place the chicken directly on the grates and cook for about 8 minutes per side, or until fully cooked through. If you have a food thermometer, the temperature at the center of the chicken should be 165°F. Remove the chicken from the grill and let it rest for a few minutes.

While the chicken is resting, lightly grill your sliced bread.

Spread some chipotle mayo on each slice of grilled bread. Layer 4 slices with the lettuce, tomato, chicken, cheese, and avocado then top with another slice of grilled bread (see Activity: Build Your Food, page 81).

We first made this recipe with our girls when they were about five and seven years old. All you have to do is take an avocado, slice it in half, remove the pit, sprinkle it with a little salt, and serve. Everyone loves scooping the fruit out of the skin when eating this healthy, nutritious light lunch or snack. Best of all, you only need two ingredients to make your boat.

**INGREDIENTS**

| 2 | avocados |
|---|---|
| 2 pinches | **fine sea salt** |

**SERVES 2**

# AVOCADO BOATS

For directions on how to cut your avocado in half, see the Avocado Toast recipe (page 76). Once you have two halves of the avocado, hold the half containing the pit in your non-dominant hand (e.g., if you're right-handed, hold it in your left hand).

Please be careful not to stab your hand. (There was a condition in the United Kingdom called "avocado hand" because so many people hurt themselves while trying to remove avocado pits.)

Being careful—and we recommend using a fork rather than a knife for safety (although still take precautions)—skewer the pit and twist it so it releases from the avocado. If this feels too risky, an alternative is to slice the avocado in half around the pit, separating the two halves. Then scoop out the pit with a spoon. You now have two halves of avocado, which represent your two boats. Season the flesh of the avocado with a sprinkle of fine sea salt and dig in or top with your favorite filling. The following two recipes, Egg Salad with Chive, and Tuna Salad, make great fillings to float your boat! But you can improvise and experiment with whatever you think will taste good.

You can also make sandwiches with these fillings. You can serve egg or tuna salad on a good quality bread, including multigrain, whole wheat, sourdough, or even an English muffin or a bagel, depending on what you have available or what you're in the mood to eat.

For avocado boats or sandwiches.

## INGREDIENTS

| | |
|---|---|
| 8 | large eggs |
| ½ cup | good-quality mayonnaise |
| ¼ cup | chopped fresh chives |
| 1 tsp | Dijon mustard |
| | fine sea salt and freshly ground black pepper |

## FOR SANDWICH

| | |
|---|---|
| 8 slices | bread |

**SERVES 4**

# EGG SALAD WITH CHIVES

See pages 59 and 60 for how to hard-boil and peel an egg.

Place your peeled, hard-boiled eggs in the refrigerator for about an hour to make sure they are absolutely cold. After an hour, chop the eggs and put them in a bowl. Stir in the mayonnaise, chives, and mustard. Season with salt and pepper and stir once more.

### TO MAKE AN EGG SALAD AVOCADO BOAT

Scoop your egg salad into the cavity that was left from having removed your avocado pit. You are now ready to eat this yummy, healthy lunch or snack.

### TO MAKE AN EGG SALAD SANDWICH

Lay out 4 slices of bread on your cutting board. Divide your egg salad onto each of the 4 slices. Spread out the filling and top with another slice of bread. Cut in half and serve.

## top tips!

It's really unpleasant to crunch down on a forgotten piece of eggshell while enjoying your egg salad. A good way to make sure there's no shell on the egg is to run your finger over the surface of the peeled egg. Another tip is to rinse the peeled egg under cold running water.

The phrase "bring the water back to a boil" means that after you add an ingredient to boiling water, you return it to a boil. For hard-boiled eggs, when you put the eggs in the boiling water, the water temperature drops and the water stops boiling. Bringing it back to a boil requires you to increase the temperature after adding the eggs so that the water starts boiling again.

For avocado boats or sandwiches.

## INGREDIENTS

| 2 | 6-oz cans white meat tuna packed in water |
| 2 Tbsp | diced red bell pepper |
| 1 Tbsp | chopped fresh basil leaves |
| ⅓ cup | good-quality mayonnaise |
| | zest of ½ lemon |
| | fine sea salt and freshly ground black pepper |

## FOR SANDWICH

| 8 slices | bread |

## FOR TUNA MELT

| | English muffin |
| | Cheddar, Swiss, or mozzarella cheese |

**SERVES 4**

# TUNA SALAD

Drain the tuna in a strainer, pressing it well to remove as much water as possible. Transfer the tuna to a small bowl and break it up with a fork. Mix in the red bell pepper and basil. Add the mayonnaise and lemon zest, season with a little salt and black pepper, and stir to combine.

### TO MAKE A TUNA SALAD AVOCADO BOAT

Scoop your tuna salad into the cavity left from having removed the pit from your avocado.

### TO MAKE A TUNA SALAD SANDWICH

Take 4 pieces of bread and lay them out on your cutting board. Divide the tuna salad on top of the bread and spread it evenly. Top with the remaining 4 slices of bread and cut the sandwiches in half.

### TO MAKE A TUNA MELT

If you feel like something warm, make a tuna melt. An English muffin is a nice bread for this option. Put a spoonful of tuna salad on a toasted English muffin, top with cheese—cheddar, Swiss, and mozzarella are all great choices. Now place your open sandwich under a medium heat broiler until the cheese melts.

### TO MAKE A TUNA SALAD DIP

As another alternative, serve the tuna salad like a dip with your favorite vegetables cut into strips.

# Listen for the Moment

There's a lot of creativity involved in making these light lunches. We get to build our own sandwiches, make onions sweat, create boats for our food, and explore lots of ways to enjoy tuna salad. Just as we can listen to what our hearts and minds tell us about being creative, we can also listen for the moment to tell a loved one our feelings, share something we're going through, or encourage our loved one to share their thoughts.

**YOUNG HELPERS**

## SHARE YOUR FAVORITE SPECIAL MOMENT WITH YOUR GROWN-UP HELPER

There are so many special moments to share with your grown-up helper. Which are your favorites? Share them and make a plan to talk about them again.

**PRETEEN + TEEN HELPERS**

## TALK WITH YOUR GROWN-UP HELPER ABOUT SOMETHING YOU'VE BEEN MEANING TO SHARE

Is there something you've wanted to tell your grown-up helper but didn't know how to say it? Maybe you were afraid of the reaction or response. Listen for the moment when your intuition tells you it's the right time to share what you want to talk about with your grown-up helper.

**GROWN-UP HELPERS**

## SEE WHAT THE SILENCE IS SAYING

Silence can tell us a lot. When you listen for the moment, you allow for those pauses that signal it's the right time to share something with your helper. You might segue from the pause asking questions like: "What are you thinking about?" or "What was your day like?" You might punctuate the pause by saying something that shows your love: "It's really nice to be together" or "It's been so fun cooking with you today—let's do it again soon." Or, you might just reaffirm the pause, saying something like: "You know I'm always here for you if you ever want to talk."

**CHAPTER 5**

# Soup

*Giving Love by Sharing Goodness*

Soup means many things to people. For some, it's a cozy food to eat and enjoy on cold days when you can snuggle at home and watch your favorite show. Soup can also be refreshing, like cold gazpacho soup on a warm summer day. For others, soup is something you eat when you're not feeling well, or something you prepare for loved ones who are under the weather. Soup is a special kind of food because it has many significant meanings attached to it.

In Chapter Four we talked about how having an honest food conversation can invite openness and transparency about a whole host of things going on in our kids' lives. One way to engage in a dialogue with our kids is to start the conversation by not starting it. Instead, stand back and listen for cues about what's going on in your young person's life. Be curious. Ask about the small things they bring up and see where the conversation leads you. Whether you have a toddler or a teen, being open to hearing their experiences builds trust.

Some conversations are harder to have than others. Loss, sadness, and sickness are difficult topics to confront, especially with the youngest members of our families. It's natural and expected that we want to protect our kids from the sad realities of life. During the pandemic, and the insurmountable loss we've experienced globally, these topics could be overwhelming and stressful. As parents/guardians/caregivers, bringing up such topics may be anxiety provoking for us as well; we undoubtedly can recall a moment when loss and sadness have had an impact on our own lives.

These realities are quietly present. They sit in the room with us. They take up space even though we aren't giving them any airtime. It is so vital to engage our kids in difficult conversations, to address how they're feeling in the moment but also as a protective measure for the future.

In October 2019, a few months before COVID-19 hit the world, my mom passed away. She had been sick for some time, but we never imagined she would leave us so quickly. We had just seen her the day before. We had gone to my parents' house to visit with them and to give my dad a break. He'd been doing all the caregiving, and we could tell he was exhausted. Julian took him out to run errands while Olliver and I stayed with my mom.

Olliver loved his grandmother. He knew exactly where to find her, sitting in her big comfy armchair as he bounded up the stairs to the living room each time we arrived. To get the call the following evening, that Grandma had died, seemed unbelievable. We had just been with her. Amid our own grief, we wondered what we should tell Olliver, who was three years old at the time. Julian and I spoke with each other and sought guidance from Olliver's preschool. We decided that an honest, up-front approach was going to be the most appropriate.

Young children are egocentric—not in the sense of being selfish, but in a developmental way; their experiences are markers to understand other experiences. Given this developmental egocentrism, we were concerned that if we weren't up front about Grandma's death, Olliver might think he was responsible. It could be, for instance, that he thought a prank he played at her house the week before had somehow led to this tragic outcome.

We were clear about what happened when we spoke with Olliver. We used the word *died*. We didn't say Grandma "went to sleep" or was going to return. This gentle and straightforward dialogue opened up a conversation that continues to this day.

As parents we can model care and kindness in the face of fear and sadness. Several years ago, a close friend reached out to Julian. Her daughter was diagnosed with an advanced cancer. She was undergoing chemotherapy and struggling to eat and keep food down. The processed foods that had previously tasted great now tasted awful. They left a tinny taste in her mouth.

Our friend asked if Julian knew of anyone who could cook meals for her daughter while she was undergoing treatment. "Well, I can," he said.

She offered to pay, but Julian wouldn't accept. "No way," he said. "We're here to help. This is the least I can do."

"Soup is what she's really craving," our friend shared.

"Sounds good," said Julian. "I'll make soup."

Julian made soup every Sunday for the next few months. Our house smelled cozy and delicious as he prepared our friend's daughter's choice each week: tomato, butternut squash. And each week we received a package from our friend—a box of pears or fresh quince. "Perfect!" Julian would exclaim as he added it to the soup.

Julian made enough soup for the week and set aside an extra small bit for us to eat for lunch. Looking back, we underestimated the impact that Julian's modeling of care had on our family. When our daughter Sabrina wrote her high school application essay, she talked about how her dad cooked soup on Sundays for a friend with cancer. Julian started to make the soup recipes at work, and unexpectedly received an award for being a best soup spot in New York City. Most important, our friend's daughter got more of the nutrition she needed to help her fight this devastating disease. It was as though the nutrition extended beyond the soup and included an awareness of being cared for and loved as key ingredients.

Modeling care and support for others is a wonderful message for our families. Among families with children of any age, we can incorporate food to show we care in countless ways. Your helpers can bake cookies for Grandma, collect goods for their school's food drive, learn about food insecurity, volunteer at a food pantry, or cook for a friend who's sick.

Just as this chapter encourages us to connect by having painful but important conversations, Chapter Six focuses on how snacks can also be a catalyst for connection. The next chapter is all about expanding our options to consider new alternatives. While we might think snacks are limited to store-bought options, in reality there are many tasty treats we can make and enjoy with our family.

And our friend's daughter survived and is living her best life.

I have to be honest: although the rest of my family loves soup, I'm not the biggest fan. But Rustic Tomato and Basil Soup is one soup I really enjoy. It's so simple and quick to make. There's no mixing, no blending, just a little chopping and heating, and presto, delicious soup that can be enjoyed anytime of year.

This recipe is also a great way to use up stale bread. And helpers of all ages will have so much fun crushing the canned peeled plum tomatoes in their hands. Let's get to it.

## INGREDIENTS

| | |
|---|---|
| ¼ cup | extra-virgin olive oil |
| 1 | small onion, finely diced |
| 3 cloves | garlic, crushed |
| 3 | 14½-oz cans peeled plum tomatoes |
| 4 cups | stale sourdough or semolina bread cut into cubes |
| ½ cup | coarsely grated Parmesan cheese |
| ½ bunch | fresh basil leaves, roughly chopped |
| | granulated sugar |
| | fine sea salt and freshly ground black pepper |

**SERVES 4**

# RUSTIC TOMATO & BASIL SOUP

Warm the olive oil in a large saucepan over medium heat, add the onions and garlic, and cook for about 5 minutes, or until soft. Be careful not to brown the onion and garlic. If they start to brown, reduce the heat and cook them more slowly (see Activity: Sweat Your Onions, page 83).

Meanwhile, open the cans of tomato and pour them into a large bowl. With clean hands, squash and crush the tomatoes into small pieces. Add to the onion mixture in the saucepan and bring to a low simmer. Season with salt, pepper, and a little sugar. Continue simmering for 10 to 15 minutes.

Add the bread, Parmesan cheese, and basil and continue cooking, stirring occasionally with a wooden spoon, for about 5 minutes to warm all the ingredients. If your soup is too thick, you can always add a little water and reheat. Your soup is now ready to be devoured.

This soup is perfect for a cold fall evening and is actually quite easy to make and always delicious.

## INGREDIENTS

| 4 lb | whole butternut squash (this equals about 2 medium squash) |
| 4 Tbsp | extra-virgin olive oil |
| ⅓ cup | maple syrup |
| 1 Tbsp | ground cinnamon, plus more for dusting |
| 1 | medium yellow onion, diced |
| 4 cloves | garlic, chopped |
| ½ cup | Greek yogurt |
| | fine sea salt and freshly ground black pepper |

**SERVES 4**

# ROASTED BUTTERNUT SQUASH SOUP

Preheat the oven to 400°F.

Peel the butternut squash, remove the seeds (see Activity: Prepping Your Ingredients, page 94), and cut into roughly 1-inch cubes. In a large bowl, toss the squash with 2 Tbsp olive oil and season it with salt and pepper. Spread the squash on a baking sheet and roast for 25 to 30 minutes, or until tender and lightly browned. Scrape the squash into a large bowl, add the maple syrup and cinnamon, and toss to fully coat the squash.

Meanwhile, warm the remaining 2 Tbsp olive oil in a large saucepan over medium heat. Add the onion and garlic, season with salt and pepper, and cook, stirring occasionally, for about 5 minutes, or until soft. Add 5 cups of water and the squash and stir to incorporate. Raise the heat to medium-high and bring to a boil. Reduce the heat to medium-low and simmer, stirring occasionally and breaking up any large pieces of squash, for about 15 minutes. Remove from the heat.

All your soup won't fit in your blender at once, so please hear this really important point: only fill your blender halfway and then place the lid on top. Next, cover the lid with a dry towel and hold it down with your hand. This is important for safety because sometimes the force of the engaging blades will push your hot soup to the top of the bowl and it might escape, resulting in painful burns. This job is for grown-ups only. With these safety measures, you can use your blender to purée the soup in batches until it's smooth. Alternatively, use an immersion blender (a blender on a stick), once again being careful of the hot liquid.

If the soup is too thick, add a little water. (see Activity: Learn about Consistency with Puréed Soups, page 101). Experiment with seasoning as you figure out how much salt and pepper is needed (see Activity: Taste as You Go, page 68).

Portion out the soup into four warm bowls. It's fun to add the finishing touches by floating some Greek yogurt in the soup and sprinkling a little ground cinnamon on top. A warm, hearty creation!

# Prepping Your Ingredients

Part of the fun of cooking is prepping your ingredients for your recipe. For these soup recipes, you squash the tomatoes and deseed the squash to get these ingredients in the right form for the dish you are about to create. Prepping ingredients is a wonderful way to engage our senses. It's like mixing paints, only the paints are food!

### SQUASH AND SCOOP
Squash those tomatoes and scoop out those seeds!

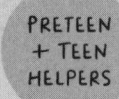

### GET OUT YOUR FRUSTRATIONS
Is there something you're upset about? Get out your frustrations by thinking about what's bothering you while you squash the tomatoes. It's like screaming in a culinary way.

### ENGAGE IN TACTILE PLAY
Did you know that tactile play promotes learning and development? As kids learn through their senses, they're expressing their curiosity about exploring the world around them. Sensory play helps develop fine motor skills, language skills, and even nerve connections in our brains. Sensory play also encourages sensory memory as information received from the environment gets sent to the brain. Ask your helper what it feels like to squash the tomatoes or scoop out the seeds. Are the tomatoes squishy? Do the squash seeds feel slimy?

This is a yummy, colorful, all-year-round soup. Make a double batch and freeze half for the next time you're in a pinch and need to put something on the table quickly. It should last up to two months in the freezer.

From the middle of spring through late summer, use fresh corn, which should be easy to find at farmers' markets or at your local grocery store. If you and your family want to have corn chowder out of season—it will happen—you can easily use canned whole corn kernels or frozen corn for great results.

### INGREDIENTS

| | |
|---|---|
| 5–6 ears | fresh corn or 2½ 15-oz cans whole corn kernels, strained |
| 4 cups | chicken or vegetable stock |
| 1 | bay leaf |
| 2 Tbsp | unsalted butter |
| 1 | small white onion, cut into a ¼-in dice |
| 1 | whole medium leek, washed and cut into ¼-in dice |
| 1 | medium carrot, cut into a ⅛-in dice |
| 2 | medium red bell peppers, seeded and cut into ¼-in dice |
| 3 | celery ribs, cut into ¼-in dice |
| ¾ lb | waxy potatoes, such as Yukon gold, peeled and cut into ¼-in dice, washed in cold water after being cut and peeled |
| 2 cups | half-and-half |
| | fine sea salt and freshly ground black pepper |
| | chopped fresh flat-leaf parsley leaves (optional) |
| | fresh chives (optional) |
| | sour cream (optional) |

**SERVES 4 TO 6**

# CREAMY CORN CHOWDER

Remove the husks and silk from the corn and set side. They're key ingredients and not to be thrown out! Hold an ear of corn upright and with a serrated knife (a knife with teeth), carefully slice off all the kernels from the cob. Put the cob to the side with the husks and silk. Keep the kernels to one side. Repeat with the other ears of corn. Place the peeled cobs, husks, and silk in a medium saucepan. Add the stock and bay leaf and bring to a boil. Reduce the heat and simmer for about 30 minutes while you prepare the other ingredients.

Melt the butter in a large pot over medium heat. Add the onion and cook, stirring occasionally, for about 5 minutes, or until soft. Add the corn kernels, leeks, carrots, red bell peppers, celery, and potatoes. Season with salt and pepper to taste. Cook, stirring occasionally, for 5 more minutes. Strain the stock over the vegetables and add the half-and-half. Gently simmer your chowder for about 15 minutes, or until the potatoes are soft. Serve your creamy corn chowder and, if desired, top with parsley or chives and a dollop of sour cream.

### top tips!

There is a lot of cutting in this recipe, but depending on how old your helpers are, you could have some great assistance. Many hands make easy chopping, and helpers of any age love peeling corn and removing the silk.

### fun fact!

The United States is responsible for about forty percent of the world's corn production. It's grown in all fifty states.

# Use All Parts of a Food Item and Reduce Waste

This corn chowder recipe is another great example of how we can use all parts of a food item (see how the fennel fronds are used in the Roasted Beet Salad, page 64). Not only does this reduce food waste but it also makes the soup taste amazing. Using every part of the corn is a great teachable moment. It shows that sometimes what we think is waste, is actually quite flavorful.

 **ASK QUESTIONS ABOUT HOW TO USE YOUR FOOD**
Husk the corn and remove the corn silk and put on a plate. Ask your grown-up helper questions about what they think it can be used for, and what it tastes like.

 **EXPLORE TASTE BY COOKING PARTS OF CORN ON THE COB WE WOULDN'T EXPECT TO USE**
Watch how the peeled cob, husks, and silk cook on the stove and taste the corn cob broth. What does it taste like?

**IDENTIFY FOODS YOU CAN USE IN VARIOUS WAYS**
This recipe shows us how all parts of a food item can be used in cooking. With your helper, do an inventory of food items in your fridge, shelves, and pantry to identify foods that have various components you can use in cooking.

Now there's a name! Your kids will be curious to know what this dish is all about! Made with fresh seasonal vegetables, chicken, barley, and a sweet twist of prunes (one of our son's most favorite foods when he was a baby), this is a classic Scottish soup—the national soup of Scotland. And although it dates from the sixteenth century, it's still cooked today.

This is a wonderful warming soup that showcases delicious leeks, celery, and carrots, which are all in season during the spring. We encourage you to take your helper to the farmers' market to pick out these fresh, healthy ingredients together.

For those who prefer a vegetarian option, it's just as easy to make a vegetable stock and lose the chicken to create a Veggie-Leekie Soup!

## INGREDIENTS

| | |
|---|---|
| 2 Tbsp | **extra-virgin olive oil** |
| 1 | **whole chicken, about 3 lb, cut into 8 pieces** |
| 1 | **small onion, peeled** |
| 2 | **large celery ribs, cut crosswise in half once** |
| 2 | **medium carrots, peeled** |
| 2 cloves | **garlic, peeled** |
| 2 | **bay leaves (fresh or dried)** |
| 6 | **sprigs fresh thyme** |
| 10 | **whole peppercorns** |
| 1¼ Tbsp | **fine sea salt, plus more as needed** |
| 6 | **leeks (white and light green parts only), halved lengthwise and thinly sliced crosswise** |
| 12 | **prunes, pitted and cut into thin strips** |
| ½ cup | **pearled barley** |

**SERVES 6**

# COCK-A-LEEKIE SOUP

Place a 6-quart stock pot over medium-high heat. Add the olive oil and then the chicken legs and cook for about 4 minutes, or until lightly browned on the bottom. Turn the chicken legs and cook for another 4 minutes, or until lightly browned on the other side. Remove the chicken legs from the pot and set aside on a plate. Repeat with the chicken breasts. If you prefer a vegetarian option, you can skip this step and go right to the next set of instructions. You might even want to add some extra vegetables that you and your helper find at the farmers' market.

Add 2½ quarts of water, along with the whole onion, celery, carrot, garlic, bay leaves, thyme, peppercorns, and salt to the stock pot. Bring to a boil, scraping any browned bits from the pot with a wooden spoon. Return all the chicken to the pot, reduce the heat, and simmer for 45 minutes, skimming any fat off the top as necessary. After 45 minutes, remove the chicken and set on a plate to cool. Scoop the celery and carrots out of the pot and set on a plate to cool.

Meanwhile, strain the stock and discard the onion, thyme, bay leaves, and peppercorns. Return the strained stock to the stock pot then add the leeks, prunes, and barley. Bring to a boil, then reduce the heat and simmer for about 40 minutes, or until the barley is fully cooked; it will be tender when you bite into it.

When the 8 pieces of chicken have cooled, remove the meat from the bones; discard the bones and skin. Next, have your helper shred these pieces of chicken (i.e., the chicken breast and leg meat that you cooked at the beginning of the recipe) while you finely dice the celery and carrots. To finish your soup, stir the shredded chicken, celery, and carrots into the pot. Add extra fine sea salt to taste. Heat through and serve.

Delicious! Cock-A-Leekie Soup is a meal in and of itself for lunch or dinner. It can also be prepared in advance and refrigerated for up to a week.

# Visit Your Local Farmers' Market

Cock-A-Leekie Soup provides a wonderful reason to visit your local farmers' market, where you are likely to find the onion, celery, carrots, garlic, thyme, and leeks. You may find fresh bay leaves at the farmers' market, but if not, you can buy dry bay leaves at the store. There are so many positive aspects of going to your local farmers' market. You're supporting local farmers and getting to know the community. You're also making less of a carbon footprint because your vegetables are traveling from a shorter distance to get to you. This means your trip to the farmers' market supports the environment. Hopefully your groceries will be fresher and taste better, too.

**YOUNG HELPERS**

### FARMERS' MARKET SCAVENGER HUNT
Find all the items on your list.

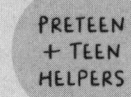

**PRETEEN + TEEN HELPERS**

### EXPLORE AND EXPERIMENT
Look around the farmers' market to identify new foods you want to try.

**GROWN-UP HELPERS**

### PLAY THE COMPARISON GAME: FOOD DIFFERENCES BETWEEN THE FARMERS' MARKET AND THE SUPERMARKET
Organize a trip to the farmers' market with your family. There are a couple ways to plan your trip. You can look online to see which fruits and vegetables are in season. You can also write a list of ingredients to get for a specific recipe like Cock-A-Leekie Soup. Once you're at the market, look around and show your helpers produce that's in a more natural state than it may be at a supermarket. For instance, carrots might be presented as bunch carrots with their stalks instead of cellophane-packed table-ready carrots. Leeks might still have dirt on their roots and longer green leaves. Have a conversation about these differences, asking your helper questions like: "Do you notice how the carrot is actually the root and the stalk is what we see coming out of the ground?" or "What do you think about the dirt on these vegetables? What does that tell us about where they grow?"

This is another simple and tasty soup. Chickpeas, or garbanzo beans, are full of dietary fiber, protein, and vitamins, so not only is this soup delicious, it's also quite filling.

## INGREDIENTS

| | |
|---|---|
| ½ cup | extra-virgin olive oil |
| 1 | small white onion, diced |
| 5 cloves | garlic, chopped |
| 1 cup | tomato sauce |
| 1 tsp | saffron pistils |
| 5 cups | vegetable stock or water |
| 1 | 15-oz can chickpeas, drained |
| 8 oz | dried short pasta of your choice, such as elbows, small shells, cavatelli, or alphabet shapes |
| 2 Tbsp | chopped fresh cilantro leaves |
| | fine sea salt and freshly ground black pepper |
| | grilled pita bread (optional) |

**SERVES 6**

# CHICKPEA & PASTA SOUP

Place a large saucepan over medium heat. Add the olive oil and then the onions and cook, stirring occasionally, for about 5 minutes. Add the garlic and cook, stirring occasionally, for a few more minutes—be careful to not let the garlic brown. Add the tomato sauce, saffron, and 3 cups of the vegetable stock or water. Bring to a gentle simmer.

Meanwhile, place half of the drained chickpeas in a food processor with the remaining 2 cups of vegetable stock or water. Use the pulse setting to purée the chickpeas until smooth. Add the chickpea purée, along with the whole chickpeas, pasta, and cilantro, to the soup. Season with salt and pepper. Continue cooking for 12 to 15 minutes, or until the pasta is tender.

Taste your soup once more to check the salt and pepper and add more if necessary (see Activity: Taste as You Go, page 68). Also check for consistency. If your soup is too thick, you can add a little more stock or water (see Activity: Learn about Consistency with Puréed Soups, page 101). Make sure your soup is hot, then serve immediately with some grilled pita bread, if desired.

## top tips!

When you strain a food item, you separate it from the liquid around it. When you strain a hot food item, it's better to use a colander in the sink for safety. A colander has a stable base and allows you to keep a safe distance from the hot liquid. If you're straining something cold, you can use a hand-held strainer or sieve because you won't get burned.

## fun fact!

Saffron is made from the pistil of the crocus flower. It's the most expensive spice in the world. This might be because it takes about two hundred flowers to make one gram of saffron. We could describe saffron as more of a perfume, getting us back to how smell influences taste. While there is no substitute for this soup ingredient (you either add it or you don't) just a little pinch of saffron goes a long way.

Gazpacho is a simple cold Spanish salad soup that was possibly introduced to the southern Spanish peninsula by the Romans. There are so many variations with different ingredients, but you should really try this one, especially in the summer, when it's hot outside, and this delicious soup will cool, refresh, and nourish you all at once. At the core of this soup are fresh, wonderfully ripe salad ingredients, including tomatoes, peppers, and cucumber, plus stale bread (see Activity: Decrease Food Waste, page 34).

I like to use a blender for this recipe, as it makes for a smoother soup, with an almost creamy texture. You can also use a food processor or, if you're up for it and have the time—lots of time!— do it the old-fashioned way with a mortar and pestle.

### INGREDIENTS

| | |
|---|---|
| 2 lb | ripe vine tomatoes |
| 1 | cucumber, peeled and seeded |
| 1 | medium red bell pepper, stemmed and seeded |
| ½ | red onion, peeled |
| 3 cloves | garlic, peeled |
| ¼ cup | sherry vinegar |
| ¼ cup | extra-virgin olive oil |
| 6 oz | stale bread, crusts removed and diced |
| | fine sea salt and freshly ground black pepper |

SERVES 4 TO 6

COLD SOUP

# GAZPACHO

Bring a kettle or saucepan of water to a boil. Fill a large bowl with ice water.

Take the tomatoes off the vine and then use a sharp knife to remove the eyes (where the stalk meets the fruit). Place the tomatoes in a large bowl and add enough boiling water to completely cover them. After about 30 to 60 seconds, use a slotted spoon to carefully transfer the tomatoes from the hot water to the bowl of ice water. This technique is called "blanching." Once the tomatoes are cold, you can easily peel off the blistered skins.

Working in batches, blend the peeled tomatoes with the cucumber, red bell pepper, onion, garlic, sherry vinegar, olive oil, and bread. Be sure not to overfill the blender, as your ingredients might try to escape. Once everything is liquefied, combine in a large bowl and mix to fully combine. Season with salt and pepper so that the gazpacho is to your liking (see Activity: Taste as You Go, page 68). If your soup is too thick, you can add a little water to thin it out (see Activity: Learn about Consistency with Puréed Soups, opposite). Cover your soup and place it in the refrigerator for a few hours to completely chill before serving. Get ready to be refreshed and nourished at the same time!

### top tips!

Blanching is used in this recipe to remove the tomato skin from the fruit. To successfully blanch the tomatoes, make sure your water is boiling and make sure you have ice cold water nearby to stop the cooking process.

### fun fact!

The mortar and pestle have been helping us create food since the Stone Age. The mortar is the bowl in which your ingredients go and the pestle is the cylindrical tool used to crush and mix the ingredients in the mortar together.

# Learn about Consistency with Puréed Soups

Consistency, as it relates to soup, is about thickness versus thinness. You don't want your soup to be thin like water, but you also don't want it to be thick like porridge. Consistency is particularly relevant for puréed soups, where you blend the ingredients by suspending a solid in a liquid, which can make your soup thick. Examples include Roasted Butternut Squash Soup (page 93), Chickpea and Pasta Soup (page 99), Gazpacho (page 100), and Iced Watermelon, Cucumber, and Ginger Soup (page 102). You want to create that balance between too thick and too thin, having it right in the middle.

YOUNG HELPERS

### TAKE A CONSISTENCY TASTE TEST
Test the thickness and thinness of your soup by adding water as needed. Which consistency tastes best?

PRETEEN + TEEN HELPERS

### IMPLEMENT A PERSONAL CONSISTENCY QUIZ
Consistency here refers to thickness versus thinness in soup. In life, consistency means how constant, regular, or reliable something—or someone—is. Conduct a consistency quiz to explore who's a consistent, supportive presence in your life.

GROWN-UP HELPERS

### REVIEW YOUR PERSONAL CONSISTENCY ASSESSMENT
Are there areas in your life where you'd like to be more consistent? Maybe with exercising, diet, or spending time with your kids? Conduct a consistency assessment to learn more about where in your life you want to create more balance.

The key to this soup is, of course, the ripeness of the watermelon. Part of this recipe involves learning how to choose fruit at the store or farmers' market. When you shop for the watermelon, be sure to choose your fruit carefully. See the opposite Activity: Which Watermelon Is Best? This soup's ingredients usher in interesting flavor combinations. You have the sweetness of the watermelon, the coolness of the cucumber, the spiciness of the ginger, the acidity of the lime juice, and the freshness of the mint. The culmination is a lovely, satisfying, cooling soup for the summer. It can be served as an appetizer or a snack.

## INGREDIENTS

| | |
|---|---|
| 4 | prunes, soaked in cold water overnight |
| 1 | small seedless watermelon, peeled and cut into 1-in pieces (about 5 cups) |
| 1 | English cucumber, peeled and seeded, then cut into 1-in pieces |
| 8 | large fresh mint leaves, plus 4 leaves for garnish |
| ¼ cup | fresh lime juice |
| 2 tsp | peeled and grated fresh ginger |
| 10 | ice cubes |
| 1 tsp | fine sea salt |

**SERVES 4**

# ICED WATERMELON, CUCUMBER, & GINGER SOUP

Drain the prunes, remove their seeds, and discard the water.

In a large bowl, combine the prunes, watermelon, cucumber, mint, lime juice, ginger, and ice.

Working in batches, use a blender to purée the watermelon mixture for about 30 seconds, or until there are no lumps. Pour the puréed mixture through a fine-mesh sieve into a bowl. It's fascinating to see how this process removes seeds or anything big that could potentially go into your soup. Next, experiment with taste, as you season your soup with salt (see Activity: Taste as You Go, page 68). Cover your soup and chill in the refrigerator for at least 2 hours. Serve this delicious, pink soup garnished with a mint leaf. Refreshing!

# Which Watermelon Is Best?

Sometimes we think the shiniest things are the best things. They catch our eye and attract our attention. The watermelon challenges this way of thinking. It's the dullness of the watermelon, not the shininess, that tells us it's ripe and ready to eat. Read below to find out more!

**YOUNG HELPERS**

### LOOK AT THE PILE OF WATERMELONS AT THE STORE OR FARMERS' MARKET
Which one looks the least shiny? Pick that one to take home!

**PRETEEN + TEEN HELPERS**

### TAKE YOUR CUES FROM THE WATERMELON AND LOOK BEYOND THE EXTERIOR
Are there classmates you'd like to meet but don't extend yourself because they seem different than who you would usually connect with? Look beyond the exterior and reach out to make a new friend.

**GROWN-UP HELPERS**

### RECOGNIZE THAT WHAT LOOKS SHINY ISN'T ALWAYS THE BEST
The less shiny your watermelon, the better it will taste. Less shiny watermelons have ripened which means that the flavors have developed within the fruit. And the heavier your watermelon, the better it will taste. Heavier watermelons have more water, making them juicy and delicious as a result.

# Give Love by Sharing Goodness

It's easy to get so caught up in day-to-day living that we forget to share our goodness with others. Especially during times of crisis and confusion like a global pandemic, it may simply be all we can do to negotiate each day as it comes. This is completely understandable. When we're intentional about giving love by sharing goodness, we get to tap into the side of our humanity that's inherently designed to reach out. Our commitment to connect allows us to engage in ways that extend across boundaries and separations, letting others know we care about them.

Tap into your creativity to develop new ways to give love by sharing goodness.

**YOUNG HELPERS**

### SEND YOUR LOVE IN THE MAIL

Share your creativity! Draw a picture for someone you care about. Your drawing can reflect whatever comes to mind. If the person you're drawing the picture for lives far away, ask your grown-up helper to get an envelope and send it through the mail.

**PRETEEN + TEEN HELPERS**

### ADVOCATE FOR SOCIAL JUSTICE

What's the community issue you care about the most? Hunger and food insecurity, animal rights, climate justice? Once you identify what you're passionate about changing, engage in volunteer work focused on the issue.

**GROWN-UP HELPERS**

### DECREASE ISOLATION WITH AN IN-PERSON VISIT

Is there a friend or family member you haven't visited for a while? Maybe so much time has elapsed that you don't even know where to begin the conversation. Make that your starting point—telling your loved one there's so much to share. Take it a step further and organize a trip to visit your loved one with your family or even on your own. Make your trip as extensive or as simple as you want it to be. You can get on a plane and travel to another state, take a simple day trip in the car, or ride the subway for an afternoon visit.

**CHAPTER 6**

# Snacks

*The Snack Dilemma: Are They Good or Bad for Our Families?*

Chapter Five focused on how we can share love by giving goodness. Nourishing foods like soups can be a great way to do that. We can show our love and offer support through a nutritious gesture like making soup for someone who's sick. We extend this idea in Chapter Six, where we talk about how snacks can provide a way to connect with others.

However, of all the eating options presented in *Eating Together, Being Together*, snacks present the biggest dilemma. Are they good for us or bad for us? Healthy or unhealthy? Some parenting books tell us to get rid of snacks altogether. Others say to keep them. And the science about whether snacks are helpful or harmful is inconclusive. According to an article published by the Harvard T. H. Chan School of Public Health, this indecisiveness may relate to the fact that there's no one definition in the scientific community about "what is a snack."[1]

What's a parent to do? Perhaps we're missing the bigger question. Maybe it's not about an all or none approach—that you're either a snack-eating family or you aren't. Maybe there's a middle ground that considers what you snack on, when you snack, and how often this occurs.

Regardless of the limitations of knowing whether snacking is good for us, the reality is, American kids eat snacks. Snacking among kids has increased in the past few decades and makes up about 27 percent of our children's calorie intake.

And guess what? The research says snacking has increased for parents, too. During the COVID-19 pandemic, "parents with children under eighteen years have reported snacking more than usual."[2]

So what are we snacking on? American children tend to eat snacks that are high in calories and low in nutritional value. We agree with the Harvard article's concern about this finding, given that 30 percent of U.S. children and adolescents are overweight or obese. This worry is echoed by the National Health and Nutrition Examination survey that found children don't get enough vitamin D, fiber, calcium, and potassium in their diets. Instead, the survey found that kids have a large intake of calories, carbohydrates, and sodium.[3]

We eat snacks for a number of reasons. We may get hungry a few hours after a meal, feel tired and crave a snack as a pick-me-up, or simply enjoy the snack's taste—wanting more of it. We may be part of a group that shares social time while snacking together—like snack time at Olliver's school.[4]

Some of us eat snacks when we're stressed, depressed, anxious, or bored. Life can be lonely, and food provides an instant comfort, like a close friend—even if it doesn't solve the problem. Most of us have engaged in emotional eating at some point in our lives. Emotional eating can fill a void or manage an emotional reaction. Emotional eating often involves foods that are high in sugar and fat. This makes sense. I've never engaged in emotional eating with baby carrots.

I can turn to a bag of sweets and eat the whole thing when I'm feeling overwhelmed. Just the repetitive movement of taking each piece of candy out of the bag makes me feel like I'm getting something done, even though all I'm doing is eating sweets out of a bag.

When I was a teen there were never snacks in my house. At best we had saltine crackers and peanut butter in the pantry (and it was the smooth peanut butter, not the crunchy kind that I prefer). I craved the taste of chocolate or cake. We lived in the suburbs, and there was no store within walking distance to go to for snacks. I used to get on my bike and ride the two-plus miles to my best friend's house for snack support. She had the best snacks, and they were unlimited. We would open the cupboards, go through the shelves, and select whatever we wanted. There was something so special about eating these delicious, rare commodities, leaning on the counter in her bright, shiny kitchen with her sisters and brother. Not only was I meeting my craving but also I felt like part of a group. We were connected in our shared snacking experience.

It turns out that snacks, like so many things in life, have positive and negative aspects. The science of snacks shows that they can actually increase our energy if we're feeling tired between meals. Snacks can help us not overeat at our next meal by having something to eat between them. Healthy snacks can provide important dietary nutrients. And if someone has an illness and can't manage big meals, snacks are a way to maintain nutrition in response to the impact the illness has on appetite.

You may recall how your child ate as a baby. Infants have such small stomachs that they only eat a little bit at a time. To make up for not being able to eat much at one sitting, they feed often, like every two hours. Biologically, this is how babies get enough nutrition to survive. It doesn't seem that different from snacks, as we may need more nourishment outside of meal time.

On the negative side, if we're eating a lot of snacks that are high in calories, we may gain unwanted weight. Eating a snack before a meal may make us full and not hungry when it's time to eat. We recently realized this was going on with Olliver. We'd come home from after-school activities exhausted and literally roll into the house, throwing all our stuff on the floor. There was no way I had the energy to make dinner at that moment.

"Can I have a snack?" Olliver would ask.

"Sure," I'd say. And prepare something for him.

I'd take a break before making dinner. By the time dinner was served, Olliver would say he wasn't hungry anymore. Or he would eat a little bit and say, "I'm full, I can't eat anything else."

It wasn't until I learned more about the science of snacking that I realized what was happening. Olliver was filling up on snacks, to the point where dinner became secondary. Realizing this increased our eating mindfulness. We changed our schedule so that we started to make dinner right when we got home. The snack that Olliver used to have before dinner is now something he eats afterward as dessert, or a treat, or not at all.

There's another negative aspect to snacking, and this one's kind of scary. Did you know that eating ultraprocessed, hyperpalatable snacks with lots of calories, carbs, fats, salt, sugar, and very little nutritional value can lead us to prefer these foods so much that our eating behaviors change?[5]

"What the heck does *hyperpalatable* mean?" you ask. It's when the calories, carbs, fats, salt, and sugar align in such a way that our brains tell us to keep eating the food, even when we're full, and even when we know we should stop. Put simply, these are cravings!

Who has ever eaten just one potato chip? If you say, "Me!" you are not being truthful!

Jokes aside, there's something liberating about knowing that our brains are wired to eat hyperpalatable foods. It makes me feel a little less guilty. At the same time, it screams eating mindfulness as we need to fight against something that tastes so great our brains tell us to keep going.

I'll be honest: throughout the years, snacks have been a way to connect in my family. When Sabrina and Izzy were growing up, every Friday night was movie night. We'd eat dinner and then I'd make homemade popcorn. With only three ingredients, it was so easy to make. It was also much more affordable than store-bought popcorn and devoid of the processed chemicals these snacks often contain. And this popcorn is delicious. People can't believe it has only three ingredients. We have many wonderful memories of watching our favorite shows while passing the popcorn bowl, a tradition that continues to this day.

Our popcorn snack gained traction. I used to make it for my daughter's friends when they came over, and it left the best aroma in the house. During a celebratory luncheon with former students of mine, one of them said, "Remember when Dr. CC brought her amazing popcorn to class for us?" I had completely forgotten about that. But my student hadn't. And this was years ago.

Recently Izzy returned home for Thanksgiving during her first year away at college. "Mom," she said when I met her at the airport, "We need to watch a movie and eat our popcorn." This popcorn is unforgettable. It's a connector.

Snacking plays such an important role connecting my family that it's something we definitely plan to keep doing. However, while popcorn is one snack we have down, we've struggled to find other healthy snack options. The recipes in this chapter aim to expand snack choices—not just for our kids but for all family members. By increasing the snack repertoire, our hope is to provide more choices, rather than feeling we always end up with the same old thing. Chapter activities present ways we can pack up snacks to take with us (see Activity: Pack Your Snack, page 115, and Activity: Go on an Adventure, page 122). This decreases the cost of buying outside snacks, increases nutritional value, and even helps our kids develop planning and organizational skills.

Chapter Six focuses on how snacks can be a catalyst to make connections. But how do we keep these connections going? Chapter Seven talks about the very important skill of listening and explores how to create safe spaces for listening to occur in our relationships.

| | |
|---|---|
| 2 | avocados, ripe but not too ripe |
| 1 | plum tomato |
| ½ | red onion, finely diced |
| 2 Tbsp | chopped fresh cilantro leaves |
| 1 tsp | finely diced jalapeño |
| | juice of ½ lime |
| | fine sea salt and freshly ground black pepper |

**SERVES 4**

# THE BEST GUACAMOLE EVER

With a knife, cut around each avocado, all the way to the pit. Hold the avocado in both hands and twist the halves to separate them. With a spoon, scoop out the avocado flesh and place it in a small bowl. Repeat with the other avocado. Have fun mashing the avocado flesh with a fork until there are no large pieces left.

Use a sharp knife to cut the tomato into quarters. Use a spoon to scoop out and discard the inside flesh and the seeds. Cut the tomato into small squares.

Add the tomato, red onion, cilantro, jalapeño, and lime juice to the avocado. Experiment with taste to figure out how much salt and pepper you want to add (see Activity: Taste as You Go, page 68). Serve with tortilla chips. This guacamole is good for you and good for your taste buds!

We rediscovered homemade popcorn one night when we ran out of the microwave kind. Thank goodness! This secret recipe is so simple and healthy. It's cheaper than store bought microwave packets and healthier than potato chips. Homemade popcorn has become a staple at our house—and not just for movie nights.

## INGREDIENTS

| | |
|---|---|
| 1 cup | **popcorn kernels** |
| ¼ cup | **vegetable oil** |
| | **fine sea salt** |

**SERVES 8**

# THE MOST AMAZING HOMEMADE POPCORN

Pour the vegetable oil into a large saucepan and place over medium heat. As the oil heats, add just 2 or 3 kernels of popcorn and cover the pan with a lid. Listen. It will get surprisingly quiet just before you hear the kernels pop. Right after that happens, add the rest of the kernels and put the lid back on.

Here's the trick: remove the pan from the heat for about 45 seconds (count down from 45 to 0 with your helpers). This will help all the kernels reach the same temperature to be able to POP at the same time. It also avoids burning the popcorn that has already popped.

When your countdown reaches 0, return the pan to medium heat, and, holding the handle, move the pan in a circular motion over the stove top. In about 1 minute, you will hear the newly added kernels begin to pop. If you have a glass lid, it's especially fun to watch the kernels turn into popcorn. When the popping has stopped, remove the pan from the stove. Pour into one or more bowls and sprinkle with salt. Enjoy your movie!

# Movie Night

Watching a movie together is a very bonding experience. It's a time when everyone puts away homework, work, and their other screens and gathers to watch something together. When you watch a movie there's no agenda and nothing you have to do—you can just be yourselves together.

**YOUNG HELPERS**

**PICK A MOVIE NIGHT WITH YOUR HELPERS**
Make your popcorn and get ready to watch with your helpers!

**PRETEEN + TEEN HELPERS**

**HOST A MOVIE NIGHT WITH YOUR FRIENDS**
Invite your friends over for a movie night.

**GROWN-UP HELPERS**

**RECOGNIZE THE IMPORTANCE OF MOVIE NIGHT AND THE IMPORTANCE OF OUR KIDS GETTING A GOOD NIGHT'S SLEEP**
Pick a weekend night when the whole family can watch a movie together and eat The Most Amazing Homemade Popcorn (opposite). If there isn't enough time for an entire movie, watching a TV show is a good alternative. If the episode is part of a series, this can be a great backup for those movie nights when it's close to bedtime. Getting a good night's sleep is essential for positive childhood development. Research shows that for kids, getting enough sleep improves mental and physical well-being, as well as cognitive skills such as memory, attention, and the ability to learn.[6] Another research study shows that among eight-to-twelve-year-old children with obesity, bedtimes that were later and inconsistent related to "greater adiposity [i.e., obesity], independent of other obesity-related behaviours."[7]

**DEVELOP A PROCESS TO CHOOSE YOUR FAMILY MOVIE**
Make choosing a family movie a fun process. This can get tricky for us because of the wide range of ages among our kids. We take a verbal survey to see what people want to watch. Then we check to see that the movies suggested are appropriate for all the different ages in our family. If we're still undecided, we watch the trailer to see which movie best fits our mood at the moment. Once decided, if there are other suggestions we're excited about, we add them to a running list of must-see movies for the future.

This recipe makes two great snacks using the exact same ingredients. What's especially fun is that even though they are so similar, they are also quite different: one snack is crunchy, dry, and takes hours to make, while the other is crisp, juicy, and takes just a few minutes to prepare. Let's get started!

## INGREDIENTS

| 2 | Granny Smith apples |
| 1 Tbsp | granulated sugar |
| 1 tsp | ground cinnamon |

**SERVES 2**

# APPLE CINNAMON WEDGES & CHIPS

### SNACK 1: APPLE WEDGES

Using a sharp knife, cut each apple in half, from top to bottom, then cut each half into 6 wedges. Repeat this process until you have 24 wedges. Use a small knife to remove the central core of each apple wedge—this is the part that contains the stem and seeds. Place your wedges in a bowl and sprinkle with the sugar and cinnamon. Mix everything together. Eat immediately or place your apple wedges in a container and take them on the road!

### SNACK 2: APPLE CHIPS

Preheat the oven to 225° F. Line a few baking sheets with parchment paper.

Using a sharp knife, cut each apple in half, from top to bottom. Use a small knife to remove the central core of each apple half—this is the part that contains the stem and seeds. Slice each apple half really thinly with either a very sharp knife or a mandoline slicer. Remember: if you use the slicer, be very careful, as it's very sharp. Lay the apple slices on the lined baking sheets and sprinkle with the sugar and cinnamon on both sides. Bake for about 1 hour, then turn the apple chips over and bake for another 45 minutes to an hour. Remove your baking sheets from the oven, place the apple chips on a wire cooling rack, and let cool to room temperature. When they've cooled and are ready, dive in!

### fun fact!

Making apple chips is really about dehydrating or removing all the moisture from the apples. This not only makes the apple chips crisp but it also concentrates the flavor of the apple. Which one do you prefer—the apple chips or wedges?

You can store your apple chips in a sealed container at room temperature for up to a week.

# Experiment with Food Versatility

The recipes to make Apple Wedges and Apple Chips show the versatility available to us when cooking. We can use just a few of the same ingredients and come up with something so different. The versatility of these apple recipes corresponds with versatility in life. When something is versatile it has many uses and can do many things. Family members face the challenge of being versatile and juggling life tasks. For young children, versatility shows up in situations like dealing with a separation from parents, guardians, caregivers, and grandparents when going to school for the first time and other adjustments like welcoming a new sibling. Preteen and teen helpers are pushed, sometimes even pressured, to be versatile in their abilities to make friends, adjust to school, and figure out a life course while developing a sense of identity and personhood. Versatility as applied to adults is reflected in our being called to many roles: parent, guardian, caregiver, grandparent, partner, friend, adult child, sibling, extended family member, colleague, employee...the list goes on. It can easily become overwhelming.

Even more, it seems these roles are always changing. Our relationship with our own parents or guardians may be different as they age, putting us in a caregiver role. We certainly saw this during the pandemic when there were mounting concerns about health, safety, and loneliness for our older loved ones.

As parents and guardians of our kids, our role is always shifting in response to changing developmental needs. Parenting a five-year-old looks and feels different than parenting an eighteen-year-old. The needs of our kids at age five require a different skill set in which we try to encourage adjustment to school, support identification of feelings, set limits, and model relationships. When they are eighteen, we may show up for our kids as consultants, as someone they can turn to when they have a question, someone who supports their transition to adulthood, and listens as they explore what they want their own lives to look like.

**YOUNG HELPERS**

### CONDUCT A VERSATILITY TEST

Which do you like better, apple wedges or apple chips? Why?

**PRETEEN + TEEN HELPERS**

### ENGAGE IN A VERSATILITY CHALLENGE

Find ingredients in your kitchen to make something new.

**GROWN-UP HELPERS**

### EXPLORE DIFFERENT WAYS TO USE FOOD

Reclaim unused food items by exploring new ways to use them in your cooking.

Our kids love snack bars. Whether on a trip, for school lunch, or when heading to an after-school activity, it's always time for a delicious and healthy snack bar. Instead of picking up ready-made bars, make your own. Tweak the recipe, adding your favorite nuts or fruit, to make it perfect for your family. Your snack bars will keep in the refrigerator for four or five days and even longer in the freezer, so make a big batch and have these bars on hand whenever you need them.

### INGREDIENTS

| | |
|---|---|
| 1½ cups | old-fashioned rolled oats |
| ¼ cup | chopped almonds |
| ¼ cup | chopped pecans |
| 3 Tbsp | chia seeds |
| 2 Tbsp | sesame seeds |
| 1 Tbsp | poppy seeds |
| ¾ cup | raisins |
| ¼ cup | chopped dried cherries |
| ¼ cup | semisweet chocolate chips |
| ¼ tsp | fine sea salt |
| 2 Tbsp | unsalted butter |
| ¼ cup | honey |
| ¼ cup | crunchy peanut butter |

**MAKES 12 BARS**

# CHIA SEED FRUIT & NUT BARS

Preheat the oven to 350°F. Line an 8-×-8-inch baking dish with parchment paper.

Place the rolled oats, almonds, and pecans on a baking sheet and bake for 12 to 15 minutes, or until lightly brown. Remove from the oven and set aside to cool.

Once the oats and nuts are cool, place them in a large bowl, add the chia seeds, sesame seeds, poppy seeds, raisins, cherries, chocolate chips, and salt, and stir to combine.

In a small saucepan, gently melt the butter over low heat. When it's completely melted, add the honey and peanut butter. Warm and mix the ingredients together for a few minutes, then pour it over the dry ingredients and mix thoroughly.

Transfer your mixture to the lined dish, cover it with another sheet of parchment paper, and press down evenly with your hands to pack the mixture tightly. Level out the top with something flat and cylindrical like a can of vegetables. Refrigerate your mixture for at least 2 hours.

After 2 hours, remove the top piece of parchment paper. Cover the dish with a cutting board and turn everything upside down, so that the dish is now on top of the cutting board. Carefully ease the solid mixture from the dish and remove the other sheet of parchment paper.

With a long sharp knife, cut the mixture into 12 equal-sized bars. Wrap each bar individually and store in the refrigerator or freezer. You're ready to pack your snack (see Activity: Pack Your Snack, opposite)!

# Pack Your Snack

The goal of making your own snacks is to have more healthy, affordable options available. Making your snacks portable is key to making them accessible for you and your helpers. Snacks aren't just eaten at home; they're also eaten when you're on the move.

**YOUNG HELPERS**

### GET YOUR SNACK READY
With your grown-up helper, organize a snack to take to your next after-school activity. You can reduce the impact on the environment by packing your snack in a reusable container.

**PRETEEN + TEEN HELPERS**

### PREPARE FOR SNACK TIME
Pack up your favorite snacks for school, after school, sports practice, and any other time you need something to eat on the go.

**GROWN-UP HELPERS**

### GET SNACK CONTAINERS
Help your helpers be prepared, by having containers and lunch bags on hand for packing portable snacks.

Fruit salad is a great snack. It's healthy, easy to prepare, and delicious to eat. On Sundays, we often make fruit salad for brunch. We always make too much of it on purpose. When brunch is done, the extra goes into the refrigerator and within days, it's vanished. It's far better to snack on fresh fruit than to reach for a candy bar.

The key to a great fruit salad is, of course, great fruit! Take a few minutes when you select your fruit in the store. Pineapples should be a little soft at the base; mangoes should resist a gentle squeeze but shouldn't be hard like a stone; cantaloupe melons should be a little soft around the top indent and smell like a melon when you give them a good sniff; and strawberries should be dark red all over, not green or white.

When you make fruit salad at different times of year, use fruit that's in season. This is when they're both more affordable and at their most delicious. The ingredients below are just one suggestion for fruit salad—you can make up your own as well!

## INGREDIENTS

| | |
|---|---|
| 1 | pineapple |
| 2 | mangoes |
| 1 | cantaloupe melon |
| 1 lb | seedless red or green grapes |
| 1 lb | strawberries |
| 6 oz | blueberries |

**SERVES 6**

# FRUIT SALAD

With a serrated knife, slice the top and bottom off the pineapple. Place the pineapple on a cutting board with the bottom flat end you have cut on the board. Starting from the top, use a sawing motion as you cut from top to bottom, down the side of the pineapple, to remove the skin. Turn the pineapple a little and repeat the sawing motion until it's completely peeled. Cut the pineapple, from top to bottom, in half and then into quarters. Lay 1 of the pineapple quarters on its skin side and use a sharp knife to remove the hard center core. Repeat with the remaining quarters, then cut the quarters into ½-inch slices, then ½-inch squares, and place them in a large bowl.

Next, place a mango on your cutting board. Use a sharp knife to cut off the top and bottom and then stand the mango up on its base. Remove the skin by cutting a slither from the top down to the base. Turn the mango a little and repeat. Make small turns and continue slicing down the sides until the mango is completely peeled. While the mango is still standing up, look down on the mango, you'll see that it's slightly oval in shape. This is because the stone inside the mango is a flat oval shape. Keeping this in mind, cut about ¼ inch from the center of the mango down to the bottom to remove the flesh from the stone. Rotate the mango 180 degrees and slice down, about ¼ inch from the center, to remove the flesh from the other side of the stone. There will be 2 other thinner slices remaining on the mango; use the knife to remove them from the stone. Cut the mango flesh into ¼-inch strips then ¼-inch squares. Repeat the process with the other mango and then add all the mango to the bowl with the pineapple.

## top tips!

Sometimes we avoid making foods like fruit salad because we don't know how to prep the ingredients. By going step by step, this recipe tells you how to cut a pineapple, slice a mango, and remove the skin of a melon. Now you're ready to make this delicious and healthy snack!

## fun fact!

This recipe only uses one bowl for all the ingredients, which simplifies the process and makes for very little clean up (see Activity: Add to Your Bowl, page 56).

The method to remove the melon skin is similar to the pineapple and mango. Place the melon on a cutting board and use a sharp knife to cut off the top and bottom. Stand the melon on its base and cut slithers, from top to bottom, to remove the skin. When the melon is completely peeled, cut it in half from top to bottom. Inside you'll find a cavity filled with a bunch of seeds and some strands. Use a tablespoon to scrape everything out of this cavity. Cut the melon halves into ½-inch strips and then into ½-inch squares. Add the melon to your bowl.

Remove the grapes from their stems and wash them in fresh cold water. Then add the grapes to your bowl.

Wash your strawberries and use a sharp knife to remove the green stems, then cut them into halves or quarters depending on their size. Add half the strawberries to your bowl. Place the other half aside.

Wash your blueberries and add half to the bowl. Place the other half to the side.

Gently mix all the fruit in your bowl. Sprinkle your creation with the remaining strawberries and blueberries.

# Develop Your Team-Building Skills

We might avoid making fruit salad because of all the fruit we need to prepare. Enlist your team of helpers to work together. This is a great way to minimize prep time and develop team-building skills.

 **YOUNG HELPERS**

### LEAD THE GROWN-UP HELPERS
Ask your grown-up helper to prepare various fruits with you. Let the grown-up helpers do the slicing!

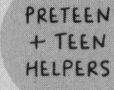 **PRETEEN + TEEN HELPERS**

### EXERCISE LEADERSHIP
It's often the case that students have to complete group assignments. These can get tricky. A group member may not want to do their share of the work and you might get stuck doing most of it. Practice your leadership skills and assign your helpers to the various tasks of making a fruit salad. Manage the process by checking in to see how everyone's doing. How can this apply to that group project you're trying to finish?

 **GROWN-UP HELPERS**

### GIVE AN ASSIGNMENT
Assign each of your helpers something to prepare in the kitchen, with grown-ups using the knives!

Hummus is another household favorite, although with Olliver, "not so much." It's a perfect snack or party item. I have one simple tip that makes this hummus exceptional—freshly ground cumin seeds. It might sound odd, but they make a huge difference to the taste of this dish (see Top Tips, at right).

In *Eating Together, Being Together*, we use freshly ground black pepper a lot. It's the same principle for freshly ground cumin seeds. Like black pepper, cumin seed has a far stronger, brighter, and more intense flavor when it's freshly ground, which dramatically adds to the overall flavor profile of whatever dish it's being used in.

When possible, always buy whole spices and grind them yourself. Fennel seeds, coriander seeds, nutmeg, and allspice, among many others, are so much tastier when freshly ground. Not only does this make them taste better, it's also economical because you only need a little to get an intense flavor.

## INGREDIENTS

| | |
|---|---|
| 1 cup | dried chickpeas (garbanzo beans) or 15-oz can chickpeas, strained |
| ½ tsp | baking soda |
| 2 Tbsp | tahini paste |
| 4 cloves | garlic, peeled |
| | juice of 2 lemons |
| 3 Tbsp | extra-virgin olive oil |
| 3 Tbsp | freshly ground cumin seeds |
| | fine sea salt |
| | grilled pita bread (optional) |
| | vegetables (optional) |
| | bagel chips (optional) |

SERVES 4

# HUMMUS WITH GRILLED PITA

If you're using canned chickpeas, skip to the paragraph (marked with an *) where you put them in a food processor.

If you're using dried chickpeas, the day before you make your hummus, wash the dried chickpeas in cold water and place them in a medium bowl. Cover the chickpeas with 1 inch of cold water, then cover the bowl with a plate and place it in the refrigerator overnight.

The next day, strain and rinse your chickpeas and place them in a medium saucepan. Cover the chickpeas with 1 inch of cold water and add the baking soda. Place the saucepan over medium-high heat and bring to a boil. With a slotted spoon remove any scum that may form on top of the water. Add 1 Tbsp of salt, reduce the heat, and gently simmer your chickpeas for 45 minutes to an hour, or until soft but not mushy. Drain the chickpeas but reserve some of the water in the saucepan for later use. Allow the chickpeas to cool completely.

*Once cool, place the chickpeas in a food processor. Add the tahini paste, garlic, lemon juice, olive oil, and cumin. Blend all the ingredients together. If you like your hummus a little chunky, blend it a little less. If you want it smooth, blend it longer. Check for salt and cumin, adding a little more if necessary (see Activity: Taste as You Go, page 68). If your hummus is too thick, you can add a little of the reserved cooking liquid (see Activity: Learn about Consistency with Puréed Soups, page 101). Mix everything again. Enjoy your hummus with grilled pita bread, vegetables, or bagel chips.

## top tips!

To make freshly ground cumin, all you need to do is clean out your coffee grinder and add the whole cumin seeds. Put on the lid and turn the grinder on. Grind for just a minute and you'll have freshly ground cumin. If you don't have a coffee grinder, no worries— you can purchase ground cumin at the store.

## fun fact!

The scum (or white foam, to put it nicely) that can appear on top of the water while you cook your chickpeas is a combination of proteins, saponins, and carbohydrates released by the chickpeas while they cook.

A quick, healthy, nutritious dish, this parfait has just a few ingredients. In a few minutes you can make a delicious snack, breakfast, or even a light lunch.

## INGREDIENTS

| | |
|---|---|
| 1 cup | blueberries or sliced strawberries |
| 1 | ripe banana, peeled and sliced |
| 2 cups | Greek yogurt |
| 1 cup | Homemade Granola (see page 41) |
| ¼ cup | honey |

**SERVES 4**

# THE PERFECT PARFAIT

Wash your berries. Divide half of the berries evenly among four wide-mouthed glasses or small bowls. Divide the sliced banana among the four glasses. Top the fruit in each glass with ½ cup of yogurt. Sprinkle the remaining berries on top of the yogurt, again dividing them evenly among the four glasses. Add ¼ cup of Homemade Granola on top of the fruit in each glass. Finish each parfait with a drizzle of honey. Easy peasy. Oh, and yummy, too.

Foods you can take with you for sustenance and energy have an important history. Take, for example, pemmican, which includes ingredients such as buffalo meat, berries, and fish. Indigenous people of North America used pemmican as "great portable sources of food energy on long hunts or while doing any task where energy was needed."[8] It continues to be made today. Trail mix is helpful to bring on long journeys given that it's lightweight, easy to carry, easy to eat, and lasts a long time. It can be a handy portable snack to take with you on your next journey.

When making trail mix, you can select your special ingredients at the store and then mix everything together at home to create your own unique blend. A word of caution: mixed nuts, seeds, and dried fruit are full of healthy nutrients like protein, vitamins, Omega-3 fatty acids, and fiber, but chocolate candy is not. Although adding some 70 percent cacao dark chocolate is great, go easy on store-bought candies or peanut butter pieces. And remember that while nuts and dried fruits are full of goodies, they are also full of calories, so be aware of portion size. This trail mix is a great snack if you're out and about engaging in physical activities, but it may not be the perfect option if you're lounging around watching a movie.

## INGREDIENTS

| | |
|---|---|
| ½ cup | cashews |
| ½ cup | pecans |
| ½ cup | peanuts |
| ½ cup | pumpkin seeds |
| ¼ tsp | fine sea salt |
| ½ cup | raisins |
| ½ cup | dried apricots, each cut into 6 pieces |
| ¼ cup | 70% cacao chocolate chips |

**SERVES 8**

# FAMILY TRAIL MIX

Preheat the oven to 300°F.

Place the cashews, pecans, peanuts, and pumpkin seeds on a baking sheet and sprinkle with the salt. Bake for about 10 minutes, or until lightly toasted. Remove them from the oven and let cool completely.

Once the nuts and seeds are cool, place them in a large bowl. Add the raisins, apricots, and chocolate and mix to combine. Store your trail mix in an airtight container at room temperature for up to 2 weeks. When you're ready for your adventures, portion your trail mix into small reusable containers for on-the-go snacking.

### top tips!

This recipe is, again, an outline or suggestion. Have fun as you and your helpers create your own unique Family Trail Mix (see Activity: Do Your Own Thing, page 42).

### fun fact!

August 31 is National Trail Mix Day in the United States.

You've got your Family Trail Mix, now where do you want to take it?

# Go on an Adventure

Is there an adventure you've always wanted to go on with your family? Hiking, driving, climbing, boating, skiing, travel…the options are endless. Life can sometimes get in the way of the best adventures we dream of for our families. This has certainly been the case with restrictions imposed by the pandemic and the struggle to stay safe. This activity encourages you to revisit those dreams. You've got your Family Trail Mix now. Where do you want to take it?

**YOUNG HELPERS**

### PICK YOUR ADVENTURE
If you could go on any adventure, where would it be? Tell your grown-up helper and make a plan.

**PRETEEN + TEEN HELPERS**

### FOLLOW YOUR DREAM ADVENTURE
What's a place you've always wanted to visit? Discuss with your grown-up helper.

**GROWN-UP HELPERS**

### PLAN YOUR ADVENTURE
Plan a day trip adventure with your family based on their responses or get out the map (or the GPS on your phone) and daydream.

Our kids have always loved raw carrots. My go-to raw veggie is cauliflower and CC's preference is, without question, cherry tomatoes. Veggies and dip are a healthy and satisfying snack. If you want to make it sound more fancy, call it crudités, which is a French dish of raw vegetables. Crudités are fun to serve when you have both adults and kids around. This recipe is a wonderful combination of easy to prepare, delicious to eat, and good for you.

I will include a few dips for this recipe, but you can dip your veggies into many things, including cottage cheese, whipped cream cheese, yogurt, Hummus (page 119), or The Best Guacamole Ever (see page 109).

### INGREDIENTS

| | |
|---|---|
| 8 oz | **peeled baby carrots** |
| 12 oz | **cherry tomatoes** |
| ½ head | **cauliflower, cut into florets** |
| 1 | **small head broccoli, cut into florets** |
| 1 | **large red bell pepper, stemmed, seeded, halved, and cut into ¼-in strips** |
| 1 | **large yellow or green bell pepper, stemmed, seeded, halved, and cut into ¼-in strips** |
| 5 | **celery ribs, cut into 3-in lengths, then cut into ¼-in strips** |
| ½ bunch | **asparagus, cut into 3-in lengths, starting from the top of each spear** |
| 1 | **English cucumber, peeled, seeded, and cut into 3-in lengths, then cut into ¼-in strips** |

**SERVES 8**

# VEGGIES & DIP

Set your prepared veggies to one side as you make your dip. Ingredients for each dip are listed on the next page.

## TO MAKE THE CREAMY CHIVE DIP

In a large bowl, mix together the mayonnaise, sour cream, chives, garlic powder, and pepper. Season with salt. Refrigerate for at least 1 hour.

## TO MAKE THE ROASTED RED PEPPER DIP

Preheat the oven to 450°F. Line a baking sheet with parchment paper.

Lay your peppers, skin-side up, on the lined baking sheet. Add the garlic and lightly drizzle everything with a little olive oil. Roast for 20 to 30 minutes, or until the garlic is soft and the pepper skins are blistered. Remove from the oven, then place in a bowl, cover, and let cool completely.

Once the peppers are cool, you should be able to peel the skins off with your fingers. Discard the skins.

Place the roasted peppers and garlic in a food processor with the 1 tablespoon of olive oil and the red pepper flakes. Pulse until the mixture turns into a chunky purée. Be sure not to make your dip too smooth.

Pour your dip into a small bowl. Add the basil. Taste to check the seasoning and add salt and more red pepper flakes until the flavor works for you (see Activity: Taste as You Go, page 68). Cover your dip and chill in the fridge for 1 hour.

Now for the fun part. With your helpers, arrange your prepared veggies around a large round serving platter, mixing the different colors. For example, a block of green, then a block of red, and then a block of orange. Continue around the platter until all your veggies are used up. Choose your veggie and dunk it in your dip!

### top tips!

The bulb of garlic is the whole piece of garlic that you buy in the store. A clove of garlic is a piece of the bulb. For this recipe, remove three cloves from the bulb. You can remove the skin from each clove by carefully peeling it off with a small, sharp knife.

## CREAMY CHIVE DIP

| | |
|---|---|
| ½ cup | good-quality mayonnaise |
| ½ cup | sour cream |
| ¼ cup | chopped chives |
| 1 Tbsp | garlic powder |
| ¼ tsp | freshly ground black pepper |
| | fine sea salt |

## ROASTED RED PEPPER DIP

| | |
|---|---|
| 3 | large red bell peppers, halved and seeded |
| 3 cloves | garlic, peeled |
| 1 Tbsp | extra-virgin olive oil, plus more for drizzling |
| 1 pinch | red pepper flakes |
| ¼ cup | chopped fresh basil leaves |
| | fine sea salt |

# Make a New Connection or Renew an Old One

Chapter 6 is all about finding ways to connect with others. Snacks can provide a catalyst for that—whether they're enjoyed when watching a movie with friends and family, while playing a sport, or even when preparing them together. During the pandemic, and all its variations of quarantine, we've seen how important it is to connect with others. Connection is a fundamental part of our humanity.

**YOUNG HELPERS**

**PLAN THAT VISIT**
Visit a friend or family member you miss, either in person or virtually.

**PRETEEN + TEEN HELPERS**

**CONNECT WITH A CLASSMATE**
Reach out to a classmate you'd like to know better.

**GROWN-UP HELPERS**

**REACH OUT TO YOUR LOVED ONE**
Is there a friend or family member you haven't seen for a while? Which of these snacks would be their favorite? Spend an afternoon making it with your helpers, then deliver your snacky treat to your loved one by planning a visit or sending it in the mail. If you send it in the mail, schedule a call or virtual visit when your package arrives to say how much your loved one means to you and how important it was to send something to show how much you care.

# CHAPTER 7

# Chicken and Meat

*Build a HAVEN to Listen*

Chapter Six focused on how we can improve our connections with others. Chapter Seven takes this a step further by looking deeply at a critical parenting skill. This is the chapter many families might turn to the most. Meat and chicken are key staples for dinner—foods that many of us eat again and again. You may have certain recipes you use when it's "time to have chicken for dinner" or you want to "have something with meat in it." The salience of chicken and meat in nonvegetarian households makes me think about whether there's a particularly significant corresponding parenting skill. Listening comes to mind. Listening as a parenting ingredient is like the chicken in chicken parm, the meat in meatballs, or, for vegetarian households, the macaroni in mac 'n' cheese. The humbling thing is, while listening is so essential to parenting, it's also something many of us struggle with. We underestimate how complicated it is to truly hear someone.

Listening is elusive. We often think we're doing it, when actually we aren't. Does the phrase "You're not listening to me!" sound familiar? We can listen to a loved one and not understand the words. Perhaps we have our own agenda for the words. Or we might criticize the words, perhaps without even meaning to, shutting down further opportunities to listen.

HAVEN is a model I'd like to introduce to support our listening to loved ones. A haven is a safe place, a place where people seek refuge and support. As parents/guardians/caregivers, we want to be a haven for our kids—we want them to feel safe and to be able to come to us with anything.

The very process of child development makes our being a haven complicated, however. Our toddlers shift between having the strong desire to be with us and pushing us away to explore their worlds. This dual ability to both connect and be independent is key for toddler development.

Similarly, our teens fluctuate between dependence and distance. One minute they seem like they're five again; the next minute we don't even know who they are anymore. These shifts are critical as our teens navigate the road from childhood to adulthood.

Because being a good listener is so complicated, it's something that I aspire to. Every day I try to be a good listener. And guess what? Everyone in my family knows I'm going to get it wrong a lot of the time. That's just how it goes. But I keep trying. Sometimes I get it right, sometimes I get it right just enough. My HAVEN model is a reminder of what I need to focus on to truly hear those around me. HAVEN is an acronym for five key words and phrases: *Hear with no agenda*; *Anticipate the moment*; *Validation*; *Empathy*; and *Not jumping in to problem solve*. HAVEN skills are a process, not an outcome.

**H—Hear with no agenda.** We've all been here before. Our child is saying something and we hear the words. Of course we understand what's being said. Of course we're listening. But then, slowly, our own thoughts about those words start to cloud what we're hearing. Our understanding creates an agenda in our heads. This agenda is about the things we think our loved one needs to be doing based on the very words just spoken. Consider the following exchange:

"Mom, I want to take a gap year after high school. I'm tired and stressed. Going to school is a lot of work and it's kind of boring."

We didn't see this coming. All those years of academic support and goal setting. A gap year? What does that even mean?

We quiet our thoughts and ask aloud, "What are you thinking about?"

"I'm not sure. I might work at a café, get a job as a barista. I can practice being more social by interacting with customers."

"But you're so good with people," we can't resist exclaiming. "College is so much more interesting than high school. You'll have a major with classes that focus on your interests."

We all can guess where this conversation is going:

"You're not listening to me. You're not hearing what I'm saying. I'm telling you I don't want to go to college next year."

And then we apologize and feel bad. We're confused—we offered support, care, motivation. Our teen stomps off and the conversation is over—leaving us standing there, wondering what even happened. Where did we mess up?

When we listen with our own agendas, we stop hearing what the other person is saying. We get so caught up in responding to what our agenda is telling us that we stop being able to hear the true experience of the person talking to us. We approach the conversation with the outcome that we want, without recognizing and respecting the different experience and outcome desired by our loved one.

I'm not saying don't have your own agenda. This is natural and expected—we're human, after all. What I'm saying is to listen with an awareness of it and work to not let it take over the conversation. Here's what can happen instead:

"I'm going to take a gap year next year."

Our minds are running fast—we weren't expecting this. All that work, the effort—on our teen's part and on ours as well. "We weren't expecting you'd be interested in a gap year. Can you tell us more about what you're thinking?"

"I want to work at a café. Take a break from schoolwork and just be in the world."

"We hear what you're saying. You've definitely been working really hard."

"It just seems like the right thing to do right now. When I go to college, I want to appreciate it, not feel like it's something I have to do."

"That makes sense," we say. "Let's keep talking."

**A—Anticipate the moment.** When we anticipate the moment, we listen out for the conversation. It's like the idea of "having the conversation by not starting it" in Chapter Four. When we anticipate the moment, we give up control, we listen, and we let the conversation happen when our kids are ready to have it. This allows us to take a developmental approach to parenting. As our kids grow, we have to grow, too, adjusting our skills to meet them where they're at developmentally. To anticipate the moment, we have to seize it. This may mean giving up what we planned to do so that we can be a listening presence for our kids. Consider the following scenario that presents a family situation that might reflect some of your own experiences:

Your teenage son surprises you when he asks if you want to watch a movie with him. His younger sister is already asleep. You have so many plans—laundry, folding, sending emails, doing more laundry.

"Yes," you say. "I'd love to. Would you like me to make some popcorn?"

As you watch the movie, you're aware of the urge to start folding clothes. But you don't. In the spirit of anticipating the moment, you are present to respond to any possibility that your son might share something about his life. And even if he doesn't, you want him to know you're focused on the two of you spending time together.

This example shows how we can be ready to respond when we anticipate the moment. The kitchen provides a natural place to do this. It's hard to know exactly why—but kitchens present their own brand of safe haven. In graduate school I threw a party every summer in my small, one bedroom apartment with no AC. Each year guests would crowd into the tiny galley kitchen—a kitchen so small that if I lay down on the floor my feet could touch one wall and, arms outstretched, my hands the other.

What is it that makes the kitchen such a special place? Maybe it's the aromas that are surprising and inviting, the lure of what will be created, the space for food where conversations nourish others?

The other night Izzy was baking before taking a late-night flight back to school. I just happened to be in the kitchen cleaning up (sure I was!). Organically, she started to talk about missing home, worries about grades, and whether she would be able to get a cab to campus from the airport. Just being in the kitchen together allowed this conversation to happen.

**V—Validation.** When we validate someone, we acknowledge their feelings. There's no right or wrong; we simply seek to understand what someone experiences at that moment. Validation is a skill that allows us to listen to the emotional undercurrents of what our kids are going through.

Validation is tricky. We may disagree with the behavior we see. Your teen might be upset because he thinks he failed a test, but you know he didn't study. The dialectical behavioral therapy (DBT) approach provides a nice way to handle this dilemma.[1] It says that validation doesn't have to mean we agree with the behavior. We may fully disagree with it, and even feel angry about it. That's okay. We can disagree with the behavior and still acknowledge and hear more about the feelings connected to it.

Consider the following scenario that presents what the conversation might look like:

"I'm so stressed. I think I failed my chem test."

"You've been going out a lot lately. Did you study for it?"

"I got so caught up in being out with friends that I didn't study at all. I think I really messed it up."

"Well, as you know, it's important to study, and it sounds like you're really stressed. I can imagine how anxiety provoking this situation must be."

Validation is freeing for parents. We can still listen and be present, even if we oppose the behavior. Consider this scenario that provides an example of how we might unintentionally engage in invalidating behavior:

A father and son were sitting on the subway. Their seats were next to each other. The father had his eyes closed. The son kept tapping his shoulder, "Dad, dad, dad," he said, as he repeatedly stood up and sat down.

The dad didn't move. He kept his eyes closed. "Dad, dad, dad!!"

Finally the dad opened his eyes. He turned to look at his son and said sternly, "Can you please relax and sit down?"

We've all been here, tired, stressed, just trying to have a quiet moment. When we offer validation to show we are listening, not only do we validate our loved one, we can also validate ourselves. The following scenario shows what this might look like:

"Dad, dad."

"Dad, dad."

"Dad, dad."

"I hear you want my attention. I'm tired and just taking a moment to close my eyes. Is there something you wanted to share with me? Do you need a hug?"

**E—Empathy.** When we really try to hear someone's experiences, to understand their feelings and where they're coming from, we bring empathy to the interaction. Empathy helps us listen by virtue of working to understand where someone is at from their point of view. We may not even say anything while we actively try to hear and understand the other person's perspective.

When Olliver was three, Sabrina was thirteen, and Izzy was fifteen, we drove three hours to pick up a forty-pound puppy. It was dark and cold by the time we arrived. The puppy's parents were there. We bundled up the puppy and put her in the back seat with the kids, stretched out across their legs. Over the squeals of excitement of our new family member, I heard Olliver say to the puppy, "It must be hard leaving your mama and papa. I'll take care of you."

**N—Not jumping in to problem solve.** A natural inclination for parents is to jump in with a solution when our kids are struggling. The tendency to problem solve can show up in daily activities:

"I hate my haircut. It looks awful!" our daughters say.

We say, "Don't worry, it will grow back. Let's get some hair clips to put it up."

And in larger scenarios:

"I don't have any friends at school."

"What about the new boy who joined your class? Can you connect with him?"

It's understandable that we want to jump in. It's painful to see those we care about hurting. Problem solving as parents makes us feel like we're helping, that we're not powerless.

A caveat of course is that we absolutely have to problem solve if there's a crisis situation, medical emergency, or other urgent situation that calls on us to think in the moment and make active decisions. In day-to-day life, however, a problem-solving approach can bring the risk of not hearing what our kids are experiencing. Even more, we risk invalidating their experience. Regardless of whether the hair will grow back, she's upset about it. Having a new kid at school doesn't necessarily translate into instant friendship.

I love to problem solve—and I'm good at it. I've learned to brace myself in these situations, however. If I find myself reaching for a solution, I emotionally pull back to regroup so that I can come to the moment with a listening-to-understand approach. This is hard. It takes courage. It takes trusting ourselves and, more importantly, trusting our child to be able to handle the situation and all the emotions it ushers in. Stepping back before stepping in might look like this:

"I hate my hair. It looks awful."

"I'm so sorry that you feel that way."

Or this:

"I don't have any friends at school."

"That must feel so lonely."

And even though the problem isn't solved, there's a connection, a safe space, a place where just through listening we're indicating that we are there for our child.

It's from this place that the conversation can grow.

## INGREDIENTS

| | |
|---|---|
| 4 Tbsp | olive oil |
| ⅔ cup | chopped red onion (about 1 medium red onion) |
| ⅓ cup | chopped smoked bacon (about 3 strips) |
| 1 cup | chopped white mushrooms |
| 2 cups | fresh breadcrumbs (about 6 slices of bread, crusts removed and lightly pulsed in a food processor) |
| 2 Tbsp | soft brown sugar |
| 1 tsp | fine sea salt |
| ½ tsp | freshly ground black pepper |
| 4 | chicken breasts, about 8 oz each, boneless and skinless |
| 1 Tbsp | unsalted butter |

**SERVES 4**

CHICKEN

# ROAST SUPREMES OF CHICKEN WITH SMOKED BACON STUFFING

Preheat the oven to 350°F.

Get started by warming 2 Tbsp of the olive oil in a sauté pan over medium heat. Add the chopped red onion and cook for a few minutes making sure it doesn't brown. Add the bacon and continue cooking, stirring continuously, for 3 more minutes. Add the mushrooms and cook for a few more minutes, or until they change color; they will turn darker while they cook. Remove the pan from the heat.

In a large bowl, have fun mixing together the breadcrumbs and brown sugar. Add the cooked red onion mixture, season with salt and pepper, and mix everything together. Set aside.

Arrange the chicken breasts so that the tenders (the thin strip of meat between the chicken breast and the chicken bone) are facing up. Push the chicken tenders away from the center of the chicken breast. Then make a small incision into the thickest part of the chicken (this will be on the other side of the chicken tender). Fill that pocket with the stuffing and then fold the chicken tenders back to seal the incisions. Season the chicken breasts all over with salt and pepper.

In a large, ovenproof sauté pan, heat the remaining 2 Tbsp of olive oil and the butter over medium heat. Add the chicken breasts and sear, turning, for about four to five minutes, or until browned all over. Place the pan in the oven and bake the chicken for 8 to 10 minutes. Then turn it over and continue to bake for another 8 to 10 minutes or until the internal temperature reaches 165°F. Serve immediately. Delicious!

I created this recipe when I was looking for an oven-ready meal during a particularly busy time in our lives. It needed to be a dish that was prepared either the day before or in the morning, so that CC could simply throw it in the oven when she got home with the kids. And that's what this is: forty-five minutes later, a complete hot and nutritious meal emerges from the oven ready to serve hungry mouths. The hands-off nature makes this recipe even more enjoyable, as CC can get on with other things, like helping with homework or checking in with the kids after their school day, while dinner is cooking.

## INGREDIENTS

| | |
|---|---|
| 1½ lb | Idaho potatoes |
| 4 | large, whole chicken legs, bone-in and skin-on |
| 1 | large red onion, peeled and thinly sliced |
| 1 | green bell pepper, stemmed, seeded, and thickly sliced |
| 1 | red bell pepper, stemmed, seeded, and thickly sliced |
| 3 cloves | garlic, minced |
| 1 Tbsp | chopped fresh thyme leaves |
| 1 Tbsp | chopped fresh rosemary needles |
| 1 tsp | dried oregano |
| ¼ cup | extra-virgin olive oil |
| | fine sea salt and freshly ground black pepper |

**SERVES 4**

CHICKEN

# ROAST CHICKEN LEGS WITH POTATOES, VEGETABLES, & HERBS

Line a roasting pan with parchment paper.

Place the potatoes in a large pot, cover with cold water, and add 2 Tbsp of salt. Place over high heat and bring to a boil, then reduce the heat and simmer for 10 minutes only. Drain the potatoes, then run them under cold water for a few minutes. Once the potatoes are cool enough to touch, remove the skins and cut them into roughly 1½-inch squares. Place the potatoes in a large bowl and set aside.

Leave the skin on the chicken legs but cut them in half. You can do this by laying the chicken legs, skin-side down, on a cutting board, and then, with a sharp knife, cutting down through the joint where the two leg bones meet in the center of the leg. It might take a few tries, but you'll find the sweet spot and the knife will go straight through the joint, separating the thigh from the drumstick. Place the 8 pieces of chicken in the bowl with your potatoes. Add the red onion, green and red bell peppers, garlic, thyme, rosemary, oregano, and olive oil. Season with salt and pepper and mix everything together. Spread the chicken mixture in the lined roasting pan, making sure the chicken legs are skin-side up. Cover your roasting pan with aluminum foil and refrigerate until it's time to cook dinner.

Once dinnertime is approaching, preheat the oven to 350°F.

Once the oven is up to temperature, place the roasting pan on the middle rack and bake for 30 minutes. Carefully remove the aluminum foil and continue baking for another 15 to 20 minutes, or until the chicken is cooked through and the vegetables are golden brown. Tasty and convenient!

We often hear that fried food is not good for us, but this is all relative.

Firstly, moderation in all things is a great rule to eat by. Consuming a pound of candy every day may not be such a great idea, but having some candy from time to time is okay. We feel that having a varied and balanced mix of different foods is the cornerstone of a healthy diet.

The following recipe is fried, but we like to use organic chicken, whole wheat flour, multigrain breadcrumbs, and extra-virgin olive oil. That's not so bad!

We use canned tomatoes for the sauce. It's similar to using fresh tomatoes because there are no preservatives. Canned tomatoes are harvested when they are perfectly ripe and then immediately canned, so you will make a wonderful sauce with delicious tomatoes.

**TOMATO SAUCE**

| | |
|---|---|
| 1 | **28-oz can whole peeled plum tomatoes** |
| ¼ cup | **extra-virgin olive oil** |
| 6 cloves | **garlic, minced** |
| 1 tsp | **fine sea salt** |
| 1 | **medium bunch fresh basil** |

**CHICKEN**

# CLASSIC CHICKEN PARMESAN

## TO MAKE THE TOMATO SAUCE

If you have a food mill, pour the tomatoes and ¾ cup of water into the mill, turn the handle, and collect the crushed tomatoes in a stainless-steel bowl underneath. Alternatively, pour the tomatoes and water into a large stainless-steel bowl and crush them with your hands. Young children—and perhaps children of all ages—will love doing this messy part of the recipe (see Activity: Prepping Your Ingredients, page 94).

### fun fact!

A food mill is a kind of sieve with a paddle inside of it that moves and pushes food through the sieve part. This removes large lumps to make your food item smoother.

Warm the olive oil in a medium (not aluminum or iron) saucepan over medium heat. Add the garlic and let it cook but do not let it brown.

Add the crushed tomatoes and salt and stir everything together.

Place the bunch of basil, including the stems, on the surface of the sauce. It will wilt and then submerge into the sauce. This can be really fun for kids to watch. Simmer the sauce over low heat for about 15 minutes, or until it's slightly thickened. Taste the sauce and add salt if needed. Cook for 5 more minutes, then remove and discard the basil. Your tomato sauce is ready!

## CHICKEN PARMESAN

| | |
|---|---|
| 4 | chicken breasts, about 6 oz each, boneless and skinless |
| ¼ cup | whole wheat flour |
| 2 | large eggs, lightly beaten |
| ½ cup | multigrain breadcrumbs (see directions at right) |
| ½ cup | freshly grated Parmesan cheese |
| 2 Tbsp | extra-virgin olive oil |
| ¼ cup | torn fresh basil leaves |
| 1 cup | freshly grated low-moisture mozzarella cheese |

**SERVES 4**

## TO MAKE MULTIGRAIN BREADCRUMBS

Dry out 4 slices of stale multigrain bread for 24 hours then grind in a food processor to make the crumbs.

## TO MAKE THE CHICKEN PARMESAN

Preheat the oven to 375°F.

Using a sharp knife and starting at the thickest part of the breast, cut 1 of the chicken breasts almost in half horizontally then unfold the 2 halves open like a book so you have 1 large flat piece. Repeat with the other chicken breasts and place between 2 sheets of parchment paper. Gently pound the chicken with a mallet or rolling pin until evenly flattened to about ⅛ inch thick.

Now for the breading. You will need 3 shallow bowls: 1 for the whole wheat flour, 1 for the beaten egg, and 1 for a mixture of the multigrain breadcrumbs and Parmesan cheese. Take each breast, one by one, and dip in the flour, covering both sides, followed by the egg, covering both sides, and lastly in the breadcrumb mixture, making sure the chicken is evenly coated. Kids will love all this dipping!

Heat the olive oil in a large frying pan over medium-high heat. Add the chicken, 1 or 2 pieces at a time, depending on the size of your frying pan, and cook, turning, for about 3 minutes on each side, or until brown on both sides. Repeat as needed to cook the remaining chicken and set aside.

Spread some of the tomato sauce in a 9-×-13-inch baking dish. Arrange the chicken in a single layer in the dish. Spread more tomato sauce on top of each chicken breast and then sprinkle with the fresh basil. Finally, evenly distribute the mozzarella cheese on top of each chicken breast.

Place the baking dish in the oven and bake for 25 to 30 minutes, or until the chicken is cooked through and the mozzarella is slightly browned.

Fried but not so bad!

# Coordinate Movements and Make Time for Self-Care

Life is a busy balancing act with many moving parts. Just like dipping the chicken in the flour, the egg, and the breadcrumbs requires coordination, so too does the management of the many movements in our lives. Sometimes we need to speed up, to move quicker to get everything done. But sometimes we need to slow down, to calm ourselves so that we can relax and focus. If we dip the chicken too quickly, it might not be fully covered in the flour, egg, and breadcrumbs. If we intensify and rush, we might accidentally drop the chicken in the egg and then have to scoop it out. Coordinating movements is a lot like HAVEN. We need to slow down and put our agendas aside to be present and empathic.

To support this openness, and the coordination of our movements, self-care is critical. Self-care looks like many different things for people: going to the gym, doing yoga, going for a run, watching football, getting together with a group of friends, cooking—the possibilities are endless. This activity is all about identifying self-care strategies that ultimately support your role as a listener who reflects the HAVEN model. It's important to take care of ourselves so we can take care of others. For me, one of the best things about self-care is the perspective it provides. When I step away from the movements that coordinate what needs to be done, and go to dinner with friends, for instance, I return home feeling that whatever I was so worried about doesn't seem so important. Self-care is about gaining perspective.

### YOUNG HELPERS

### TAKE A BREAK
Once a month, invite your grown-up helper to join you on an afternoon adventure that's focused on an activity of your choice. Pick something that will make you feel happy: Miniature golf? Crafting? Playing in the park? Going on a bicycle ride? Ice skating in the winter? You and your grown-up helper can choose a different outing each month and explore where you live.

### PRETEEN + TEEN HELPERS

### DE-STRESS
Did you know that states including Arizona, Connecticut, Colorado, Maine, Illinois, Nevada, Oregon, and Virginia passed bills that allow students to miss school for mental or behavioral health-related concerns? These bills have been largely supported by youth advocating for change. School work and after-school expectations can be overwhelming and relentless. Coordinate consistent times when you allow yourself to take a break.

### GROWN-UP HELPERS

### FIND TIME TO STOP
In the midst of movement coordination, sometimes it's important to simply STOP. Take a moment away from the day-to-day to regroup and reclaim calmness. "But how can I do this?" you ask. After all, you have a family and a demanding job. Find the moments, or pockets of time, when you can make time for you. Do you have a couple of free hours on Tuesday afternoon? Do something fun for you. And don't check work email or respond to work-related texts or messages. Don't feel that you need to do an errand for someone else during that time. It's just two hours—do only what you want to do.

Chicken pot pie is quintessential comfort food and a one stop meal with protein, vegetables, and starch. Although it takes some preparation, the results are well worth the effort. Making pot pie can be quite interactive, too. Our kids especially love to roll out the pastry and paint the top with egg. The pastry dough is a rough puff pastry. It's flaky and light and, as you will see, can be made without spending the hours it takes to make traditional puff pastry.

Chicken pot pie was a lunchtime favorite at my restaurant in England. A few years later, after I arrived in New York, I put it on my menu at a restaurant in Union Square. To my great surprise and pleasure, people loved it. So much so that it even received a wonderful write up in the *New York Times*. The article came out around Thanksgiving and all day cabs drove up to the restaurant. Passengers would jump out to pick up their pot pies and then get back in their cabs to go to the airport, taking their pot pies with them for the Thanksgiving weekend. So from a small village near Oxford to one of the largest cities in the world, Famed Chicken Pot Pie delights and nourishes.

## ROUGH PUFF PASTRY

| | |
|---|---|
| 3 cups | all-purpose flour, plus more for dusting |
| 2 tsp | fine sea salt |
| ¾ cup | unsalted butter, cold |
| ¾ cup | lard or vegetable shortening, cold |
| ¾ cup | ice-cold water |
| 1 Tbsp | white vinegar |
| 1 | large egg |

## CHICKEN

# FAMED CHICKEN POT PIE

### TO MAKE THE ROUGH PUFF PASTRY

Place the flour and salt in a large bowl.

Cut the cold butter and lard into ¼- to ½-inch squares and add to the flour mixture. Mix everything with clean hands and then add ½ cup of the ice-cold water and the vinegar and mix. The dough should be a dry paste, but if all the flour is not incorporated, add a little more of the ice-cold water until you get a uniform dry dough. Flatten the dough into a disk, wrap it in plastic wrap or parchment paper, and refrigerate for 30 minutes.

*top tips!*

You can make the pastry one or two days before you need it. Just keep it in the fridge, snuggly wrapped in plastic wrap or parchment paper until ready to use.

### TO MAKE YOUR FILLING

Put the chicken on your cutting board, breast-side up. With a large serrated knife, cut the chicken along the breast bone, moving the knife back and forth. You will first go through the breast cavity and then continue cutting through the chicken back. This will separate the chicken into two pieces. Now place your two chicken halves, along with the celery, carrots, onions, garlic, thyme, bay leaves, salt, pepper, and 2½ quarts of water, in a large pot. Bring to a boil over high heat, then reduce the heat and very gently simmer the chicken and vegetables for about 45 minutes, or until the chicken and vegetables are cooked. To check whether your chicken is cooked, you can use a pair of kitchen tongs to pull out one of your chicken halves. Poke the chicken leg joint with a knife. If there's no blood coming from it, your chicken will be cooked. If the chicken is cooked, the vegetables will be cooked. If blood does come out, continue to cook for another 15 minutes. While simmering, use a large kitchen spoon or ladle to remove and discard any impurities and fat that may rise to the surface.

Set a large colander in a large bowl and strain the chicken and vegetables, reserving all the cooking liquid—this becomes an important ingredient as you will see. Set the chicken and vegetables aside to cool.

## FILLING

| | |
|---|---|
| 1 | whole chicken, about 3½ lb, cut in half (see directions opposite) |
| 6 | large celery ribs, cut crosswise in half |
| 4 | medium carrots, peeled |
| 2 | small onions, peeled |
| 2 cloves | garlic, peeled |
| 4 sprigs | fresh thyme |
| 3 | bay leaves |
| 2 Tbsp | fine sea salt |
| 1 tsp | freshly ground black pepper |
| 4 Tbsp | unsalted butter |
| 8 oz | white mushrooms, sliced |
| ½ cup | all-purpose flour |
| ¼ cup | heavy or whipping cream |

**SERVES 6**

## fun fact!

What's the difference between puff pastry and rough puff pastry? Puff pastry is a flour-based dough that is folded with butter to create alternate layers of dough and butter. This is called lamination. Rough puff pastry is also a flour-based dough, but it's made with chunks of butter and/or lard that when rolled out create a less evenly laminated dough. The good news is that rough puff pastry is still flaky when baked.

Melt the butter in the same large pot over medium heat. Add the mushrooms and cook for about 5 minutes. Use a slotted spoon to transfer the mushrooms to a bowl and set aside. Add the flour to the butter left in the pot and cook over medium heat, stirring with a wooden spoon, until all the butter is absorbed and you have a kind of firm paste—this is called a roux. Slowly add the reserved cooking liquid and gently simmer for about five minutes. The liquid will slowly thicken. Add the cream, stir briefly, and remove from the heat. This now becomes your sauce.

Once the chicken is cool enough to touch, remove and discard the skin and bones. Cut or tear the chicken meat into bite-size pieces and add to your sauce. Cut the celery, carrots, and onions into bite-size pieces and add to your sauce. Add your mushrooms and gently mix everything together. Place the filling in a deep 12-×-8-inch baking dish and set aside.

### TO ROLL AND FOLD THE ROUGH PUFF PASTRY

Remove the plastic wrap or parchment paper from your dough and place it on a lightly floured surface. Dust the top with flour and use a rolling pin to roll it out into an even rectangle that is about ¼ inch thick. Fold the top third of the dough toward the center, then fold the bottom third so it's on top of the first third. Turn the dough 90 degrees and repeat the rolling and folding once more. Wrap your rough puff pastry in plastic wrap or parchment paper and refrigerate for another 30 minutes.

### TO BAKE YOUR POT PIE

Preheat the oven to 375°F.

On a floured surface, roll out your pastry to fit the dish you are using—it will be placed over the filling. Break the egg into a cup and whisk it with a fork. Using a pastry brush, paint the top edge of the pie dish. Carefully place the pastry over the dish, then use a sharp knife to remove any excess pastry hanging over the sides of the dish—reserve any extra dough for decoration (see Activity: A Heart of Dough, page 138). Paint

## fun fact!

A roux is a thickening agent consisting of equal parts (by weight) of a fat and flour. We typically use butter as the fat, melting it in a saucepan, then adding flour and mixing them together. We can make a white roux, which has no color. If we cook it a little longer it becomes a blond roux, which is a biscuit color. A brown roux is cooked the longest and is a brown color.

## top tips!

Use a little extra dusting flour if the dough sticks to the rolling pin or the work surface while you are rolling it out.

What's the difference between butter and lard? Butter is made from cow's milk. When you whip heavy cream, the fats clump together into a solid—this is the butter. The liquid that separates out is the buttermilk. Lard is a by-product of pork. It's pig fat that has been melted and clarified and when cooled, turns into a solid.

the entire top of the pastry with the beaten egg. Using the back of a knife, mark but don't cut the top of the pastry into 6 equal portions. This makes it easier to cut the pot pie when it's time for you to portion it for your family. Add your decorations (see Activity: A Heart of Dough, below) then place the dish in the oven and bake for 45 minutes to an hour, or until the pastry is golden brown and crispy. Sit down, relax, eat, and be comforted.

# A Heart of Dough

HELPERS
OF
ALL AGES

You can paint and decorate your pot pie! Let your pastry be your canvas and your pastry brush your paint brush. Use your dough trimmings as decor, like the acrylic gems you stick on drawings. As described above, once your pie crust covers your pie, paint the whole of your "canvas" with your egg. Now is the time to make and place your designs on top of the crust canvas. If you want your design to be shiny, you can paint it with the egg. If you prefer an un-shiny look, leave it "unpainted." The egg acts as both paint and glue to secure your dough decorations.

As you paint your dough with your egg paint, consider the following: How do I hold the pastry brush? What kinds of brush strokes do I make? Is painting something I want to do more of? Now you're ready to decorate.

Pick up that extra pastry dough and knead it in your hands. What will you sculpt? How will you decorate your pot pie? You can make shapes that reflect something about the season, like leaves if it's fall and the trees are changing colors. Or you could make a chicken shape. You can even create the initials of the person you're making the pot pie for and place them in the center. Is it Valentine's Day? Pot pie is a wonderful Valentine's Day treat. Make a heart shape and put it front and center on top of your pie. A heart of dough!

This recipe is a really interactive dish to make as a family, as there is a lot of cutting and assembly involved. It's a perfect meal for "al fresco" dining in the spring, summer, and early fall.

## MARINADE

| ¼ cup | extra-virgin olive oil |
| | zest and juice of 1 lemon |
| 2 cloves | garlic, minced |
| 1 Tbsp | chopped fresh basil leaves |
| 1 Tbsp | chopped fresh thyme leaves |
| | fine sea salt and freshly ground black pepper |

## SKEWERS

| 1 lb | chicken breast, boneless and skinless, cut into ½-in squares |
| 1 | skinny green zucchini (or pattypan squash), cut into ¼-in slices |
| 1 | skinny yellow squash (or sunburst squash), cut into ¼-in slices |
| ¼ head | cauliflower, cut into small florets |
| 8 oz | small to medium cremini mushrooms |
| 1 | large red onion, peeled and cut into ½-in squares |
| 16 | cherry tomatoes |
| 1 | red bell pepper, stemmed, seeded, and cut into ½-in squares |
| 1 | yellow bell pepper, stemmed, seeded, and cut into ½-in squares |
| 1 | green bell pepper, stemmed, seeded, and cut into ½-in squares |
| 8 | 10-in bamboo skewers, soaked in cold water overnight |

**SERVES 4**

CHICKEN

# GRILLED MARINATED CHICKEN & VEGETABLE SKEWERS

If you use bamboo skewers, plan ahead and soak them in fresh water overnight. This will give your skewers time to soak up the water, which means they'll last longer on your grill before burning, though you still need to be careful. If you use metal skewers, they are, of course, not combustible, but when you pick them up, they can be very hot. Be careful!

### TO MAKE THE MARINADE

In a small stainless-steel bowl, whisk together the olive oil, lemon zest and juice, garlic, basil, and thyme. Season with salt and pepper and set aside.

### TO MAKE THE SKEWERS

Thread the chicken, zucchini, squash, cauliflower, mushrooms, onions, tomatoes, and bell peppers onto the skewers, alternating the various ingredients and having fun with colors and patterns (see Activity: Thread Your Skewers to Learn about Pattern and Design, page 141). Once all the skewers are made, brush your marinade over them. If you're using an outdoor grill, heat it to medium. Alternatively, if you're cooking inside, preheat a grill pan over medium heat and preheat the oven to 350°F.

If cooking on the outdoor grill, set the skewers directly on the grill grate and cook, occasionally turning and basting with more marinade, for 15 to 20 minutes, or until the chicken is cooked through and the vegetables are tender. (To test the chicken to see if it's done, cut into a piece and make sure it's uniformly white inside.)

*top tips!*

Serve your skewers with a super fresh tomato salad. Slice ripe vine tomatoes, then drizzle with extra-virgin olive oil and balsamic vinegar and finish with a twist of black pepper and a sprinkle of coarse sea salt.

Alternatively, serve your skewers with a delicious potato salad. Boil fingerling potatoes in their skins, then drain, cool, and slice before mixing with good-quality mayonnaise, chopped fresh chives, a touch of sweet pickle relish, salt, and pepper.

The whole family can sit outside enjoying the weather while threading the delicately prepared ingredients onto bamboo skewers before a grown-up helper places them on the grill (see Activity: Thread Your Skewers to Learn about Pattern and Design, opposite).

Skewers are a fun and delicious way of cooking many different foods. Thread your bamboo skewers with vegetables only or mix them up with jumbo shrimp, tender beef, marinated pork, Italian sausage, or a combo of your family's favorites.

These skewers can be fully cooked outside on the grill or started in a grill pan on the stove and then finished in the oven. I recommend serving the skewers with a super fresh tomato salad or, if you prefer a starch, a delicious potato salad (see Top Tip, previous page).

Alternatively, if you are cooking inside, place the skewers in the preheated grill pan and cook, occasionally turning and basting with more marinade, until you see what we call "marks" in the professional kitchen. These brown stripes will appear on the chicken and vegetables where the food has gotten hot on the raised grill bars. You may need to "grill" your skewers in batches, depending on the size of your grill pan. Once you've put grill marks on all your skewers, place them on a baking sheet and bake in the oven for 10 to 15 minutes, or until the chicken is cooked through and the vegetables are tender.

Enjoy this colorful meal outside or indoors—either way, it's delicious!

## fun fact!

Sunburst squash are small, only about ½ inch, and can be left whole for your skewers; yellow squash are larger and need to be cut.

## fun fact!

Is squash a fruit or a vegetable? We often think of squash as a vegetable, but it has seeds, which makes it a fruit.

# Thread Your Skewers to Learn about Pattern and Design

Extend your creativity as you thread your skewers. Consider the fruits, meat, and vegetables for your skewers to be like the beads for beading a necklace. They're all different shapes and colors: green, yellow, white, gray, purple, red. Which colors will you choose? What order will you put them in?

 **YOUNG HELPERS**

**CREATE YOUR PATTERN**
Make a pattern with color, shape, or size on your skewers. Be sure to ask your grown-up helper to supervise.

 **PRETEEN + TEEN HELPERS**

**SHARE ON SOCIAL MEDIA**
Photograph your skewers and share your creation on social media.

**GROWN-UP HELPERS**

**HOST A DESIGN CONTEST**
Have everyone decorate their skewers and vote to see which is most creative.

Homemade burgers are a great dinner for the whole family. This recipe is full of taste and texture. Burgers consist of very few ingredients. Let's start with the most important: the meat. Purchase freshly ground meat from a reputable store and select the best quality like CAB (Certified Angus Beef) or even USDA Prime, if it's available. I'll be honest here: usually, the more expensive the beef, the better the quality. That being said, what's even more important is the fat content. If your meat is too lean, your burgers will be dry and tasteless. Select a 75 percent–25 percent blend. This means the meat is 75 percent lean and 25 percent fat, which is perfect for delicious, flavorful, juicy burgers.

The other main ingredient is bread. I encourage you to avoid traditional precut, white sesame burger buns and instead choose something a little different. How about a brioche bun, a potato roll, or even an English muffin? Explore what looks inviting at your store and try something new.

Now that the basics are covered, you can finish your burger in your own unique way—cheese, lettuce, tomato, mustard, bacon, ketchup, mushroom, good-quality mayonnaise, pickle chips, onion—all or nothing. Go wild!

## INGREDIENTS

| | |
|---|---|
| 1½ lb | freshly ground beef |
| 1 Tbsp | olive oil |
| 4 | buns, halved horizontally |
| | fine sea salt and freshly ground black pepper |
| | your choice of toppings (optional) |

**SERVES 4**

# HOMEMADE BEEF BURGER

Preheat the oven to 300°F.

Divide the ground beef into 4 six-ounce portions. Roll each portion in your hands to make balls. Now place the balls on a flat surface and push them down with the palm of your hand so they are about ⅓ inch thick. Fix the edges if necessary so they are not split. You should have 4 uniform beef patties. Season each patty on both sides with a little salt and pepper.

Place a skillet large enough to accommodate 4 burgers over high heat. Let the skillet get hot, then add the olive oil. Carefully add the beef patties and cook to your desired doneness. In general, you can think about cooking your burgers for 2 minutes per side for rare; 2½ minutes per side for medium-rare; 3 to 3½ minutes per side for medium; and 4 to 4½ minutes per side for medium-well. Once you've cooked the first side of your burgers, put your buns in the oven for about 4 minutes to warm through.

### NOW EVERYTHING COMES TOGETHER

Remove your buns from the oven and place each on a separate plate. Take the tops off the buns and add your perfectly cooked burgers to the bottoms. Lay the tops next to the burgers and serve with assorted toppings and sauces ready to finish your unique burgers.

Kids from 3 to 103 will love forming their own food with this recipe. The challenge is to try to get all the meatballs to be the same size, which is fun and actually not that easy. It's also interesting to compare the first few meatballs you make to the ones you make at the end. Often the ones at the end are bigger than those from the beginning. Perhaps this is because we get tired, or our eyes play tricks on us. Olliver and I made these recently. He loved the tactile sensation of rolling the meatball mixture in his hand.

## INGREDIENTS

| | |
|---|---|
| 6 oz | day-old bread (weighed when the crusts are removed and then cut into small pieces) |
| ¾ cup | whole milk |
| 1 lb | freshly ground pork |
| 8 oz | hot Italian sausage, casings removed |
| 3 cloves | garlic, thinly sliced |
| ½ bunch | fresh basil, leaves roughly chopped |
| 2 | large eggs |
| ½ cup | freshly grated Parmesan cheese |
| 2 tsp | fine sea salt |
| 1 tsp | freshly ground black pepper |
| 24 oz | tomato sauce (or use your own from the Classic Chicken Parmesan, page 133) |

**SERVES 4**

# MEATBALLS: FUN FORMING FOOD

Preheat the oven to 350°F. Line a baking sheet with parchment paper.

Soak the bread in the milk for 5 minutes, then remove the bread and squeeze out any excess milk by hand. This is a great tactile experience for kids of all ages.

Place the soaked bread in a large bowl. Add the pork and sausage and mix by hand to combine. Add the garlic, basil, eggs, Parmesan cheese, salt, and pepper, and mix well to combine.

Use your hands to form the mixture into golf ball–sized meatballs. You should be able to make about 12 equal-sized meatballs. Place the meatballs on the lined baking sheet and bake for 15 minutes. Lower the oven temperature to 325°F.

### fun fact!

When I make these at the restaurant, I weigh out each meatball so that they're all the exact same size.

Meanwhile, place the tomato sauce in a glass baking dish. Fill your sauce jar with about ½ cup of water, shake, and then pour it on top of the tomato sauce in the dish. Use a large metal stepped spatula to scoop the meatballs into the tomato sauce. Using this type of spatula reduces the risk of breaking your meatballs. Cover with aluminum foil and bake for 1 hour.

When the meatballs are ready, serve them with your favorite pasta dish, like our Whole Wheat Rigatoni alla Norma (page 177), or with plain boiled spaghetti. They also make a scrumptious lunch when served with our Spring Salad (page 50).

# Form Your Fun Food

It is so much fun to let go and create something. This makes our meatballs decidedly more than just something you eat. They're also something you make with your hands, like creating pottery—only you get to eat it, too.

**YOUNG HELPERS**

### MAKE A MESS
Get messy and form those meatballs.

**PRETEEN + TEEN HELPERS**

### EXPRESS YOUR FRUSTRATIONS
Get out your frustrations as you squish, roll, and form the mixture into meatballs.

**GROWN-UP HELPERS**

### PLAN ANOTHER MEAL
This dish freezes well if you want to double the recipe and save half for a later meal. All you have to do is use half for serving immediately. Then allow the other half to cool, place it in a freezer-safe container, and put in your freezer. It should last for up to 2 months in your freezer.

This stew is one of my favorite dishes and methods of cooking. The braised beef short ribs are succulent, tender, and packed with flavor. Years ago, I was doing a cooking demonstration in NYC, and Izzy, who was probably four years old at the time, came along to watch. She was so excited to see her dad cooking in front of a large audience that she joined me in the demonstration kitchen. Her reaction was clear: "Yum!"

## SHORT RIBS

| | |
|---|---|
| 4–5 lb | boneless beef short ribs or beef chuck flap, cut into 2-in squares |
| 2 tsp | whole coriander seeds |
| ½ tsp | whole cloves |
| ½ tsp | whole black peppercorns |
| 4 | bay leaves |
| 2 Tbsp | fine sea salt |
| 2 tsp | ground cinnamon |
| ½ tsp | ground allspice |
| ¼ cup | vegetable oil |

## SAUCE

| | |
|---|---|
| ¼ cup | vegetable oil |
| 1 | large white onion, peeled and chopped |
| 1 | large carrot, peeled and cut into ¼-in squares |
| 8 cloves | garlic, minced |
| 3 in | fresh ginger, peeled and finely chopped |
| ½ cup | tomato paste |
| 1 Tbsp | Worcestershire sauce |
| 1 | 28-oz can diced tomatoes in juice |
| 3 Tbsp | soft brown sugar, packed |
| 1 Tbsp | fine sea salt |
| 2 cups | red wine or water |

**SERVES 6 TO 8**

# BRAISED SHORT RIB STEW

Preheat the oven to 325° F.

### TO MAKE THE SHORT RIBS

In a small skillet over medium heat, gently toast the coriander, cloves, peppercorns, and bay leaves. This process is called blooming, and helps develop the flavor of the spices. Transfer the bloomed spices to a clean coffee grinder and grind into a fine powder. Place the ground spices in a large bowl, then add the salt, cinnamon, allspice, and vegetable oil. Stir to combine then add the short ribs and coat them with the spiced oil.

Place a heavy-bottomed large skillet over high heat. Working in batches, sear the ribs, turning, until dark brown and charred all over. Transfer the short ribs to a large but shallow braising pot—they should be packed together with little to no space between them—and set aside. Do not clean the skillet.

### TO MAKE THE SAUCE

In the same large skillet, warm the vegetable oil over medium heat. Add the onions and carrots and cook for about 5 minutes, or until they take on a little color. Add the garlic and ginger and cook for 5 more minutes. Add the tomato paste and continue cooking, stirring constantly for one minute. Add the Worcestershire sauce, diced tomatoes and their juices, brown sugar, salt, and the red wine or water. Bring to a boil, then pour over the short ribs.

Cover the braising pot with a tight-fitting lid or aluminum foil and cook your ribs for 3 to 4 hours, or until soft when touched with a fork. Remove the braising pot from the oven and use a ladle to remove as much cooking fat as possible. Serve the ribs with the vegetables and cooking juices. This stew is delicious when accompanied with Broccoli (page 181), Brussels Sprouts and Cauliflower Sautéed with Garlic and Olive Oil (page 187), or Mash for All (page 189). Go ahead, experiment!

# Ad-*Rib*: Create Something Spontaneously

There are so many ways to create something spontaneously with our Braised Short Rib Stew recipe. Express yourself and do something different. We present some ideas below, but trust that you will bring your own to the mix as well!

**YOUNG HELPERS**

### CREATE AN INGREDIENT INVENTION
If you could make anything else out of the ingredients for this stew, what would it be?

**PRETEEN + TEEN HELPERS**

### PUT TOGETHER A BRAISED SHORT RIB PIE
Use the rough puff pastry from our Famed Chicken Pot Pie (page 136) and fill it with the braised short ribs.

**GROWN-UP HELPERS**

### MAKE A SHEPHERD'S PIE
Use the braised short ribs as the filling and cover with Mash for All (page 189)

This is a grown-up dish that uses the slow cooking method I love so much. It also introduces another food into your family's "ingredient vocabulary." Trying something new or outside your comfort zone is a great way to experience different tastes and textures. It demonstrates to younger members of your family that you too can try something new even though you might not like it. But I think—and hope—that you do like these lamb shanks.

## INGREDIENTS

| | |
|---|---|
| 4 | meaty lamb shanks, about 1 lb each |
| 4 Tbsp | vegetable oil |
| 4 | celery ribs, cut into ¼-in squares |
| 1 | large carrot, peeled and cut into ¼-in squares |
| 1 | large onion, peeled and cut into ¼-in squares |
| 3 cloves | garlic, minced |
| 1 | 28-oz can diced tomatoes in juice |
| | zest and juice of 1 orange |
| | zest and juice of 1 lemon |
| 2 Tbsp | chopped fresh thyme leaves |
| | fine sea salt and freshly ground black pepper |

**SERVES 4**

MEAT

# BRAISED LAMB SHANKS

Preheat the oven to 325°F.

Generously season the lamb shanks with salt and pepper.

In a large skillet, heat 2 Tbsp of the vegetable oil over high heat and let the oil get really hot. Carefully add 2 lamb shanks to the skillet and brown the meat, turning the shanks a quarter turn at a time, until browned all over. Transfer the lamb shanks to a deep ovenproof baking dish large enough to fit all the meat. Return the skillet to high heat, add the remaining 2 Tbsp of vegetable oil and let it get really hot. Brown the remaining 2 shanks, then add them to the dish and set aside. Do not clean the skillet.

Place the same skillet over medium heat. Add the celery, carrot, and onion and cook for about 5 minutes. Then add the garlic and cook for 3 more minutes. Add about 2 cups of the diced tomatoes and their juices. Reduce the heat to low and add the zest and juice of the orange, the zest and juice of the lemon, and the thyme. Cook, stirring occasionally, to warm the ingredients. Taste your sauce and season with salt and pepper if necessary (see Activity: Taste as You Go, page 68). Carefully pour the mixture over the lamb shanks, then add the remaining diced tomatoes. If necessary, add a little water to make sure the shanks are totally submerged in liquid.

Cover and seal the baking dish tightly with aluminum foil and cook your lamb shanks in the oven for 3 to 4 hours, or until soft when touched with a fork. Remove the baking dish from the oven and use a ladle to remove as much cooking fat as possible. Serve the lamb shanks with the vegetables and cooking juices. They are delicious paired with some Broccoli (page 181), Brussels Sprouts and Cauliflower Sautéed with Garlic and Olive Oil (page 187), or Mash for All (page 189). Be adventurous: enjoy something new.

# Build a HAVEN to Listen

When we commit as parents to providing a safe HAVEN to listen, we acknowledge that hearing the authentic experiences of our loved ones is a really important way to validate them and let them know they're heard. At the same time, this commitment acknowledges that we are imperfect people. We won't always get it right. We can just keep trying to have empathy and understanding, knowing that sometimes we will get it wrong. In building a HAVEN to listen, we make ourselves available for all that parenting encompasses, working to hear our kids' authentic experiences, and recognizing that we're doing our best to do so.

**YOUNG HELPERS**

### SHARE YOUR FEELINGS WITH YOUR GROWN-UP HELPER
Share how you feel about your day with your grown-up helper. Here are some prompts to help you:

The best part about my day was _____ .
The worst part about my day was _____ .
Three words that describe how I felt today are _____ .
When I talk with you about how I feel it's _____ .

Grown-up helpers, you can support these prompts with your young helper by turning them into questions: What was the best part about your day? What was the worst part? What three words describe how you felt today? What is it like for you when we talk about your day together?

**PRETEEN + TEEN HELPERS**

### COMMUNICATE YOUR CONFLICT
If you have a conflict in a relationship that's important to you—and most of us do—take a moment to check in with that person in an effort to understand where they're coming from and to share your own experience.

**GROWN-UP HELPERS**

### STEP BACK TO STEP IN
The next time your child tells you about a day-to-day experience they're upset about (note: crisis moments not included here), step back from problem solving and step in to hear and validate their experience.

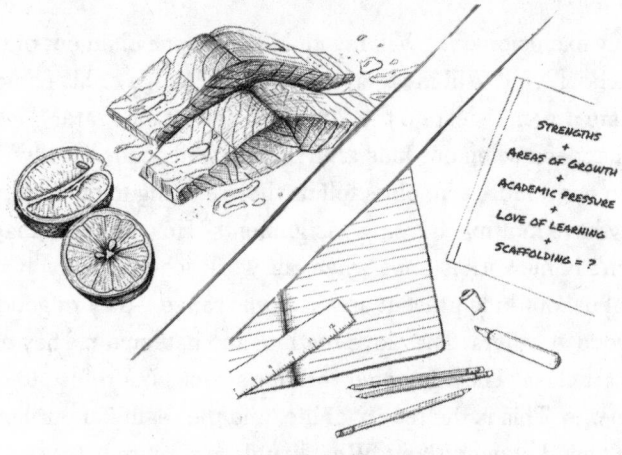

**CHAPTER 8**

# Dinner: Fish

*Brain Food, Pain Food*

Why is it that we call fish "brain food"? Oily fish has omega-3 fatty acids that help build brain cell membranes, supporting neurons so that our brains function better. But despite being aware that fish is good for us, we often put it aside as a regular cooking ingredient. We assume that preparing a fish dish will be complicated or unwieldy. I'll admit, the smell of fish and touching fish don't really work for me. And with fish I always wonder: Will I be able to cook a dish that actually tastes good, or will it taste fishy?

Chapter Eight is full of recipes that address these concerns with food creations aimed to support our brains and the brains of our loved ones. Fish is not only really healthy to eat but also really quick to cook. Most fish should be eaten when just cooked, meaning that it's warm in the center but still moist. A few exceptions are salmon and tuna, which can be eaten cold after being cooked and put on something like a salad, rare or even raw. When fish is cooked for too long it can be dry and less appetizing. The recipes that follow don't require many ingredients, and we promise that the prep time is quicker than you think. It also turns out that the dishes are delicious.

As parents, when we think about brain development, academic success immediately comes to mind. Are our kids doing well at school? How can they do better? Will they be successful? What does success look like? So much of our angst is around whether our kids will manage in a competitive world that, let's face it, can be incredibly exclusionary. "Will my child be the one child out of three thousand who gets into school X?" "Will my teen get into the college of his choice—his complete ultimate dream—despite the 2 percent acceptance rate?"

And what happens when our kids aren't doing well academically? What do we do as parents when our middle schoolers tell us they're doing their work and the school calls to say they have multiple missing assignments? How do we manage making sure our preteen's homework is done when our work schedules involve long hours?

For many of us, our kids present an academic range—they're good at some things, not so good at others. They love reading and hate math. They excel at sports but can't stand art class. They do homework for science but refuse to complete history assignments. This is the reality of life, and the reality of our humanity— most of us aren't good at everything. Why would we want to be?

The problem is that the system is set up so that we feel our kids have to excel at all things academic. Standardized testing presents questions that reflect a combination of skills for which students need to indicate some level of mastery. The SAT has a reading/writing section and a math section, but we can't ask an admissions office to just look at one set of scores—to consider the math score, for example, and leave out the reading/writing. The whole package is evaluated.

Many kindergarten to grade 12 parents can now opt out of having their kids tested. COVID-19 ushered in significant change as colleges and universities made standardized testing optional for admissions (although there has already been a shift back to a preference for SAT or ACT test scores). Where does the love of learning go in all this? How can we help our kids preserve it?

But wait—the focus on excelling at everything is even more pronounced when we think about the scholarships at stake. Maybe your child is seeking a merit scholarship for a private high school or a scholarship for college. These possibilities make getting good grades and high test scores essential for the affordability of college, particularly when the Education Data Initiative tells us that the cost of college has increased threefold over the past twenty years.[1] In 2021, the average cost for each year of college in the United States was $35,720. And that's for just one year!

These realities make it difficult for us as parents to approach academics in a laid-back manner. Instead, we understandably become overwhelmed with worry for how it's ever going to all come together: getting into a college of choice and being able to afford it. We may find ourselves wanting to pinpoint how our child is special to seize opportunities and ensure academic success and scholarship support. Wouldn't that be nice!

While providing academic success strategies is beyond the scope and purpose of this chapter, we can talk about how to try to stay grounded in the midst of a loaded academic playing field. This is just one perspective; yours might differ substantially. Take what works for you and leave the rest.

Brain food becomes pain food when our kids stop loving learning. As mentioned earlier, Olliver called preschool "school party!" Each day he bounded up the sidewalk to join his friends and teachers for another round of active, engaged play. His excitement was infectious. We saw a shift away from that when Olliver started kindergarten, however. He seemed "too cool for school" and talked about missing his family during the school day.

The transition from preschool to kindergarten is huge for our little ones. Olliver went from a play-centered environment to a school setting with expectations for learning. I assume that's the case for most of us, and not necessarily a bad thing. We want our kids to start to learn to read and do math. They need to be developing these skills. So what do we do as parents? Here are some ideas of how the kitchen can help.

Scaffolding allows us to structure our kids' learning by breaking down bigger learning tasks into smaller, more edible bites. Scaffolding involves both hands-on support, such as helping your child pronounce a word, and more independent support, like being on hand to respond to questions while your child engages in independent reading.

For working parents, it can be challenging to think about providing homework scaffolding after returning home from a tiring workday. One of our strategies is to invite our kids to sit at the kitchen table to work on homework while we make dinner. Between peeling and frying, we can check in and say, "How's it going?" Or they can reach out to us and ask, "Dad, I don't know this word." By scaffolding while cooking, we provide our kids a consistent routine and setting for homework.

Just as Chapter Seven talks about listening as an essential parenting skill, Chapter Eight presents reading as a critical academic skill. Of all the academic skills, reading is the most important. If our kids can't read, they can't acquire information to learn other subjects. Reading aloud to kids encourages their cognitive development and language skills. As we cook with our young helpers, we can read the recipes out loud to them. We can intersperse reading out loud with hands-on activities like finding ingredients or mixing things together. This incorporates other types of learning styles, like auditory and tactile learning. It also furthers the bond between us as parents and our young helpers.

Things change in the preteen years. Our kids may pull back more and appear to need our help less. Interestingly, this developmental shift often begins at the very same time that school expectations start to ramp up. We pull back while our preteens get pulled forward into greater academic responsibility.

As we notice our preteens and teens balancing greater academic demands alongside feeling they need to be less dependent on their grown-up helpers, we can support them in subtle ways such as inviting them to do homework while we're preparing dinner or asking them to make dinner with us or do the dishes together. Even if they don't have much to share about their day or their feelings, our presence shows we're open to listening when they're ready. Positive peer pressure is a great tool to use in the preteen and teen years. If friends are invited over to do homework and have dinner together, the hard work suddenly becomes more fun and less isolating.

School attendance is one of the most important predictors of school success or school failure. Kids who ultimately drop out of high school tend to have had more school absences throughout their childhoods in comparison to their graduating peers.[2] Attendance is key. Every day our kids learn new material that builds on what they learned the day before.

So what does this have to do with cooking? There are so many parallels between what goes on at school and what happens in the kitchen. Consider the following:

Our kids read assignments at school and recipes in the kitchen.

Our kids are challenged to focus at school and focus on following a recipe in the kitchen.

Our kids benefit from being organized at school and face having to organize ingredients, cooking supplies, and the cooking process in the kitchen.

Our kids are given directions to follow at school and have directions to navigate if they want their cooking creation to flourish.

Our kids are multitaskers who manage a range of classes, teachers, and schedules and have to balance different ingredients, a range of utensils, and how the recipe will be cooked or chilled.

We've come full circle and return to scaffolding—only this time it's self-scaffolding. We learn these skills in the kitchen by practicing them over and over again. Just like our kids learn skills at school by attending day after day. By breaking them down, whether at school or in the kitchen, we improve our ability to read, focus, organize, follow directions, and multitask.

The contrast in the kitchen between Julian, a professional chef, and myself, a novice, is enormous. When Julian cooks, the kitchen looks clean—it's like he didn't even cook anything. The utensils are hardly used and everything gets stored right away. When I cook, there are loads of pots and pans and extra ingredients on the counter. The kitchen is messy, with egg whites on the stove or butter on the oven door. Dishes are piled up in the sink and nothing gets cleaned until cooking preparations are done. And that's when I make scrambled eggs.

Breathe. And stir.

I love fish but was unsure whether our kids would enjoy it, too. One Sunday, I decided our dinner would be pan-roasted salmon—prepared in a simple way, as described in this recipe—and it was met with such delight that it's now become a staple family meal. Otherwise known by our kids as "pink fish," this dish can be prepared, from fridge to table, in less than ten minutes. Healthy, quick, easy, delicious—all ingredients that make this recipe a must for your cooking repertoire.

## INGREDIENTS

|   | |
|---|---|
|   | extra-virgin olive oil |
| 4 | salmon fillets, skin-on and scaled, about 6 oz each |
| 1 | lemon |
|   | fine sea salt and freshly ground black pepper |

**SERVES 4**

# PAN-ROASTED SALMON FILLET

Heat a little olive oil in a large nonstick frying pan over high heat. Generously sprinkle the salmon with salt and pepper. Place the fish skin-side down in the pan, and reduce the heat to medium-low. Cook the fish, without moving the fillets, for about 5 minutes, or until well browned on the bottom and cooked about halfway through. Turn the fillets over and cook for another minute or so. Remove the fish from the pan and place, skin-side up, on paper towels. If you cook the salmon skin-side down, as directed here, it becomes crispy. Serve your salmon skin-side up, so you present a crispy top with tender salmon below. For those hesitant about eating the skin, you can easily remove it with a knife and fork. However, model trying it first—it is crispy, healthy goodness at its best.

Squeeze a little lemon juice onto the salmon. Your Pan-Roasted Salmon goes well with our Spring Salad (page 50) and Mash for All (page 189).

# Meet the Challenge

It's so often the case in life that something we assume will be so difficult, like making salmon, turns out to be easier to do than we thought. It makes one wonder: "Why didn't I do this earlier?" This activity is all about meeting challenges and discovering that sometimes things are more achievable than we think.

### TALK TO YOUR TEACHER

**YOUNG HELPERS**

Talk to your teacher about something you're struggling to learn in school.

### PROCRASTINATION STATION

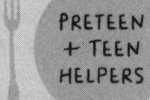

**PRETEEN + TEEN HELPERS**

Is there something you've put off doing? Set aside time to get it done. Was it as difficult as you imagined?

### SHARE YOUR CHALLENGE

**GROWN-UP HELPERS**

Set a challenge for yourself and let your helpers know about it. Talk about the struggles and strengths you bring to meeting this challenge so they have an inside understanding of your experience. Your challenge could be as simple as making your bed in the morning or more complicated, like balancing work and family life. By sharing your experience with your helpers, you model effort and coping.

I was thinking this might be a great way to introduce younger kids to fish. It's easy to prepare and easy to eat. Dare I say this can be eaten with some of the dipping sauces kids love to eat? Ketchup, mayo, or even tartar sauce—kids love to dip food. Alternatively, you can simply squirt your fish fingers with fresh lemon juice. The sour flavor and crunchy texture go really well together.

## INGREDIENTS

| | |
|---|---|
| 1½ lb | flat white fish fillets, such as flounder, sole, plaice, or dabs |
| 1 cup | all-purpose flour |
| 1 tsp | onion powder |
| 1 tsp | garlic powder |
| ½ tsp | Spanish paprika |
| 3 | large eggs |
| 2 cups | plain breadcrumbs (homemade or store-bought) |
| 2 Tbsp | olive oil, plus more as needed |
| 2 Tbsp | unsalted butter, plus more as needed |
| | fine sea salt |
| | lemon (optional) |
| | Dipping Sauces (optional; see Activity: Dip Your Crisp, page 156) |

**SERVES 4**

# CRUNCHY FISH FINGERS

With a sharp knife, cut the fish fillets into strips that are about 4 inches long and ½ inch thick. This is a guide; if they are a little longer or shorter, that's fine. Place the fish in a large bowl and sprinkle with a little salt. Gently mix to make sure all the fish is seasoned.

To prepare the coating, combine the flour, onion powder, garlic powder, and paprika in a medium bowl and whisk together. In a separate bowl, combine the eggs and 3 Tbsp of water and whisk to combine. Put the breadcrumbs in a third bowl.

Place half the fish in the flour and toss to make sure it's completely coated. Take out the fish, shaking off any excess flour. Next, add the fish to the egg mixture. Turn the fish to make sure it's well coated. Finally, add the fish to the breadcrumbs and toss well to completely coat. Place the breaded fish on a large plate. Repeat the flour, egg, and breadcrumb process with the remaining fish.

In a large skillet, heat the olive oil over medium-high heat. When the oil is hot, add the butter. Add half the breaded fish and cook, carefully turning occasionally, for 5 to 8 minutes, or until cooked through and golden brown all over. Gently remove the fish from the skillet and place it on a paper towel to absorb any excess oil. Cook the remaining fish, adding a little more olive oil and butter as needed. Serve immediately with a dipping sauce or lemon wedge.

# Dip Your Crisp

This recipe encourages you to dip your food. It's so fun and delicious to dip crispy, crunchy food in a salty, creamy, or spicy dip.

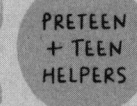 **YOUNG HELPERS**

**TASTE TEST**
Dip your fish stick into different sauces and decide which tastes best for you.

 **PRETEEN + TEEN HELPERS**

**MAKE TARTAR SAUCE**
Tartar sauce is easy to make. In a medium bowl, combine 1 cup good-quality mayonnaise, 1 Tbsp chopped red onion, 1 Tbsp chopped capers, 1 Tbsp chopped gherkins or dill pickle, and 2 dashes Tabasco sauce. Mix all the ingredients together. Try your tartar sauce with your crunchy fish sticks!

**GROWN-UP HELPERS**

**ORGANIZE A DIP SCAVENGER HUNT**
Create a scavenger hunt for helpers of all ages to identify and find possible dips in the fridge.

One of the many things I love about this dish is that everything goes together in one big pot. All the ingredients cook together, and when the paella is ready, it all gets spooned out into waiting bowls. This dish isn't fancy or sophisticated, but it does taste good. It includes ingredients that we don't usually combine like fish, chicken, rice, and sausage. Don't be afraid of all the ingredients; this recipe is quite straightforward and worth the effort. And once you make it for the first time, it will be easy after that!

## INGREDIENTS

| | |
|---|---|
| 4 | chicken thighs, boneless and skinless, each cut in half, totaling 8 pieces |
| 8 | jumbo shrimp, peeled and deveined |
| 4 Tbsp | olive oil |
| 8 oz | Spanish chorizo sausage, cut into 8 pieces total |
| 1 | small Spanish onion, peeled and cut into ¼-in squares |
| 1 | small red bell pepper, stemmed, seeded, and cut into ¼-in squares |
| 1 | small green bell pepper, stemmed, seeded, and cut into ¼-in squares |
| 4 cloves | garlic, minced |
| 2 cups | Spanish short-grain rice, such Bomba or Calasparra |
| 1 cup | finely chopped fresh tomato |
| 1 pinch | saffron pistils |
| 2 tsp | Spanish paprika |
| 4 cups | chicken stock |
| 8 oz | fresh mussels in the shell, beards removed |
| 1 | lemon, quartered |
| | fine sea salt and freshly ground black pepper |

**SERVES 4**

# PAELLA

Season the chicken and shrimp with salt and pepper.

Heat a large, high-sided skillet over medium-high heat. Add 2 Tbsp of the olive oil and let it get hot. Add the chicken and cook, turning, for about 4 minutes on each side, or until browned. Remove your chicken from the skillet and set aside. Add the shrimp to the same skillet and cook, turning, for about 2 minutes per side, or until browned. Remove the shrimp from the skillet and set aside. Add the remaining 2 Tbsp of olive oil to the same skillet. Add the chorizo and cook, stirring, for about 3 minutes. Add the onion and bell peppers and cook, stirring, for 2 minutes. Add the garlic and cook, stirring, for 2 minutes. Add the rice and mix well to combine with the vegetables and chorizo. Add the tomato, saffron, paprika, chicken stock, and chicken thighs. Season with some salt and pepper and bring to a gentle boil.

Taste the liquid to check the seasoning and add more salt and pepper as needed (see Activity: Taste as You Go, page 68). Reduce the heat to very low and gently simmer, uncovered, for 10 minutes. Add the mussels and shrimp, cover the skillet with a lid, and give it a good shake. Do not stir, as we want to create a lightly toasted crust on the bottom of the skillet. This is called socarrat. Cook for another 10 minutes, then check to see if the rice is cooked— it should be soft but still have a little resistance. If it's too hard, add another ¼ cup of stock or water and continue cooking until the liquid is absorbed but the mixture is still moist.

### fun fact!

The socarrat adds another layer of texture and flavor to your paella.

Once your paella is cooked, remove it from the heat and let it rest for 5 minutes. There are several reasons why we want the paella to cool for a few minutes. We want to make sure it's not too hot to eat. We also want all the proteins to be cooked through and to give the flavors time to meld together. After 5 minutes, divide the paella among 4 plates and serve with a lemon wedge. Enjoy!

# Play the Ingredients Game

Because there are so many ingredients to add to this paella dish, it's fun to think about incorporating games centered on how much you're including. As you add everything to the big pot, think about the many ways you can play games while making your creation. We present some ideas below.

### COUNTING GAME
Count your ingredients as you and your helper add them to the pot. How many are there? If you take one ingredient away, how many will you have left?

### PERSONAL GOALS GAME
Being an adolescent can be overwhelming. It's easy to get caught up in an intense schedule of schoolwork, extracurricular activities, and thinking about the future. With all this activity going on, it's understandable that you may forget what's important to you. Play a game as you prepare your dish. For each ingredient added, identify a goal that's wholly something you want to do for yourself. Don't hold back—no one's here to judge. These are your goals for yourself.

### FACILITATE AN INGREDIENTS-BASED GAME WHILE COOKING WITH YOUR HELPER
For the Ingredients Adding game, young helpers can add up the number of each ingredient they add to the paella. Ask your young helper to write an equation that represents the number of ingredients added.

For the Ingredients Storytelling game, help build executive functioning by asking your young helper to tell part of a story each time an ingredient is added to the pot.

Play a Name-that-Emotion game with your young, preteen, and teen helpers. Each time one of you adds an ingredient to the paella, name an emotion you experienced that day. Because you and your helpers are playing together, everyone gets a sense of what others have been experiencing emotionally.

This recipe reflects Izzy's creativity and love of cooking. Now a teenager, she will quite happily run out to the store, select her ingredients, come home, and prepare this delicious meal for the whole family. I used her basic recipe as a guide and gave it my own twist, but I credit her for all the inspiration.

## INGREDIENTS

| | |
|---|---|
| 1½ lb | medium shrimp, peeled and deveined |
| 2 Tbsp | vegetable oil |
| 1 | small onion, peeled and cut into ¼-in slices |
| 1 | red bell pepper, stemmed, seeded, and cut into ¼-in slices |
| 1 | green bell pepper, stemmed, seeded, and cut into ¼-in slices |
| 2 cloves | garlic, minced |
| 3 tsp | peeled and freshly grated fresh ginger |
| 2 Tbsp | Thai red curry paste |
| 1 | 13½-oz can coconut milk, unsweetened |
| 1 Tbsp | light brown sugar |
| 8 oz | rice noodles (1 packet) |
| ⅓ cup | chopped fresh cilantro leaves |
| 4 | scallions, finely sliced |
| | juice of 3 limes |
| | fine sea salt and freshly ground black pepper |

**SERVES 4**

# THAI COCONUT CURRY SHRIMP WITH NOODLES

Season the shrimp with salt and pepper.

Place a large, deep, preferably nonstick pot over high heat. Add the vegetable oil and when it's just beginning to smoke, add the shrimp. Cook, moving the shrimp around with a wooden spoon, for a few minutes, or until slightly brown. Scoop out the shrimp with a spoon and set aside. Do not clean the pot.

Place the same pot over medium-high heat. Add the onion, bell peppers, and garlic and cook, stirring occasionally, for 5 minutes. Add the ginger and curry paste and mix well to coat all the vegetables. Pour in the coconut milk and 2 cups of water. Add the brown sugar and season with some salt and pepper (see Activity: Taste as You Go, page 68).

Simmer your sauce for 5 minutes, then add the rice noodles and shrimp and cook for about 7 minutes, or until the noodles are soft. Finally, add the cilantro, scallions, and lime juice. Remove the pot from the heat and serve in bowls.

# Who Inspires You?

People who inspire us are people we look up to and admire. These are the people we want to be like or the objects, like works of art, that make us want to do something new and different. To be inspired, whether in or out of the kitchen, is to forward our creativity. We can look to a person or a creation as an inspiration, and then move from that toward something we want to bring to the world.

**YOUNG HELPERS**

**WORDS OF INSPIRATION**
Come up with three words that describe someone you look up to.

**PRETEEN + TEEN HELPERS**

**INSPIRATION CONTEMPLATION**
What can you do to be more like the person who inspires you?

**GROWN-UP HELPERS**

**INSPIRATION INCORPORATION**
Make a list of the qualities you like about the person who inspires you. How can you incorporate these qualities into your life?

I have fond memories of trout. Growing up in England, just outside of London, we had many trout fisheries and farms close to home. And in the stream going by our house, we would often see whopping trout meandering at their own pace, feeding and exploring the banks of our little waterway.

Trout is a delicious freshwater fish. It needs little to make it even more tasty than it already is. The key to trout is freshness. Just add a few simple ingredients and dinner is served.

## INGREDIENTS

| | |
|---|---|
| 4 | whole rainbow trout, 10–12 oz each, gutted and cleaned |
| 1 Tbsp | freshly ground fennel seed |
| ½ | small white onion, peeled and finely chopped |
| 2 cloves | garlic, minced |
| 4 sprigs | fresh thyme |
| 2 Tbsp | olive oil |
| 1 | lemon, quartered |
| | fine sea salt and freshly ground black pepper |

**SERVES 4**

# BAKED RAINBOW TROUT

Preheat the oven to 425°F. Line a rimmed roasting pan with parchment paper.

Head on, head off? Your choice! If you decide to take the heads off your trout before cooking, just place the trout on a cutting board and with a sharp knife, cut down as close to the head as possible. Your knife will cut through the backbone of the fish, removing the head.

Season your trout inside and out with the fennel, salt, and pepper. You can season the inside by simply opening the cavity (where the guts were; this cavity is created when the fish is gutted) of the trout to sprinkle it with fennel, salt, and pepper. Divide the onion and garlic and stuff some into each trout cavity. Stuff a sprig of thyme in each cavity.

Spread 1 Tbsp of the olive oil in the lined roasting pan. Place the trout in the pan, leaving space between each fish. Drizzle the remaining 1 Tbsp of olive oil over your trout. Place the roasting pan in the oven and cook for 5 to 8 minutes. Rotate the roasting pan and continue roasting for 5 to 7 minutes. This will ensure all your trout are cooked through and ready at the same time. After 10 minutes, check for doneness. To do this, take a sharp knife and make a small cut into the thickest part of the fish to see if it looks like the raw fish you started with or whether it looks opaque and cooked.

Serve your trout with a lemon quarter. Trout goes wonderfully with options like Spring Salad (page 50), Roasted Beet Salad (page 64), Moroccan-Style Lentil, Chickpea, and Vegetable Salad (page 66), Not French Fries (page 180), Broccoli (page 181), or Mash for All (page 189).

### top tips!

You can ask the person at the fish counter to prepare your fish when you buy it at the store, although it's usually cleaned and gutted already.

These delicious crab cakes, coated in crispy Japanese breadcrumbs, can be enjoyed as an appetizer or main course. There is plenty of mixing, shaping, and dipping involved, so everyone can take part in preparing this meal.

## CRAB CAKES

| | |
|---|---|
| 2 oz | brioche, weighed after crusts are removed and then cut into ¼-in squares |
| 2 Tbsp | fresh lemon juice |
| 1 lb | pasteurized jumbo lump crab meat (fresh works, too) |
| ½ cup | good-quality mayonnaise |
| 1½ Tbsp | Dijon mustard |
| ½ Tbsp | Old Bay Seasoning |
| 2 Tbsp | vegetable oil |
| 2 Tbsp | unsalted butter |

## BREADING

| | |
|---|---|
| 1 cup | all-purpose flour |
| 2 | large eggs |
| 1½ cups | panko breadcrumbs |

**SERVES 4** (MAIN COURSE)
**SERVES 8** (APPETIZER)

# PANKO-CRUSTED CRAB CAKES

### TO MAKE THE CRAB CAKES

Line a baking sheet with parchment paper.

Place the diced brioche in a large bowl and drizzle it with the lemon juice. Add the crab meat, along with any crab juice that might be in the can or container. Mix well but gently, so as not to break the lumps of crab meat.

In a small bowl, stir together the mayonnaise, mustard, and Old Bay Seasoning. Add to the crab meat and gently mix everything together.

Divide the crab cake mixture into 8 equal-sized balls and arrange them on the lined baking sheet. Apply a little pressure to each ball to slightly flatten them into patties. Cover and place in the refrigerator for a minimum of two hours.

### TO MAKE THE BREADING

Preheat the oven to 350°F.

Place the flour in a medium-size bowl. In a separate medium-size bowl, combine the eggs and 2 Tbsp of water and whisk together. Put the panko breadcrumbs in a third medium-size bowl.

*fun fact!*

Panko are coarse Japanese breadcrumbs.

Old Bay Seasoning is easy to buy at the store. It includes seasonings like celery salt, red pepper flakes, and paprika.

Remove the crab cakes from the refrigerator and, one by one, carefully dip them in the flour, followed by the egg mixture, and finally, the panko breadcrumbs. Make sure the crab cakes are nicely coated with each ingredient at each stage.

## NOW YOUR CRAB CAKES ARE READY TO COOK

In a large skillet, warm 1 Tbsp of the olive oil over medium heat. When the oil is warm, add 1 Tbsp of the butter and let melt. Add 4 crab cakes and cook, turning, for about 3 minutes per side, or until evenly golden brown. Return the crab cakes to the baking sheet. Repeat to cook the remaining crab cakes, adding more oil and butter to the skillet.

Place the crab cakes in the oven and cook for about 10 minutes, or until warm inside. Serve immediately with a wedge of lemon and your favorite side. We recommend Spring Salad (page 50), Summer Sun on a Cob (page 185), or Broccoli (page 181).

### top tips!

You can make these crab cakes in advance and freeze them to have for a meal on another day. Just keep in mind that it's best to freeze the crab cakes before the breading stage. This is so the panko crumbs won't get moist as the crab cakes defrost. After your crab cakes defrost, all you have to do is bread them. They will taste fresh and delicious, not soggy! Your crab cakes should last in the freezer for up to 2 months.

# Exercise Your Executive Functioning Skills

Executive functioning starts when we're babies. Whether we're zero or one hundred years old, executive functioning strategies help with school, work, friends, day-to-day activities, and even cooking. They include skills like memory, cognition, flexibility, organization, and self-control. As the activities below show, there are many ways to build executive functioning skills when you and your helpers are cooking.

 **YOUNG HELPERS**

### TAKE-A-TURN STORYTELLING GAME

This game involves taking turns to make up a story together. While cooking with your grown-up helper, start to create a story by sharing a sentence or two. Now it's your grown-up helper's turn. Your grown-up helper has to pick up at the end of your last sentence and add a sentence or two. The story line continues—who knows where it will go or how it will resolve? Your story ends when you and your grown-up helper are done preparing the dish. The Take-a-Turn Storytelling game helps with executive functioning on many levels. You and your helper create a narrative together, listen to one another, make connections between ideas, and remember each other's sentences to construct your part of the story. Consider the following Take-a-Turn Storytelling game narrative that emerged when Olliver and I played:

**Olliver:** Once upon a time, there was ice cream that mommy bought. I ran and got it from her. And then I put it in my pocket.

**CC:** We thought the ice cream might start to melt in your pocket.

**Olliver:** We hurried to get it somewhere.

**CC:** We got the ice cream out of your pocket and put it in the freezer.

**Olliver:** And then my sister sneakily got past us and ate the ice cream.

**CC:** Mama had to buy more ice cream. Which flavors should she get?

**Olliver:** Vanilla with rainbow sprinkles.

**CC:** Mama got the ice cream and put it in the freezer.

**Olliver:** Then no one got this ice cream ever again except for me. That's my treat! And I know what the last thing is—the last thing is, happily ever after!

 **GROWN-UP HELPERS**

### PLAY THE LISTENING GAME

The Listening Game is a great game to play with kids of all ages, and to be honest, with your partner, too. To play, just say three things your helper needs to do. They need to listen to what you're saying to follow in that order. For instance, you can say: "Ok, please get in your pajamas, brush your teeth, and then come find me for story time." Here's a fun variation of the game that you can play on your own to get stuff done that you've been putting off: "Ok, I'm going to fold the laundry, put it away, and go through the mail." Up your game by putting on a timer to see how fast you can complete your tasks.

**PRETEEN + TEEN HELPERS**

### CLEAN YOUR ROOM!

Yes, this is an executive functioning skill. How does it reflect memory, organization, and even self-control?

Branzino, or Mediterranean sea bass, is a delicate white-fleshed fish that is very popular throughout Southern Europe. In recent years, it's become readily available in the United States, and is a wonderful addition to your culinary toolbox of ingredients. In tribute to its origins, this simple dish incorporates tomatoes, olives, bell peppers, herbs, and olive oil—essentially, the flavor palette of Provence, a region in southern France. (Here, palette refers to ingredients rather than the paint colors on an artist's mixing tray.)

## INGREDIENTS

| | |
|---|---|
| 4 | branzino fillets, skin-on, about 6 oz each |
| 2 Tbsp | olive oil |
| 1 | medium onion, peeled and cut into ¼-in slices |
| 1 | green bell pepper, stemmed, seeded, and cut into ¼-in slices |
| 2 cloves | garlic, minced |
| 6 | plum tomatoes, cut into ¼-in squares |
| 1 Tbsp | chopped fresh thyme leaves |
| ½ cup | pitted Niçoise olives |
| 1 Tbsp | chopped fresh flat-leaf parsley leaves |
| | fine sea salt and freshly ground black pepper |
| | fresh crusty bread (optional) |

**SERVES 4**

# BRANZINO PROVENÇAL

Place a large sauté pan over medium heat. Add the olive oil, followed by the onion and pepper. Cook, stirring occasionally, for about 5 minutes—do not let the vegetables brown. Add the garlic and cook for a few more minutes. Add the tomatoes and thyme and season with some salt and pepper. Cook your sauce for about 5 minutes, or until everything is soft. Add a little water if the sauce is too dry. We do this because the liquid can evaporate if it boils too much and may need to be replaced.

Meanwhile, lay the fish fillets, skin-side up, on a cutting board. With a sharp knife make small, shallow cuts into the skin, about 1 inch apart, along the length of the fillet. This is called scoring and helps keep the fillet from curling up too much when cooking. Lightly season the branzino with salt and pepper. Gently add the fish and olives to the sauce. Carefully submerge the fillets in the sauce and slowly cook for 10 minutes.

Serve each fillet with a good spoonful of the sauce, which is full of yummy vegetables. Sprinkle some freshly chopped parsley on top and, if desired, have some warm crusty bread near at hand for mopping up all the last remnants.

Once again, for busy people, fish is a surprisingly fabulous meal choice. This dish is healthy, tasty, and quick to put on the table. There are literally five ingredients, two being salt and pepper. While your sea bass or halibut is baking for thirteen to sixteen minutes, you can set the table and find a quiet moment to individually check in with your kids about their day.

## INGREDIENTS

| 4 | Chilean sea bass or halibut, about 6 oz fillets |
|---|---|
| 2 Tbsp | extra-virgin olive oil |
| 1 | lemon |
| | fine sea salt and freshly ground black pepper |

**SERVES 4**

# BROILED FILLET OF CHILEAN SEA BASS OR HALIBUT

Preheat the broiler to low. Lightly oil an ovenproof baking dish. Place the fish in the prepared baking dish and brush it with olive oil. Sprinkle with salt and pepper and add a squeeze of lemon. Place your baking dish on the middle rack of the oven and broil for 13 to 16 minutes, or until the fish starts to flake. The cook time depends on the thickness of the fish. Watch carefully to make sure the fish doesn't burn and lower the heat as needed. (You will know if the sea bass is starting to burn because it will start to turn dark brown and eventually black.) Broiled sea bass is that easy to make! Eat with Spring Salad (page 50).

### top tips!

When your fish is ready it will flake or detach in pieces when pushed down with a fork.

Tilapia is an easily sourced freshwater fish. This means that it's likely to be at your grocery store. It's also one of the more economical types of fish to buy, contributing to its popularity in the United States. In keeping with the theme of fish being quicker to prepare than we'd imagine, this recipe can be made literally in minutes, especially if you have your Cajun spice ready. Tilapia has a mild flavor, so the Cajun spice gives it some real pizzazz. By making your own Cajun spice, as described below, you can adjust the flavor profile to make the perfect blend for you and your family.

### CAJUN SPICE

| | |
|---|---|
| 2 Tbsp | smoked paprika |
| 1 Tbsp | dried oregano |
| 1 Tbsp | garlic powder |
| 1 tsp | dried thyme |
| 1 tsp | cayenne pepper |
| 1 tsp | onion powder |
| 1 tsp | granulated sugar |
| 1 tsp | fine sea salt |
| ½ tsp | freshly ground black pepper |

### TILAPIA

| | |
|---|---|
| 4 | tilapia fillets, skinless, about 6 oz each, pin bones removed |
| 1 Tbsp | olive oil |
| 1 Tbsp | unsalted butter |
| 2 | limes, halved |

**SERVES 4**

# CAJUN-STYLE TILAPIA

## TO MAKE THE CAJUN SPICE

In an airtight container, combine the smoked paprika, oregano, garlic powder, thyme, cayenne, onion powder, sugar, salt, and pepper. Your spice mixture will keep in a dry, cool, dark place for 3 to 4 months.

## TO MAKE THE TILAPIA

Liberally season both sides of the fish fillets with the Cajun spice.

Place a large nonstick skillet over high heat. Add the olive oil and allow it to get hot. When the oil is hot, add the butter. Add the fish fillets, then reduce the heat to medium and cook for about 4 minutes. Turn the fish over and cook for 4 more minutes.

Serve your tilapia with lime halves and our Spring Salad (page 50) or Mash for All (page 189) for a super quick, super delicious dinner.

# When Our Brains Are a Pain

Sometimes things don't work out the way we want them to. We might not have gotten that job or that grade, made that friend, or had the day we hoped for. We might have forgotten about plans, forgotten an answer to a test question, or messed up in a job interview. Sometimes, our brains are a pain. Teaching our kids and ourselves how to cope when things don't work out is part of building resilience. The ability to cope can help us move forward, even when we're disappointed that things didn't go the way we hoped. Modeling coping behaviors is a powerful thing we as parents can do for our kids. It provides a perspective that encourages us to look at what happened and think it through. Coping provides hope.

**YOUNG HELPERS**

### IDENTIFY FEELING MORE THAN ONE FEELING

This may be hard to grasp, but often we can feel more than one thing at the same time. We might feel happy and sad or excited and nervous. A good way to try to identify what we're feeling is to sit with and give words to our feelings in the moment. Practice telling your grown-up helper the different ways you feel. It's also understood that sometimes we get so upset it's hard to even use our words. We just can't seem to get what we're thinking out of our brains. Take a moment, a deep breath, or have a glass of water to center yourself to share how you feel. And if it just doesn't come to you, that's okay, too.

**PRETEEN + TEEN HELPERS**

### KNOW THAT DURING ADOLESCENCE OUR BRAIN DOESN'T ALWAYS INTERNALLY COMMUNICATE

Did you know that our brains keep developing until we're about twenty-five years old? During adolescence, different parts of your brain, specifically the part that deals with emotion and the part that deals with thinking, are still learning how to communicate with one another. This can help explain why sometimes you might feel really emotional and unsure about how to develop strategies to deal with those feelings.

Sometimes feelings can be so overwhelming that there's a tendency to isolate and be alone. You might think no one understands you or that no one is going through what you're experiencing in quite the same way. Talk to a trusted friend or grown-up helper about what's upsetting you and try not to isolate. Sometimes just talking to someone brings relief.

**GROWN-UP HELPERS**

### MANAGE FRUSTRATION TO MODEL COPING

I remember waiting in line for over an hour one hot summer afternoon. Olliver was with me. He must've heard me sighing as he asked if everything was okay. "It's fine sweetheart," I replied. "I'm sighing because I don't want to say anything that will be upsetting. I'm trying to give an example of how to manage waiting for a long time." (Note: Trying is the operative word here).

Our kids are like sponges that absorb much of what we say and do. When we model a coping behavior for our kids, we give them a working example of how they can respond and manage a situation. In this scenario, I knew it wasn't the last time I'd be stuck waiting in a long line. I knew it wouldn't be Olliver's last time either. Modeling coping helps us and our kids anticipate future moments when we need to bring those skills. I think it's also okay to let your kids know if you're struggling to model coping behavior. It's okay to share with them that yes, you too are frustrated and not understanding why the wait has been so long. This lets your kids know that you're human and trying to get through as best you can.

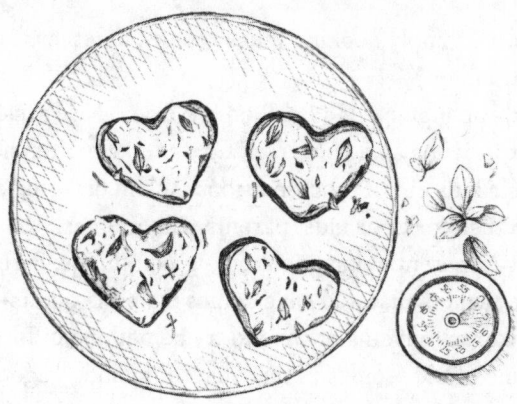

# CHAPTER 9

# Dinner: Pizza, Pasta, and Veggies

*"No Basil on the Pizza. No Parsley on the Pasta!"*

While Chapter Eight focuses on brain food, pain food, Chapter Nine says, let go of the anchor and do something different. Try something new, change it up, and see what transpires. More important than even liking a vegetable is the experience of trying a new food and making your own decision about whether you like it. It's a process that parallels life lessons, where we as parents, guardians, and caregivers want to help our kids try new things and take calculated risks. Both are critical to learning. Being curious and creative in the kitchen contributes to good problem-solving skills, decision making, and self-confidence. So much of what happens in the kitchen, like so much of what happens when we're faced with making a choice, is transformative.

As you've probably already guessed from the themes presented in this book, our view is that learning how to make healthy food choices is one of the most important tools we can give our children in life. Contrary to popular books that claim hiding healthy ingredients in food is the way to get our kids to eat healthy meals, we think it's absolutely critical that kids (and adults) are aware of what they're eating. It's through this level of awareness that we learn to make food choices. Rather than hide healthy ingredients, we can be aware of them and choose to eat them.

We want people to know what they're eating. This type of awareness encourages conversations between kids and grown-ups about food choices. When healthy ingredients are hidden in what we're eating, we never get to make the choice—it's made for us. Simply cooking these recipes together is a delicious way to start the conversation.

The subtitle for this chapter ("No Basil on the Pizza. No Parsley on the Pasta!") arose from Julian's experience as a New York City chef. He often hears from waiters that parents leave their kids out of food decisions. When ordering a margarita pizza or a fresh pasta dish for their kids, parents will often ask the chef to hold the basil and the parsley. Apparently, kids don't like green things. Perhaps what's most amazing about this request is that it always comes from the adults—never from the kids. It's as if the kids aren't given a chance to try something different—like trying something green. Some of the recipes in this chapter include vegetables, a hidden ingredient in some cookbooks geared toward family meals. By fostering choice, awareness, and conversation, *we all* have the courage to try new foods to see if they might indeed taste good.

And let's keep in mind the reality that eventually our kids grow up. At some point, they will make food choices on their own. Until then, and to prepare for this time, we can be our kids' partners not opponents in exploring making healthy choices together.

Let me confess, if you haven't guessed already: I really don't like cooking. It's not relaxing for me: I find it overwhelming, and I'm not good at it. Watching people cook on TV feels futile. They make it look so easy, and I know at the first moment of having to mix something I'll mess it up. I can't tell you how many times I've come home and just wanted to give my kids a premade meal or order takeout, again. Writing this book has been helpful because it's been so motivating to think about the benefits of creating food with my kids, not to mention that it makes it so much more fun. And I'll share a little secret: on more than one occasion, my teens have cooked dinner for all of us. Joy!

What I'm saying is that I completely understand the desire to make an easier choice in the moment, like hiding what is nutritious about the food your family is eating. I understand the appeal of not directly introducing your kids to healthful ingredients to avoid a potential conflict over eating them. Here's what I tell myself: while this seems like a big challenge now, at some point our kids find out that ingredients are being hidden in the food. The decision to introduce children to a variety of foods, involve them in food preparation, encourage good food choices, and engage in meaningful conversations throughout the process means we're raising informed eaters. This type of eating mindfulness is something we can engage in with kids and grown-ups of any age. The other thing I've learned is that the more we're open about healthy ingredients, the less we're going to encounter conflict around mealtimes. Introducing and talking about healthy ingredients normalizes this process as a part of nutrition within the family and in life.

We're always surprised to see how much kids actually like eating healthy foods. It reminds us of the playdates we hosted when our daughters were growing up.

Before a get-together, parents would often say:

"She'll eat the pasta, but she won't eat the broccoli."

Or, "He's very picky, so don't be surprised if he doesn't eat his vegetables."

Despite these alerts, the kids we were told wouldn't eat healthy foods loved them. They ate green salad, carrots, even broccoli.

What was going on? It wasn't that the parents didn't know their kids. Everything they said was absolutely true: their kids didn't eat salad, veggies, or broccoli. Perhaps the difference reflects how people respond to those expectations, a process we first mentioned in Chapter Three. Maybe kids engage in a behavior if they think it's how their parents want or expect them to behave.

Perhaps kids who came over expanded their food palates because there was an assumption that they could. And they had fun taking food risks together, simultaneously shouting out, "Yuck, that's really gross!" or exclaiming "Oh, wow, this is delicious!"

We can give our kids permission to try something to eat, while also letting them know they won't be forced to eat something if they don't like it after trying it. This builds food choice and decision making. Of course, this is often easy to say and really difficult to put it into practice. There's no one way to address this issue. A good place to start is to keep lines of communication open when it comes to food choices. Have an intentional conversation with your helpers where you talk about finding the balance between trying new foods and not forcing someone to eat something they don't like. A recent experience with Olliver might provide us with some insight:

Having recently celebrated a birthday, Olliver had his six-year-old checkup at the pediatrician's office. It was very exciting, and he was in good spirits. We decided to go out for lunch afterward. Focaccia bread was served with my order. It was delicious. "Olliver, you have to try this," I said. "It's so good."

"Ewwww," he said. "That looks gross. I'm not going to try it."

I truly believed Olliver would like the bread if he tried it, and I didn't want him to miss out. "Just give it a try and see how it goes. If you don't like it, you don't have to eat it."

"Okay," Olliver said. He wrinkled up his nose as he got ready to take a bite.

He chewed. He chewed some more. "Hmmmmmm. Okay," Olliver said. "Okay, I like it. I really like it."

Not only did Olliver end up eating most of the bread I shared with him, he was upset when I continued to nibble what was still on my plate—he wanted the rest of the focaccia for himself. So we asked the restaurant for another piece to take home.

At dinner, I said to Olliver, "Hey, I really appreciate how you tried that bread you thought you weren't going to like. That was very brave—and then you got to see that you liked it."

Of course there are countless times when things don't turn out this way. Consider the following: Olliver used to love bananas. Then one day, he decided he didn't. No matter what we said or how we tried to convince him to reconsider, Olliver wasn't having it. No bananas. But Olliver loves baking Izzy's Banana Chocolate Bread, which is full of bananas. This completely happened by accident— Olliver was just enjoying cooking with his sister. We don't point out that while he says he hates bananas, he eagerly eats them in this recipe.

I'm not sure what "solution" can fully address the struggle of giving our kids eating choices while also wanting them to eat certain foods. However, it's interesting to look at some of the factors presented in these scenarios: There was never any pressure to eat something. Choice was clearly communicated. Instead, there was encouragement in the form of "Just try it and see if you like it. If you don't, you don't." This was followed by acknowledgment of effort: "You were brave to try this." This acknowledgment also seems important for future attempts at expanding our children's food repertoire. If our kids know they'll be recognized for efforts to try something new, they might be more likely to take the risk in the future.

And finally, there were other ways to eat the foods reported as "Yucky" or "Gross" or "No way!," Olliver doesn't like bananas on their own—but he loves them when they're in Izzy's Banana Chocolate Bread. Granted, there's chocolate in this recipe; however, perhaps Olliver's enjoyment is influenced by actively helping to bake it and knowing the recipe has bananas in it. In this way, Olliver is aware of and makes a choice about how he wants to eat bananas.

Classical conditioning is a theory about a process of learning: we learn that one environmental stimulus indicates another will arrive.[1] Have you ever eaten a food and become really sick? So ill in fact that when you think about that food or someone mentions it you feel nauseous, even years later? Getting really sick after eating a food provides an intense classical conditioning situation—you now pair that specific food with being ill. My point is, and by now I'm sure you've identified your classically conditioned food nightmare, some food dislikes are simply never going to go away. For whatever reason, some people just don't like certain foods. And that's okay—we can explore substitutions for them or just let it be. By having an open conversation about food choices, we seek to avoid classical conditioning in a negative direction.

But we invite you to say yes to basil on the pizza and parsley on the pasta…

Pizza is a super fun food to make at home. Making it into a heart shape—and not just for Valentine's Day—adds an extra bit of creativity. For both kids and adults, it's interesting to see the chemical reaction of the yeast and how it interacts with the flour, sugar, and water in the dough. This recipe makes four individual heart-shaped pizzas and takes forty-eight hours in total, so let's get started!

## INGREDIENTS

| | |
|---|---|
| 1 cup | warm (not hot) water |
| 1 Tbsp | granulated sugar |
| ½ Tbsp | extra-virgin olive oil |
| ¼ tsp | active dry yeast |
| 2 cups | 00 pizza flour or bread flour (each is a high-gluten flour) |
| ¾ cup | all-purpose flour |
| 1 Tbsp | fine sea salt |
| 1 cup | good-quality pizza sauce |
| 2 cups | shredded low-moisture mozzarella cheese |
| ½ cup | diced fresh mozzarella cheese |
| 8 | fresh basil leaves, torn into small pieces |

**SERVES 4**

## fun fact!

A pizza screen is a round tray with a mesh bottom—you often see them at pizza shops. Pizza screens, along with pizza cutter wheels, can be purchased online.

PIZZA DISH

# HEART-SHAPED PIZZA

### 48 HOURS BEFORE EATING YOUR PIZZA

It takes a chemical reaction to make the dough for our heart-shaped pizza! In a small bowl, whisk together the warm water, sugar, olive oil, and yeast. Let stand for 8 to 10 minutes. It's cool to watch your yeast mixture become frothy and bubbly.

In a large bowl, combine the pizza or bread flour, all-purpose flour, and salt. Add the liquid yeast mixture and knead by hand for 5 to 8 minutes, or until smooth and elastic. Cover the bowl with plastic wrap and let stand at room temperature for 1 hour.

After 1 hour, divide your dough into 4 equal balls. Place them in a lightly floured container, cover tightly, and refrigerate for 2 days. Aggghhhhh, the anticipation!

### PIZZA DAY

After 2 days, preheat the oven to 475°F and get your container of dough out of the fridge.

On a lightly floured surface, use a rolling pin to roll out a ball of your dough until it is thin and round. It can be tricky to make it round because the dough can be thicker in some places than others. Once you've made the best circle that you can, fold your circle in half. With a pizza cutter wheel, trim the folded dough to form the shape of half a heart, then unfold the dough to reveal your full heart-shaped pizza base. This is kind of like making paper snowflakes. Put your heart-shaped dough on a pizza screen. With a spoon, spread your pizza sauce over the dough but leave a ½-inch border around the edge. Sprinkle the grated mozzarella cheese over the tomato sauce and top with a few chunks of fresh mozzarella. Repeat the rolling and topping process until your 4 heart-shaped pizzas are ready to cook.

You're almost there. Depending on the size of your oven, you may need to bake the pizza in batches. Place your pizza screens (see Fun Fact, left) in the hot oven and bake for 5 to 8 minutes, depending on your oven. Your pizzas are ready when the dough is lightly brown and the mozzarella is bubbling. Carefully remove your pizzas from the oven and finish with the fresh basil. You did it—no need for pizza delivery!

# Learn about Transformation

Watching ingredients change into something else is a magical process. When we make Heart-Shaped Pizza, helpers of all ages see transformations that they've created themselves, including making shapes with the dough or the chemical reactions that take place in the dough-making process. Both are transformational.

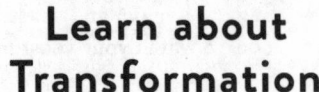

**YOUNG HELPERS**

### NAME THE SHAPE
As you make your pizza, tell your helper the names of the shapes you're creating.

**PRETEEN + TEEN HELPERS**

### PUT YOUR SCIENCE HAT ON
What is the scientific process you observed while making your pizza dough?

**GROWN-UP HELPERS**

### SHOW YOUR WONDER
Let your helpers know how cool you think it is to witness these transformations.

This recipe helps you create your own homemade mac and cheese. The mac here is macaroni—usually a short tube-shaped dried pasta—but you can experiment with different shapes of dried pasta, such as penne, mezzi rigatoni, small shells, or even alphabet. You can also try whole wheat, gluten free, or fresh pasta. In addition to changing up the mac, you can swap out different cheeses and add things like crispy bacon, cooked shrimp, breaded chicken, chopped tomatoes, caramelized onions, sautéed mushrooms, fresh asparagus, basil leaves, and on, and on, and on.

## INGREDIENTS

| | |
|---|---|
| 12 oz | elbow macaroni or pasta of your choice |
| ⅓ cup | unsalted butter |
| ⅓ cup | all-purpose flour |
| 3 cups | whole milk |
| 1 Tbsp | Dijon mustard |
| ½ tsp | fine sea salt |
| 3 cups | freshly grated cheddar cheese or your favorite semihard cheese |
| ½ cup | panko breadcrumbs |

**SERVES 4**

# BAKED MAC & CHEESE

Preheat the oven to 350°F.

Bring a large pot of lightly salted water to a boil. Add your pasta, stir, and cook for 8 to 10 minutes (check the directions on the box to determine how long your pasta shape should be cooked). You'll know when your pasta is ready when it is soft but still a little firm. This is doubly important because we will cook the pasta again in the oven with the sauce. After your pasta is cooked, drain it well (do not rinse; see Top Tips, page 179), and set aside.

Meanwhile, in a medium-size pot, melt the butter over a medium-low heat. Add the flour and whisk for a few minutes. Now that you have your roux, slowly add the milk and whisk until your sauce thickens. At this point, add the mustard, salt, and 2½ cups of the grated cheese. Continue gently whisking for a couple minutes until the cheese is completely melted. Add the cooked pasta to your cheese sauce and stir with a wooden spoon. Pour the mac and cheese into an approximately 6-x-10-inch ovenproof dish. Sprinkle with the remaining grated cheese and panko breadcrumbs and bake for 20 minutes, or until the crust is golden brown and the sauce is bubbling. Enjoy this yummy, simple, comfort food!

## fun fact!

An ovenproof dish is a dish that can go in the oven without cracking. The dish should say oven-safe on the back.

# Change It Up

This Mac and Cheese is just one example of how we can change ingredients to suit our tastes and make a recipe our own. You can change the pasta shape or the cheese, or add additional ingredients like cooked shrimp or chopped tomatoes.

**CHANGE INGREDIENTS**
If you could change anything in this recipe, what would it be and why? What would you add?

**EXPLORE YOUR CREATIVITY**
Adolescence is a time of identity development and exploration. Many of the recipes in this book encourage you to explore and develop your own creativity.

**MAKE CONVENIENT SUBSTITUTES**
It may be that you can't find all the ingredients for a recipe, or that there are other ingredients that are more affordable. Substitute ingredients as needed for convenience and to suit your budget.

Whole Wheat Rigatoni alla Norma is a vegetarian pasta that introduces kids to eggplant. Although it is often underused in cooking, eggplant is a really cool fruit. It's true: eggplant is not a vegetable. It's also shiny, oddly shaped, and purple. In addition to eggplant, our recipe also introduces (or reintroduces) your family to a lot of green things—thyme, parsley, and basil are all herbs that add flavor to your creations. This recipe sounds like it's harder to cook than it is; we provide step-by-step instructions.

## INGREDIENTS

| | |
|---|---|
| ¼ cup | extra-virgin olive oil, plus more for drizzling |
| ½ | medium red onion, peeled and cut into ¼-in dice |
| 4 cloves | garlic, thickly sliced |
| 2 | medium eggplants, cut into ½-in dice |
| 1 | 28-oz can crushed Italian tomatoes |
| 2 sprigs | fresh basil, plus more leaves for garnish |
| 1 sprig | fresh thyme |
| ¼ bunch | fresh flat-leaf parsley, leaves chopped |
| 1 lb | whole wheat rigatoni |
| 4 oz | ricotta salata, coarsely grated |
| | fine sea salt and freshly ground black pepper |
| | red pepper flakes |

**SERVES 8**

# WHOLE WHEAT RIGATONI ALLA NORMA

In a 12- to 14-inch sauté pan, heat the olive oil until smoking (this is over a medium to high heat). Add the red onion and garlic and cook, stirring, for 5 to 6 minutes, or until soft but not yet browned (see Top Tips, below). Add the eggplant and cook, stirring occasionally, for 8 to 10 minutes, or until softened and lightly browned. Add the crushed tomatoes, basil, thyme, and parsley and bring your mixture to a boil. Lower the heat and simmer for 15 minutes—your creation will gently bubble in the pan. While it's still simmering, season with salt, pepper, and red pepper flakes (see Activity: Taste as You Go, page 68).

Meanwhile, fill a large pot with 5 quarts of water (there are 4 cups in a quart, so use 20 cups of water) and 2 Tbsp of salt and bring to a boil. Add the rigatoni and cook according to the package instructions for al dente pasta. After cooking, drain your pasta well (do not rinse; see Top Tips, page 179) and add it to the pan with your eggplant sauce. Add the grated ricotta salata and stir it in thoroughly until everything is combined.

Serve equally onto 8 plates. Garnish with the additional basil leaves and drizzle with extra-virgin olive oil.

## top tips!

The reason we don't want onion and garlic to change color too much is that they will lose their delicious taste and become bitter.

Seasonings are added to your sauce while it's still simmering so that the flavors are incorporated evenly.

## fun fact!

Eggplant is called eggplant because before it was commercially grown, the original was a lot smaller and looked like an egg.

# Be a Garnisher

It's really fun to add the final touches to a recipe we've just created. Garnishes finish off a dish. They make it look pretty, even professional, and take it to another level. We can express our culinary artistic side by decorating with garnishes.

**YOUNG HELPERS**

### BE A GARNISHER
Put parsley, red pepper flakes, and basil on the rigatoni; garnish heart-shaped pizza with basil; sprinkle eggplant roll ups with mozzarella cheese; and add garlic to Brussels sprouts and cauliflower.

**PRETEEN + TEEN HELPERS**

### EXPERIMENT WITH DIFFERENT FLAVORS
Combine garnishes, olive oil, and seasoning to see which tastes you prefer.

**GROWN-UP HELPERS**

### BE CREATIVE
How food looks is an important part of appetite. If it doesn't look good, chances are we won't want to eat it. Play around with how the placement of garnishes influences the appearance of the dish you created.

This pasta dish, originally from Rome, Italy, has very few ingredients—just guanciale (cured pork), pasta, egg yolk, Pecorino Romano cheese, salt, black pepper, and water. It can be an acquired taste, as guanciale and Pecorino Romano cheese have a funky, salty flavor. The classic version can be quite difficult to make, as it requires keeping a mindful eye to add just enough pasta, water, cheese, yolk, and fat. Our version is much easier and still loaded with delicious flavors. It's also a real winner with our kids.

We've added and changed a few ingredients to the Italian original, but our pasta carbonara is still quick and easy to make—not to mention yummy. After a busy day, or when you don't have a lot of time to get lunch or dinner ready, this meal takes about 15 minutes from when you start to prepare it to when you sit down to eat.

### INGREDIENTS

| | |
|---|---|
| 1 lb | long pasta, such as spaghetti, linguini, or bucatini |
| 5 oz | smoked bacon, cut crosswise into short, thin strips |
| 1 | small white onion, peeled and cut into small square pieces |
| ½ cup | heavy or whipping cream |
| ⅓ cup | freshly grated Parmesan cheese |
| 2 | large egg yolks |
| | fine sea salt and freshly ground black pepper |

**SERVES 4**

# PASTA CARBONARA

Fill a large pot with 5 quarts of water (there are 4 cups in a quart, so use 20 cups of water) and 2 Tbsp of salt and bring to a boil. Add your pasta and cook according to the package instructions for al dente pasta. After cooking, drain your pasta well (do not rinse; see Top Tips below), reserving about ¼ cup of the cooking water, and set aside.

Meanwhile, in a large deep sauté pan, sauté the bacon over medium heat, stirring occasionally with a wooden spoon until it starts to melt— professional chefs describe this as rendering the fat. You will see the bacon reduce in size and create a liquid; this is the rendered bacon fat. Add your onions and continue cooking the bacon and onions together for 3 to 5 minutes, or until the bacon looks a little crispy and the onions are translucent (see Activity: Sweat Your Onions, page 83). Add ¼ cup of the reserved pasta cooking water and stir. Continue cooking to allow some of the water to evaporate. Add the heavy or whipping cream and bring the mixture to a gentle boil for a few minutes to slightly thicken the sauce. Add your Parmesan cheese, stirring to help it melt, and incorporate into your sauce. Taste your sauce and season with salt and pepper. Lower the heat, add the egg yolk, and stir, then immediately add your pasta (this is so your eggs don't turn into scrambled eggs, which will happen if they're overheated) and stir to coat with your carbonara sauce. It's now time to tuck into this modern classic.

## top tips!

Do not wash your pasta with hot or cold water after it's cooked, as this will remove some of its flavor and starch. You want some of the starch because it helps bind your sauce to the pasta.

If your sauce is too thick, add a little hot pasta water. If it's too thin, boil your sauce, so the cream reduces and thickens.

In this recipe you reserve some of the water used to cook your pasta and add it to your sauce. This gives your dish more taste as the water from the pasta contains salt, starch, and some flavor from the actual pasta.

When you taste a dish or sauce that is hot, always use a wooden or plastic spoon. If you use a metal spoon it will get hot and can burn your lip or tongue when you're tasting.

I was chatting with CC about dinner the other day, when she asked, "What's an alternative for French fries?" Excellent question! My first thought was, actually, nothing. Strips of potato, deep fried until golden brown, crispy, and salty on the outside yet soft and silky on the inside—French fries are rather too yummy to be replaced. Hence the reason that the United States consumes huge amounts of French fries and what's even more worrying, huge amounts of fat and grease as a by-product of the cooking process.

French fries are definitely tricky to replace. But after CC's question, I thought about a small potato that I use at the restaurant all the time. It also has quite a cute name, the fingerling potato. So here we are: a small potato that should be eaten with the skin left on (it's much healthier that way) and is versatile and delicious. Like French fries, fingerling potatoes, as the name suggests, can be eaten with your fingers. Unlike French fries, these potatoes are baked in the oven rather than cooked in a fryer, the result being beautiful baby baked potatoes. Try them with our Homemade Beef Burger (page 142) and see what a great substitute they are.

### INGREDIENTS

| | |
|---|---|
| 2½ lb | plain white fingerling potatoes |
| | drizzle of extra-virgin olive oil |
| 1 cup | sour cream |
| 1 bunch | scallions, chopped |
| ¾ cup | freshly grated low-moisture mozzarella or cheddar cheese |
| | fine sea salt and freshly ground black pepper |

**SERVES 4**

VEGGIE DISH

# NOT FRENCH FRIES

Preheat the oven to 350°F.

Involve your whole family from the outset, as you scrub your potatoes in cold water and dry them. Place them in a bowl, drizzle with a little olive oil, and sprinkle with salt and a couple turns of freshly ground black pepper. Toss together until your potatoes are covered with a thin layer of oil, salt, and pepper. Spread your potatoes out on a baking tray and bake, turning occasionally, for 15 to 25 minutes, or until soft when squeezed. Grab a clean kitchen towel and squeeze them so your fingers don't get burned.

Meanwhile, in a small bowl, combine the sour cream and scallions. Season with a little salt and pepper and set aside.

### top tips!

You can also buy confetti or rainbow fingerling potatoes; kids really like their different colors.

When the potatoes are cooked, hold each one with a kitchen towel in your hand and use a sharp knife to make a small cut just down the length of the potato. This will make a kind of pouch or pocket. Now push the sides of the potato back a little bit to open up the cut. Pack the opening with some grated cheese and a dollop (spoonful) of the sour cream and scallions. Enjoy immediately but mind your fingers!

Broccoli gets a bad rap. To start, it's green and it's a vegetable—the first two strikes against it. While it's simple to cook, broccoli is also really easy to mess up. It can be overcooked or undercooked, underseasoned or overseasoned, all of which perpetuates the idea that broccoli is just yucky. Here, we show you how to cook broccoli just right. It's one of our family favorites and very easy to prepare. Plus, broccoli is one of the least expensive veggies and has very little waste. Making great broccoli begins with your selection process. When you're at the store or market, choose only bright green and firm broccoli. This will be the freshest and therefore, the most delicious.

## INGREDIENTS

| | |
|---|---|
| 2 lb | **fresh broccoli** |
| ¼ cup | **unsalted butter** |
| | **fine sea salt** |

**SERVES 4**

# BROCCOLI

Get started by preparing your broccoli to maximize flavor. Cut bite-size florets from the stem. You do not need to waste the stem. For a longer stem, remove and discard the final inch. Peel the rest of the skin on the broccoli with a peeler and cut it into ½-inch pieces. Then add to be cooked with the florets. When you have a shorter broccoli stem, just incorporate with the florets (see Activity: Use All Parts of a Food Item and Reduce Waste, page 96). Wash your broccoli in fresh, cold water, and drain.

Meanwhile, fill a large pot with about 5 quart of water (there are 4 cups in a quart, so use 20 cups of water) and bring to a boil. Once the water is boiling, add 5 tsp of fine sea salt and return to a boil. (When you add the salt, the water may stop boiling because salty water boils at a slightly higher temperature. Because of this, you want to make sure that your water is boiling when you add the broccoli.) After checking to make sure your water is boiling again, add your broccoli— the water will stop boiling—cover immediately, and return to a boil. Once your water is boiling again (this could take about 30 seconds), immediately remove the lid. Cook your broccoli, uncovered, for 3 minutes. That's it! Immediately drain your broccoli and place it in a bowl.

Melt the butter in a small saucepan or the microwave. Pour the melted butter over the broccoli and toss. Finish it with a few pinches of sea salt. We will guarantee that if you can get your kids to try this recipe, they will think about broccoli in a different way!

## top tips!

Wash your broccoli in cold water because washing it with hot water might cook it a bit. This holds true for many raw vegetables.

The key to great broccoli is cooking it quickly in salted water.

## fun fact!

Broccoli dates back to Roman times, when it was cultivated as a food source. It was brought to the United States in the nineteen hundreds by Italian immigrants settling in Long Island, New York.

# Practice Your Time Management Skills

Most recipes involve a time limit. Two and a half to three minutes is all that's needed to make this broccoli delicious, so managing time is critical. Time management is also an important life skill. Being on time, completing assignments on time, and picking up kids on time are all tasks when showing up as planned is key.

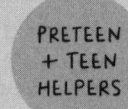

YOUNG HELPERS

### PRACTICE YOUR NUMBERS

Set a timer (the old-fashioned kind, not an electronic version) with your grown-up helper. Which number did you put it on? Which numbers does the timer pass as it counts down to 0?

PRETEEN + TEEN HELPERS

### USE COOKING TO PRACTICE TIME MANAGEMENT SKILLS

Research shows that teens naturally need more sleep, but sleeping more can interfere with doing everything you want to do. Practice your time management skills as you balance various recipe tasks within the time frame provided.

GROWN-UP HELPERS

### USE A TIMER

Most of us use our cell phones as timers these days. But there's nothing like an old-fashioned timer to encourage young helpers to learn about numbers and time. Every recipe in this chapter involves a time limit. Ask your young helper to find the number on the timer (if they're just learning numbers, you can do this together) and then watch as the timer ticks away. Young helpers will delight in hearing the timer buzz, signaling the next phase of your creation.

The Mediterranean diet, filled with vegetables, olive oil, fresh herbs, and, at times, fish, is incredibly healthy. Our Mediterranean grilled eggplant roll ups are all veggie and literally ooze Mediterranean taste. This dish has lots of color and flavor. Once the eggplant is grilled and the veggies are precooked, you can take a back seat and let your helpers do the rolling. It's easy and understandable to get overwhelmed by a recipe. We've broken this one down so you can approach each part step-by-step.

### INGREDIENTS

| | |
|---|---|
| 1 | large eggplant, cut lengthwise into 8 long slices |
| | extra-virgin olive oil |
| 1 | small onion, diced |
| 1 | red bell pepper, seeded and diced |
| 1 | yellow bell pepper, seeded and diced |
| 1 | green bell pepper, seeded and diced |
| 2 cloves | garlic, minced |
| 2 sprigs | fresh thyme, leaves removed and chopped |
| 2 sprigs | fresh rosemary, leaves removed and chopped |
| 2 | ripe vine tomatoes, diced |
| 1 sprig | fresh basil, leaves roughly torn |
| ½ bunch | fresh chives, roughly chopped |
| 4 sprigs | fresh flat-leaf parsley, leaves roughly chopped |
| | zest of 1 lemon |
| 1 cup | freshly grated low-moisture mozzarella cheese |
| | fine sea salt and freshly ground black pepper |

**SERVES 4**

# MEDITERRANEAN GRILLED EGGPLANT ROLL UPS

Preheat the oven to 375°F. If you're using an outdoor grill, heat it to a high heat. Alternatively, if you're cooking inside, preheat a grill pan over a high heat.

Brush both sides of each eggplant slice with olive oil and season all over with salt and pepper. Working in batches, place the eggplant slices directly on the grill grates or in the grill pan and cook for 3 to 4 minutes, or until you see grill marks and the eggplant is just starting to soften. Carefully flip the eggplant over and grill until there are grill marks on the other side and the eggplant is a little soft. Set aside while you grill the remaining slices.

Heat a large sauté pan over medium heat and add a good drizzle of olive oil. When the oil is hot, add the onion and cook, stirring occasionally, for about 5 minutes, or until soft. Add the red, yellow, and green bell peppers, and the garlic. Season with salt and pepper. Cook, stirring, for about 10 minutes. Add the thyme, rosemary, and tomatoes and cook for a few more minutes, then pour the mixture into a large metal bowl. Add the basil, chives, parsley, and lemon zest. Give everything a good mix to incorporate all your ingredients, then taste and season with a little salt and pepper if needed (see Activity: Taste as You Go, page 68).

### fun fact!

In cooking, to dice something means to chop it into small squares.

Now for the fun part! Helpers and grown-ups will love this. Ask your helper or grown-up to lay out the slices of eggplant, 2 slices at a time. Top the eggplant slices with the vegetable mixture and a little grated mozzarella cheese (use about ½ cup of mozzarella total for the inside of the roll ups). Now roll up the eggplant slices. Secure your roll ups with a toothpick and place them in a medium-size baking dish so they fit snugly.

When all the roll ups are rolled up, ask your helper to sprinkle the remaining mozzarella cheese on top. Bake for 10 to 15 minutes, or until the cheese is starting to brown. Remove your roll ups from the oven and carefully take out the toothpicks. Enjoy your roll ups with Spring Salad (page 50) or Mediterranean Summer Salad with Preserved Lemon Dressing and Chia Seeds (page 53).

Wonderful, juicy corn on the cob can be an entrée served with a fresh green salad. It's also so easy to make. We cover a few different cooking options. The recipe here is corn the way our family loves to eat it, which is the Mexican way, called elotes. It's topped with lime juice, a little mayonnaise, and some freshly grated Parmesan or Cotija cheese, the Mexican cheese you eat with elotes.

## INGREDIENTS

| | |
|---|---|
| 4 | large fresh local ears of corn |
| 1 | lime |
| ¼ cup | good-quality mayonnaise |
| ⅓ cup | freshly grated Parmesan or Cotija cheese |
| 2 Tbsp | unsalted butter |
| | fine sea salt |
| | extra-virgin olive oil (for grilling) |
| | cayenne pepper or sweet paprika (optional) |

**SERVES 4**

# SUMMER SUN ON A COB

### COOKING METHOD 1: BOILING

Boiling is one of the more popular ways to cook corn on the cob. Remove the husks and all the fine silk from the ears of corn. Use a pot large enough to fit 4 ears of corn and fill it with water, adding 1 quart at a time, until about two-thirds full. Add 1 tsp of fine sea salt for each quart of water. Cover the pot and bring the water to a rolling boil. Using tongs or a long, slotted spoon, carefully add the corn to the pot and cook for 4 to 5 minutes. Using the tongs or spoon, carefully remove the corn from the water.

### COOKING METHOD 2: MICROWAVING

This method is easy and quick. It is also delicious if you know how to use the microwave just right. Place 2 ears of corn (with their husks left on) in your microwave. Cook on high for 3 to 4 minutes. Carefully remove the corn from the microwave and repeat to cook the remaining 2 ears the same way. When the ears have cooled slightly, remove the husks and silk. Your corn will be perfectly cooked and very hot.

### COOKING METHOD 3: GRILLING

Remove the husks and all the fine silk from the ears of the corn. Lightly brush the corn with a little extra-virgin olive oil and sprinkle with some fine sea salt. Using long tongs, place your corn on a grill preheated to medium and cook for about 1 minute. Turn your corn about a one-fifth rotation and cook for another minute. Continue like this for 5 turns, or until the corn is cooked.

### top tips!

We might think that because corn looks big, we need to cook it for a long time. Nothing could be further from the truth. Think about it this way—you're not cooking the cob, you're cooking the corn on the cob. This means that less is more. To avoid having overcooked, dry corn (yuck!) don't cook it for more than 4 or 5 minutes. Try it—you'll see what we mean.

Leave the husks on when cooking corn on the cob in the microwave, because it will help retain the heat and keep the corn juicy.

## COOKING METHOD 4:
## REMOVING KERNELS FROM THE COB
## (CORN OFF THE COB)

Eating corn off the cob is a great way to enjoy fresh corn if your helper has braces. Remove the husks and all the fine silk from the ears of corn. Hold an ear of corn upright over a large bowl and use a sharp knife to slice down each side of the cob to remove the kernels. Repeat with the other ears of corn. Once all the kernels are removed, place them in a small saucepan, add 2 Tbsp of unsalted butter, 3 Tbsp of water, and a couple of good pinches of fine sea salt. Cover the saucepan and cook the corn over medium heat, stirring occasionally, for 4 to 5 minutes, or until the corn is cooked.

### TOPPINGS FOR YOUR CORN ON THE COB

Now for the fun part. Give each of your diners a wedge of lime. Set the mayonnaise, the grated cheese, and cayenne or paprika, if using, in the middle of the table—make sure spoons are handy. Spread the corn with a little mayonnaise (or a dollop if you're having corn off the cob), then sprinkle it with the cheese and if you like, a little cayenne or paprika pepper. Finish by squeezing fresh lime juice over the corn. Prepare to don a cheesy, mayonnaise-y smile!

### fun fact!

There are many reasons why it's a good idea to buy local corn. Corn has a lower carbon footprint when it's bought locally, making this a more environmentally friendly option. Your corn will also be fresher as it's had less distance to travel. When corn is in season, the best place to get it is at a farm or farmers' market. In this way, you really know where your corn is grown.

In the spirit of trying things we think we might not like, this recipe includes Brussels sprouts and cauliflower to create a delicious and healthy side dish. You might even be surprised to discover that Brussels sprouts are something you want to eat again. They taste really good when sautéed rather than just boiled. But go ahead, see for yourself!

## INGREDIENTS

| | |
|---|---|
| 1 head | cauliflower, cut into florets |
| 1½ lb | Brussels sprouts, stem and outer leaves removed, cut in half |
| 3 Tbsp | extra-virgin olive oil |
| 5 cloves | garlic, thinly sliced |
| | fine sea salt and freshly ground black pepper |

**SERVES 8**

### top tips!

Steam drying vegetables means that you allow the water to evaporate from the vegetables. You do this by leaving the vegetables, uncovered, in the hot pan after cooking. This is important for the vegetables you plan to sauté because you want to remove as much water as possible, so that it doesn't mix with the oil you'll use to sauté.

Your young helper may not know what three-quarters means, so you can explore the meaning of fractions as you fill the pot together.

# BRUSSELS SPROUTS & CAULIFLOWER SAUTÉED WITH GARLIC & OLIVE OIL

Fill a medium pot three-quarters full with water and add salt, little by little, until it tastes like seawater (see Activity: Test Your Taste, page 188).

Bring the water to a rolling boil. Add the cauliflower and simmer for 5 to 8 minutes, or until fork tender, which means when you stick the cauliflower with a fork it doesn't resist too much. Drain the cauliflower, then return it to the hot pan and let it steam dry for a few minutes.

Repeat the process for the Brussels sprouts but cook them for about double the time—10 to 16 minutes—or until they are tender but not mushy. Drain the Brussels sprouts then return them to the hot pan and let them steam dry for a few minutes.

You're almost done. In a large, nonstick frying pan, warm the olive oil over medium heat. Add the sliced garlic and cook, stirring, until it starts to brown a little. Using a slotted spoon, remove the garlic from the pan and set it aside. Leave the oil in the pan!

Place the pan over medium heat, then add the cauliflower and Brussels sprouts. Cook, stirring constantly with a wooden spoon, until the vegetables start to turn slightly brown. Season with salt and pepper. Use a slotted spoon to remove your vegetables from the sauté pan and sprinkle them with the garlic. This dish goes really well with Roast Supremes of Chicken with Smoked Bacon Stuffing (page 131), Braised Short Rib Stew (page 145), and Pan-Roasted Salmon Fillet (page 153).

### fun fact!

Brussels sprouts are in the cabbage family; cabbage should be cooked all the way through for the best flavor and texture. This is why the Brussels sprouts are cooked twice as long as the cauliflower in this recipe.

# Test Your Taste

We can all learn about taste and what our taste buds like. How much sea salt tastes good on broccoli? What combination of lime, mayo, and cheese tastes best for corn on the cob? What does seawater taste like?

### MAKE AND TRY SEAWATER

YOUNG HELPERS

Explore what seawater tastes like at the beginning of the Brussels Sprouts and Cauliflower recipe (page 187) when you fill the pan with water and add salt.

### EXPLORE FOOD CHOICES

PRETEEN + TEEN HELPERS

Teen and preteen years are a time of increasing independence. You'll gradually start to make more choices for yourself. Think about food choices and decide what tastes good to you. As you explore those tastes, make decisions about the kinds of foods you like and those you don't. Are there seasonings that make some foods taste better than others?

### CONDUCT A TASTE INVENTORY

GROWN-UP HELPERS

What kind of tastes do you prefer? What do you dislike? How does your taste influence your food choices?

A fabulous dish for helpers and grown-ups alike, this recipe is a real time saver because the potatoes are left with the skins on and don't have to be peeled. Removing the skins is the most time-consuming part of making mashed potatoes. Leaving the skins on also means that more of the nutrients are left intact.

### INGREDIENTS

| 2 lb | Yukon Gold potatoes |
|------|---------------------|
| 1 Tbsp + 1 tsp | fine sea salt |
| ½ cup | heavy or whipping cream |
| ¼ cup | unsalted butter |

**SERVES 4**

**VEGGIE DISH**

# MASH FOR ALL

Scrub your potatoes in cold water, then roughly cut them into 2-inch pieces and rinse in cold water. Place your cut potatoes in a large saucepan, then cover with cold water and add 1 Tbsp salt. Bring to a boil, then lower the heat and cook your potatoes for about 15 minutes, or until they are soft. You can test this by inserting a knife in the middle of a potato. If the potato falls off the knife, it's cooked.

Meanwhile, warm the cream and butter in a small saucepan over medium heat. When the potatoes are cooked, drain them and place them in a bowl. Use a potato masher to mash your potatoes while adding the hot cream and butter mixture and the remaining 1 tsp of salt. Mash for All goes great with so many dishes. Try Braised Lamb Shanks (page 147), Broiled Fillet of Chilean Sea Bass or Halibut (page 166), and Cajun-Style Tilapia (page 167).

### top tips!

It's important to scrub your potatoes in cold water to remove any dirt or sand.

Rinsing the cut potatoes in cold water removes any excess starch. This is key because if you have too much starch in your potatoes, they can become elastic and goopy.

# The Courage to Be Present

Helpers of all ages are interested in connecting and having meaningful relationships. It may not always be apparent when our kids are upset about something. They might tell us they need space while simultaneously finding it grounding to have us around as a supportive presence, even if from a distance.

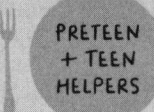

**YOUNG HELPERS**

### INVITE YOUR FRIENDS OVER TO COOK TOGETHER

It can be scary to leave family when you go to school. Sometimes having just one close friend helps ease the transition. Plan a playdate with a classmate you'd like to get to know better. Choose one of these fun recipes and cook together. Your grown-up helpers can join!

**PRETEEN + TEEN HELPERS**

### RECOGNIZE THAT ADOLESCENCE IS FULL OF CHANGES

Other than when you were a baby, there is no other time in life when you will experience so much change—physically, emotionally, psychologically, and socially. Just like the metamorphosis seen in some of these recipes, you are growing more into your new self. Who are you going to be as an adolescent? As an adult?

**GROWN-UP HELPERS**

### BE INTENTIONAL ABOUT DEVOTING TIME TO COOK TOGETHER

This will look different depending upon your helper's age. With young helpers, actively invite them to participate in the child appropriate activities our recipes present. With preteen or teen helpers, you might just sit and talk at the counter while they take charge.

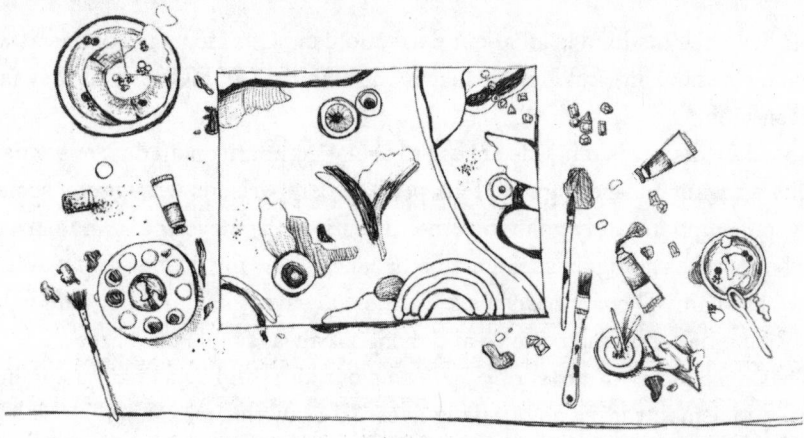

CHAPTER 10

# Dessert

*Bittersweet Perfection: The Imperfections of Living a Perfect Life*

For many, *dessert* is a loaded word. Flour, sugar, and flavors like chocolate, all leading to a craving for more, more, more. Of course this can incite guilt coupled with the feeling that we shouldn't let ourselves have these delectable items. We think they might lead us astray from our "perfect" selves.

It often feels like parenting is charged with perfectionism. We feel pressure to raise children who excel and fear for them if they don't. This overwhelming feeling leads us to overlook the beauty of mistakes and learning, the joy of upside-down cake. The main reason we didn't use photographs in this book was to avoid the sense that what you cook has to look perfect. We want you to be as imperfect as you want to be when cooking with your loved ones. Make mistakes in the kitchen, learn and laugh together, and create delectables that are delicious in their flawed unveiling: chocolate mousse that droops, cheesecake that falls over, glazed fruit and berries that are uneven in their presentation.

Perfectionism does have its place, like when making a meringue—it requires precision to transform eggs, sugar, and vanilla into a fluffy, peaked confection. If there's a little grease (from butter or oil) or even a bit of egg yolk in the mixture, it won't turn into meringue. But our expectations of our kids if we strive too hard for perfectionism can make them something else, pulling them away from who they really are or really want to be. Finding the right balance is tricky and elusive. This dynamic is even more complicated when we consider the presence of social media in their lives: the medium is all about perfectionism. Our kids gaze online at what everyone else is doing and feel the fear of missing out (FOMO) or that they fail to measure up.

Social media gives our kids access to social comparison all day, every day. Just like we want our meringue to look perfect, comparisons wrought by social media consumption rarely go in the other direction. I've never heard a teen say, "I felt better after going on social media because I saw my friends aren't able to do what I can." The comparisons are almost always about another person looking better, being better, living better—and the ideal always feels out of reach.

The sense of never measuring up leaves our kids, and us as parents, vulnerable to perfectionism intruding on our daily lives. "If I buy this makeup, I'll look as good as X does, and then life will be great." "I can't believe she got into that school. If I fit in one more extracurricular activity, maybe I'll have a chance, too." "If the kids at school don't accept me, I'll make friends through social media." And this can get scary and dangerous.

But restricting all access to social media doesn't seem realistic for preteens and teens who have access to the Internet and devices like cell phones. Research shows that kids whose parents restrict them from eating certain foods, like sweets, actually become more interested in those foods when they're available. So interested, in fact, that they may eat more than a regular portion when they have access to foods that were restricted or off limits in the past.[1] This research flies in the face of the deception approach to feeding your kids. With deception, your kids aren't aware of what they're eating because certain ingredients are intentionally hidden. By not restricting foods, and letting everyone know what they're eating, you create a balance. So too is the importance of addressing the imperfections of perfectionism.

Perfectionism correlates with depression and anxiety, mental health concerns that are on the rise for children globally. In fact, recent research shows that depression and anxiety among youth across the globe doubled during the pandemic.[2] Perfectionism can lead us to focus on the expectation, what we think other people want from us and for us, rather than tapping into an internal sense of what *we* want for ourselves.

Lately Olliver and I have been painting pictures together to give as presents. The idea first came about when Olliver and one of his sisters glued and glittered preschool drawings onto a canvas for their grandma's birthday. The result was a multidimensional collage, the last gift the kids gave her before she passed away. The artwork still hangs on the living room wall for their grandfather to enjoy. These days, as Olliver and I paint together, I'm struck by the initial urge to have the painting make sense and be liked by whoever we're making it for.

Kids are very intuitive. It's as though Olliver sensed this and rejected it when he said, "Let's make a barrier between the side you're working on and the side I'm working on. We'll paint our own sides for ten minutes and then we'll surprise each other." Whoa—what was he going to paint? How was it going to look? Would our sides be really different? What kind of a gift would that make? It was through Olliver's direction that I came to recognize the big picture (literally). We were creating something fun for someone we care about, an expression of our appreciation for that person, communicated in any way we wanted to portray it.

This realization was so freeing. It allowed me to take risks with the paints. It encouraged me to respect that we were each doing our own thing. It helped me trust the process. More importantly, it helped me trust Olliver—something we don't necessarily do when perfectionism sets in. While we were painting, I didn't peek at Olliver's side at all—I promise.

We risk losing our creativity when we're driven by perfectionism; we might not even be aware of such lost opportunities. I might not have let Olliver do his own thing—or insisted that I draw something for him to color in. If that happened, we would never have ended up with the bold combination of fluorescent colors, glitter, and sequins that adorns our painting.

This reminds me of my own first-grade experience. We had just moved to Venezuela and I was in Spanish class. We were given printed pages of outlined pictures to color in. Each picture was labeled with the Spanish word we were learning. The picture of a balloon, for instance, had the word *globo* beneath it. I remember taking the crayons and coloring outside the lines, scribbling all over the page. It felt so good to do that. But I received an NS grade—*no satisfactoria*, not satisfactory. I failed because I didn't color within the lines.

This stuff starts early.

Perfectionism is like a standard we have in our brains, something to live up to. But what is that something? And who decides what it is? Life is full of unknowns and circumstances we can't control. Sometimes we can see what's coming, but often what's put before us is unexpected and unknown—overwhelming new territory. When we focus on a perfectionism standard, we risk forgetting about the beauty of an imperfect stance that allows us to react and respond with resilience and flexibility.

Most of us can probably think of a peer who had many achievements and constantly received praise throughout their childhood. We may have even seen how this positive attention was motivating, helping the person continue to excel as they went through school. And then at some point, the real world hit. And the real world is less generous. Perhaps this person's perfectionism was derived from external things, like receiving praise, rather than developing an internal foundation of persistence and trying new things. Things might start to crumble when expectations aren't met. Sometimes perfectionism makes us unmotivated; we give up because we don't think we can meet the standard.

The truth is, it's not a bad thing to eat desserts. It becomes a negative when that's all we eat, or if we eat way too much of it, or if we have to limit our sugar intake for health reasons. But not all sweets are bad. Eating in moderation is an important skill for all of us to learn and a big part of mindful eating.

Julian made his Halloween Cheesecake when we needed to bring treats to school to celebrate Izzy's seventh birthday. The birthday was in June, by the way, not October. Julian wanted to make something sweet that kids could enjoy, but also something that included a different type of fruit for them to try, like pumpkin. To this day our daughter remembers the impact of serving Halloween Cheesecake in June: "They loved the pumpkin. Even the teachers were astonished, it was so good."

Embrace imperfectionism as you approach the dessert recipes in this chapter. It's okay if your Bittersweet Chocolate and Orange Mousse doesn't look like you imagined it would when you put it in serving glasses. Who cares if your Upside-Down British Summer Pudding falls down? The more important factor is that you connected with your helper to make it, and its deliciousness is in however it turns out. Embracing imperfectionism encourages us to be flexible as we navigate the unexpected.

Throughout COVID-19 we've tried to support my ninety-three-year-old dad, who lives independently. This often involves making the drive to his home to see him in person (initially from a distance while parked in the driveway as a social distance measure). We set the GPS to get directions for the fastest route. The route is always changing based on traffic, accidents, and road conditions. There's no one way that's going to always be the best way. It's up to us to be flexible if we want to have the most time with dad/grandpa.

*Imperfectionism can be our new GPS.*

We also lose out on making mistakes when we focus on being perfect. Our kids may be so afraid to make a mistake that they overly plan and are too diligent, all in an effort to get it right. But making mistakes is an integral part of learning how to take calculated risks. It's also central to building identity.

Consider the following: Our toddlers are likely to topple over as they learn to walk. Our preteens need to explore friendship groups to figure out where they fit in—a process that can be fraught with rejection as they learn about relationships. Our teens need to pull away from us as they test out their interests and explore their transition to adulthood.

Don't get me wrong: I'm not saying not to strive for things, and not to go for our goals. I'm actually saying the opposite—that we might be even better able to do the things we want to do, in the way we want to do them, when we're doing them from a place of what feels right for ourselves, not an imposed standard of perfectionism. Finding a balance is important.

As we start to make some of the delectable goodies that follow, here are some strategies to support imperfectionism for ourselves and our kids:

Know that it's okay, even important, to make mistakes. Ask, "What did you learn from the mistake?" "How has it changed your view?" "Is there something you would do differently?" "Is there something positive that came out of it?"

Encourage innate resilience through an approach like, "I'm sorry you didn't get into the club you wanted to join. That's really hard. What are you thinking about doing now? Are you going to try again next year or let it go?"

Reassure, reassure, and reassure with statements like, "You did the best you could—I'm proud of you."

Replace the phrase, "I tried my best, and my best wasn't good enough" with "I tried my best, and my best was good enough."

Hold on to perspective by considering the big picture: "Ten years from now, no one is going to even remember you got a 30 on your math test, not even you."

Have fun making these dessert recipes. They're sweet and messy, just like the best of life.

Most of all, paint using a barrier and see what turns out!

I originally made this dessert at my first big job in London, a long, long time ago. Over the years, I've made it and improved it, and every time I serve it, it consistently receives gushing acclaim. The recipe requires some care and uses some interesting techniques, but the key ingredient is bittersweet chocolate. Use the best quality you can find—it makes a huge difference. I hope you enjoy this dessert as much as those who have already fallen for it.

### INGREDIENTS

| | |
|---|---|
| 6 oz | **bittersweet chocolate (about 70% cacao)** |
| 1 cup | **heavy or whipping cream** |
| 4 | **large eggs, separated** |
| 6 Tbsp | **granulated sugar** |
| 1 pinch | **fine sea salt** |
| | **zest of 1 small orange** |

**SERVES 4**

# BITTERSWEET CHOCOLATE & ORANGE MOUSSE

Have at the ready 4 medium wineglasses.

Break or chop the chocolate and place in a medium metal bowl.

Fill a saucepan that is smaller than the metal bowl with 2 inches of water and place over medium heat. Set the metal bowl with the chocolate on top of the saucepan and carefully melt the chocolate without stirring it too much. This is called the water bath method. It's important to keep the chocolate dry and to not overheat it. Both of these scenarios will cause the chocolate to seize—in other words, to turn hard, lumpy, and unusable (see Top Tips, right).

Meanwhile, place the cream in a medium bowl. Use an electric mixer or handheld balloon whisk to whip the cream until firm peaks form. Divide the cream in half and place half in the fridge.

Place the egg yolks and 3 Tbsp of the granulated sugar in another medium bowl. Use an electric mixer or a handheld balloon whisk to vigorously whip the mixture for 3 to 6 minutes, or until the yolks are pale, thick, and viscous. This is called the ribbon stage (see Fun Fact, right).

Please note that this recipe involves consuming raw eggs.

## top tips!

Chocolate is very sensitive to heat, so melting it slowly with hot but not boiling water is the best approach. We place it over a water bath (a pan of water) to minimize the chance of burning it, because the water will not go above 212°F. The diameter of the saucepan that goes on the bottom should be slightly smaller than the bowl on top. This setup protects the chocolate from being in direct contact with the heat source and minimizes the risk of the chocolate getting wet.

## fun fact!

The ribbon stage of whisking egg yolks and sugar means that when you pull the whisk out of the mixture, the mixture on the whisk will fall back into the bowl, creating thick raised strands that will briefly look like ribbons on the surface of the mixture and then disappear. The mixture will also become paler in color as the sugar dissolves into the yolks and air is incorporated, increasing the volume.

Put the egg whites and a pinch of salt in a large bowl. Use an electric mixer or a handheld balloon whisk to whip the mixture. As the egg whites start to increase in volume, rain 1 Tbsp of the granulated sugar over them (see Top Tips, right, for how to do this). Continue whipping and adding more sugar, 1 Tbsp at a time, until there is no more sugar to add. Continue whipping the egg whites until firm peaks form. This is a basic French meringue.

Now we bring our four elements together. Once the chocolate is melted, add the orange zest, followed by the egg yolks, and mix together with a rubber spatula. Add the unrefrigerated portion of whipped cream and gently fold it in (see Top Tips, right). Add half of the meringue and gently fold it in. Then add the rest of the meringue and gently fold all the ingredients together until you don't see any more white meringue, then stop mixing.

Use a metal spoon to divide your chocolate mousse among the 4 glasses. Cover each glass individually with plastic wrap and refrigerate for a few hours. When you're ready to serve the chocolate mousse, remove the plastic wrap and top with the reserved whipped cream. Bittersweet imperfection!

## top tips!

To rain a Tbsp of sugar over the egg whites means that you don't just throw the sugar into your mixture in one large clump. Instead, you imitate rain, lightly sprinkling the sugar all over the egg whites. Sugar helps stabilize the air bubbles that create the volume and thickness essential to making meringue. Raining the sugar over the egg whites helps incorporate the sugar, while also avoiding breaking down the air pockets you create with whisking.

The technique of folding means to gently and carefully mix two or more separate ingredients or mixtures. This incorporates them together without breaking down the original structure of the separate ingredients or mixtures.

## fun fact!

Meringue is simply whipped egg whites and sugar. Whipping egg whites and sugar creates a firm foam that can be used in different desserts, including chocolate mousse, macaroons, and baked Alaska.

Summer pudding was a favorite of mine growing up. I loved the vibrant red color and the simple way the best summer fruits were gently enhanced with a little sugar and held together with sliced bread and some luck.

Puddings have a long history in British cooking. There are both savory and sweet types, and they can be as varied as black pudding (made with pig's blood) and steak and kidney pudding to plum pudding (known as Christmas pudding) and the more familiar rice pudding.

This dessert celebrates berries at their best. It would be perfect after a pick your own day (see Activity: Pick-Your-Own Day, opposite), when everyone collects their own berries and then prepares a special pudding to enjoy as a family.

**INGREDIENTS**

| | |
|---|---|
| 1½ lb | mixed berries (strawberries, raspberries, blueberries, blackberries, red currants, black currants), stems and leaves removed |
| ⅔ cup | granulated sugar |
| 1 pinch | fine sea salt |
| 6–8 slices | white bread, crusts removed |

**SERVES 4**

# UPSIDE-DOWN BRITISH SUMMER PUDDING

In a large saucepan, melt the granulated sugar and salt in 3 Tbsp of water over medium heat. Add all your berries, except the strawberries. Warm the rest of the fruit, gently mixing it with a rubber spatula occasionally, for 3 to 4 minutes. Remove the pan from the heat and let the mixture cool (do not strain).

Next, prepare the pudding bowl: lightly splash a little water inside a 1½ pint pudding bowl and then line it with plastic wrap (the water will help the plastic wrap stick to the sides of the bowl). Line the bowl with the sliced bread. Start this process by cutting a round piece of bread for the bottom of the bowl and then cut the bread into triangular pieces and use them to line the sides of the bowl, alternating them tip to tail. When you look into the bowl you should only see bread, with none of the bowl peeking through.

With a slotted spoon, put the cooled berries in the bowl. You can now slice your strawberries and add them as you go. If the berry filling looks dry, add a little juice from the saucepan. Cut a circle from 1 slice of bread that's the same size as the top of the bowl and place it on top of the berry filling to close the pudding. Sprinkle the bread with a little juice and cover with plastic wrap. Place a plate that is slightly smaller than the top of the bowl on top of your pudding, then place a weight (such as a pack of butter or a can of soup) on top of the plate. This will help push the fruit together and into the bread. Refrigerate overnight.

The next day, remove the weight, the plate, and the top layer of plastic wrap. Place a large plate upside down on top of the pudding bowl and carefully flip everything, so your plate is on the bottom and the pudding bowl is upside-down on the plate. Carefully remove the bowl from the pudding and then remove the plastic wrap.

Serve your summer pudding with vanilla ice cream or freshly whipped cream. A different and delicious way to enjoy the best summer berries!

# Pick-Your-Own Day

While we suggest some berries, you can also use this Upside-Down British Summer Pudding recipe (opposite) as a base and select what you prefer. This supports food choice and encourages eating mindfulness about what tastes right for you and your helpers. Have a Pick-Your-Own Day where everyone decides which berries they want for their pudding, and then brings them all together as a group. You can go to an orchard, where everyone picks the berries they want, or you can go to the grocery store together to each select your preferred berry.

**YOUNG HELPERS**

### PLAN A BERRY FUN SCAVENGER HUNT
Make a list or draw pictures of everyone's favorite berries. Go with your grown-up helper to the grocery store and participate in a scavenger hunt to find them.

**PRETEEN + TEEN HELPERS**

### ORGANIZE A GROCERY STORE OUTING
Ask your helpers, older and younger, to join you on a trip to the grocery store to each pick out your favorite berries. If you're making this dish in the summer, choose from seasonal berries like blueberries, strawberries, raspberries, and blackberries. If you decide you must have Upside-Down British Summer Pudding in the fall, consider cranberries and even blackberries that are at the end of their season.

**GROWN-UP HELPERS**

### VISIT A BERRY FARM
Did you know there are berry farms? Plan a family outing with your helpers to each pick your favorite berries.

This is a dessert that should be made at the end of the summer because cherries are at their peak this time of the year. It might also cheer everyone up when you're all thinking about the kids returning to school after a long summer vacation. Put a smile and cherry juice on everyone's face with this very yummy, very easy, very cherry pie.

Depending on your kid's age, they can help a lot or a little. They can make the dough, roll out the pastry, and remove the pits from the cherries (a job for everyone) with the aid of a handy cherry pitter tool.

## CRUST

| | |
|---|---|
| 4 Tbsp | unsalted butter, at room temperature |
| ¼ cup | soft brown sugar |
| 1 tsp | vanilla extract |
| ¾ cup | old-fashioned rolled oats |
| ¾ cup | whole wheat flour |
| ¼ tsp | fine sea salt |

## FILLING

| | |
|---|---|
| 3 cups | fresh cherries, stems removed and pitted |
| ¼ cup | maple syrup |
| ¼ cup | turbinado sugar |
| | zest of ½ orange |
| 3 Tbsp | cornstarch |
| ½ tsp | ground cinnamon |

**SERVES 6**

# VERY CHERRY PIE

## TO MAKE THE CRUST

Preheat the oven to 425°F.

In a large bowl, vigorously mix the butter, brown sugar, and vanilla with a rubber spatula until very soft and smooth. Add the oats, whole wheat flour, salt, and 3 Tbsp of water and mix by hand until everything comes together. Do not overmix, as the dough will become hard when cooked (see Top Tips, below). Wrap your dough and refrigerate for an hour.

On a floured surface, use a rolling pin to roll out three-quarters of the dough into a large circle that's about 2½ inches larger than your 10-inch pie pan. Carefully lay your dough in the pan, gently pushing down the sides and corners. With a sharp knife remove any dough hanging over the edge of the pie pan.

Roll out the remaining dough into a rough rectangle that measures about 4 × 9 inches. Use a pizza wheel cutter to cut the dough into 8 long strips. Set aside the crust and strips of dough.

## TO MAKE THE FILLING

Kids to the rescue! It's time to remove the pits from the cherries, but please make sure the kids are not wearing white or brand-new fancy clothes—cherry juice stains!

Place each cherry in the open-ended cup of an olive/cherry pitter tool and push down on the tool. The cherry will stay in the cup and the pit will be ejected. Discard the pits and place the pitted cherries in a medium bowl. Once all the cherries are pitted, add the maple syrup, turbinado sugar, orange zest, cornstarch, and cinnamon and gently toss to coat the cherries. Pour the cherry mixture into the dough-lined pie pan.

Lay 4 strips of dough evenly on top of your pie filling, then lay the other 4 strips of dough evenly in the opposite direction. Trim the overhanging dough. You should now have a lattice design on top of your cherry pie.

### top tips!

Once your mixture of butter, brown sugar, vanilla, oats, flour, and water has come together with everything incorporated, stop mixing! Mixing more than necessary will not improve the dough. To the contrary, it will make it hard when cooked.

Bake your pie for 15 minutes, then lower the oven temperature to 350° F and bake for 20 more minutes, or until the crust is golden brown. Remove your pie from the oven and let cool slightly before cutting it into wedges.

To make this an even bigger treat, serve your pie with a small scoop of vanilla ice cream or fresh Greek yogurt.

# Take a Step Back to Move Forward

Chapter Two includes an Activity called Whisk Just Right (page 40) that helps us prepare Lemon Ricotta Pancakes (page 39). It's no accident that this chapter, with its focus on imperfection, includes a couple recipes that caution us not to overmix. Have you ever really wanted something and tried and tried and tried to make it happen? Maybe the desire was for a relationship to work or for people at the office to really like you? No matter how hard you tried, those dynamics just didn't change. In fact, they may have gotten worse as your partner or your co-workers saw how hard you were trying and recognized their power. Just like overmixing, sometimes when we try too hard, it's a signal to take a step back so we can move in another direction. This might mean ending the relationship to find someone who meets you where you're at or transferring to a different department with co-workers who appreciate what you bring. Paradoxically, and as this recipe shows, sometimes not overmixing leads to a smooth and gratifying outcome.

**YOUNG HELPERS**

### START AND STOP
Once your ingredients are all mixed, stop mixing!

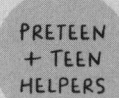

**PRETEEN + TEEN HELPERS**

### STOP BEING IN THE MIX IF IT DOESN'T WORK
If a friendship doesn't feel right to you or a relationship doesn't feel healthy, listen to your instincts and move on to a healthier relationship space.

**GROWN-UP HELPERS**

### STIR UP YOUR LIFE
Sometimes we get so used to relationships that we forget to evaluate if they're good for us. Maybe there's a friend who makes us feel worse every time we hang out. Maybe our interactions with another parent leave us feeling less-than every time. Be intentional about doing something different with relationships that don't feel right for you. If it hasn't felt right for some time, and you don't really want the relationship, consider how your precious time could be spent investing in those relationships that you care about and that are meaningful to you.

Sabrina loves to bake. Once everyone has gone to bed she will organize the kitchen, selecting her recipe, getting her ingredients together, cutting, mixing, and baking until her creation is ready for devouring. We benefit too, as we'll come into the kitchen the next morning only to be greeted by a plate of freshly baked goodies.

## INGREDIENTS

| | |
|---|---|
| 1 cup | soft brown sugar |
| ½ cup | unsalted butter, melted |
| ½ tsp | fine sea salt |
| 1 | large egg |
| 1 Tbsp | vanilla extract |
| 1 cup | all-purpose flour |
| 1 Tbsp | cornstarch |
| 1 tsp | baking powder |
| ½ cup | cashews, measured first and then toasted and roughly chopped |
| ½ cup | coconut flakes or shreds |
| ¼ cup | bittersweet chocolate chips |
| ¼ cup | white chocolate chips |

**SERVES 6**

# SABRINA'S BLONDIES

Preheat the oven to 350°F. Lightly butter and flour an 8-×-8-inch baking pan.

In a large bowl, mix the brown sugar, melted butter, and salt until smooth. Add the egg and vanilla and mix until fully combined.

In a smaller bowl, whisk together the all-purpose flour, cornstarch, and baking powder. Add the dry ingredients to the wet ingredients and mix with a rubber spatula until everything is just combined. Add the cashews, coconut, half of the bittersweet chocolate chips, and half of the white chocolate chips. Mix until combined.

Spread the blondie batter in an even layer in the prepared baking pan. Sprinkle the remaining bittersweet and white chocolate chips evenly on top. Bake for 20 to 25 minutes, or until a toothpick inserted in the center comes out clean. Place the pan on a wire cooling rack and let the blondies cool completely.

Cut the blondies into 12 pieces (cut 4 strips one way and 3 strips the other way). A scrumptious treat!

This is an individual dessert: everyone gets their own very special and delicious shortcake. With crunchy almond cakes, intensely sweet strawberries, and homemade vanilla whipped cream, this is a wonderful dessert for a memorable occasion or just because your family deserves a treat. Celebrate you and yours!

## ALMOND SHORTCAKES

| 1¼ cups | all-purpose flour |
|---|---|
| 3 Tbsp | granulated sugar |
| 1 Tbsp | baking powder |
| 1 pinch | fine sea salt |
| 3 Tbsp | unsalted butter, cold and cut into small squares |
| ½ cup | almonds, measured first and then lightly toasted and chopped |
| ⅓ cup | buttermilk (or heavy or whipping cream), plus 2 Tbsp for glazing |
| 1 | large egg |
| 1 tsp | almond extract |

## STRAWBERRIES

| 2 cups | ripe strawberries, thinly sliced |
|---|---|
| 1–2 Tbsp | granulated sugar |
| 1 pinch | fine sea salt |

## VANILLA WHIPPED CREAM

| ½ cup | heavy or whipping cream |
|---|---|
| 3 tsp | granulated sugar |
| 3 drops | vanilla extract |
| 2 Tbsp | confectioners' sugar, for dusting |

**SERVES 4**

# STRAWBERRY ALMOND SHORTCAKES

### TO MAKE THE ALMOND SHORTCAKES

Preheat the oven to 400°F. Line a baking sheet with parchment paper.

In a large bowl, whisk together the all-purpose flour, granulated sugar, baking powder, and salt. Add the butter and rub the ingredients between your fingertips for 3 to 5 minutes to create a crumb consistency. Take your time—it's important that the butter is well incorporated into the flour. Mix in the almonds.

In a small bowl, whisk the ⅓ cup of buttermilk or cream with the egg and almond extract. Add the wet ingredients to the dry ingredients and gently fold to bind them together. Don't overmix your ingredients or the shortcakes will become tough when baked (see Activity: Take a Step Back to Move Forward, page 201).

Place the dough on a lightly floured surface and pat it down a little. Using a medium-size (3¼-inch) round cookie cutter, mark out, but don't cut, 4 circles on top of the dough. If you have too much extra dough, squash it together to make it thicker. If you don't have enough dough to make 4 circles, pat it down a little more.

Use the cutter to cut the dough into 4 shortcakes, then place them on the lined baking sheet. With a pastry brush, paint the tops of each shortcake with a little buttermilk or cream (see Activity: A Heart of Dough, page 138). Bake for 15 to 20 minutes, or until a toothpick inserted in the middle comes out clean. Place the shortcakes on a wire cooling rack while you prepare the strawberries and whipped cream.

### TO MAKE THE STRAWBERRIES

In a small bowl, sprinkle the strawberries with the granulated sugar and salt. Taste your strawberries to see if they're sweet or not so sweet, and add granulated sugar accordingly (see Activity: Taste as You Go, page 68). Gently mix with a spoon. Cover the bowl and leave it on the counter for about 30 minutes. This process will draw the moisture from the strawberries and concentrate their flavor. The strawberries will also absorb the sugar, making them sweeter. As the sugar dissolves with the strawberries, there will be juice in the bowl that can be used to add extra flavor to the shortcakes.

## TO MAKE THE WHIPPED CREAM

In a medium bowl, combine the cream with the granulated sugar and vanilla. Use a balloon whisk to vigorously whip the cream until firm peaks form. Do not overwhip the cream or it will separate, and you will end up making butter and buttermilk (see Activity: Take a Step Back to Move Forward, page 201).

Cut each shortcake horizontally in half. Place some strawberries and strawberry juice on the bottom halves. Finish with some whipped cream and place the remaining halves on top. Repeat until all your shortcakes are assembled. Place each shortcake on its own plate and divide any extra fruit and juice between the plates. To complete your presentation, dust with confectioners' sugar and serve.

## top tips!

You can tell when the butter is incorporated into the flour enough, because they will look and feel like crumbs. There won't be any lumps of butter in the flour and the flour won't be as fine as it was before you rubbed in the butter.

# Work Together

Even though this Strawberry Almond Shortcakes recipe (page 203) is about making individual cakes for friends or family members, the many parts of putting it together offer a wonderful teamwork opportunity. Young helpers can let grown-up helpers know what they want to work on to make this recipe happen, and preteen and teen helpers can work together or with young and grown-up helpers. Everyone can enjoy coming together to eat these individual cakes.

**YOUNG HELPERS**

### EXPLORE LEADERSHIP

You may very well be the youngest in your family. And I'm assuming that the older members of your family might make more decisions than you do. In this activity, you get to be the leader. Tell your helper(s) which parts of the recipe you want to make and which parts you want them to make. Watch your helpers to make sure they finish the jobs you assign them!

**PRETEEN + TEEN HELPERS**

### DELEGATION STATION

Delegating is an important life skill. It's important because as you have more and more responsibilities, there are more moving parts. Doing everything on your own may not always be an option. Practice how to delegate while preparing this recipe. After you invite your helper(s) to make this dessert with you, delegate specific tasks for them to do. Supervise to make sure they're completed. What was it like for you to delegate? Did it help make the process more manageable? Where in your life can you use more delegation? Who will you delegate tasks to?

**GROWN-UP HELPERS**

### EXTEND AN INVITATION TO CONNECT

As you explore your own cooking skills, invite helpers of all ages to join. Whether it's mixing ingredients, painting dough, cutting fruit, or whisking cream, creating together makes cooking even more fun and meaningful.

Don't wait for Halloween! Although this cheesecake incorporates fall flavors (e.g., pumpkin and cinnamon), it can be enjoyed any time of year, as you will soon see. The dark cookie crust, orange center, and spider web topping transforms cheesecake into something theatrical, entertaining, and of course, scrumptious.

## COOKIE CRUST

| 3 cups | ground chocolate cookies with cream filling |
| ¼ cup | soft brown sugar, firmly packed |
| 4 Tbsp | unsalted butter, melted |

## FILLING

| 4 | 8-oz packages cream cheese, at room temperature |
| 1⅔ cups | granulated sugar |
| 1½ cups | canned pure pumpkin |
| 9 Tbsp | heavy or whipping cream |
| 1 tsp | ground cinnamon |
| 1 tsp | ground allspice |
| 4 | large eggs |
| 1–3 Tbsp | purchased caramel sauce (in a squeeze bottle) |
| ½ cup | sour cream |

**SERVES 10**

# HALLOWEEN CHEESECAKE

### TO MAKE THE COOKIE CRUST

Preheat the oven to 350°F.

In a food processor, combine the cookie crumbs and soft brown sugar and pulse to combine. Add the melted butter and blend until combined. Once that's done, have fun pressing the crust mixture onto the bottom of a 9-inch springform pan with 2¾-inch sides. Set aside.

### TO MAKE THE FILLING

In a large bowl, use an electric mixer to beat the cream cheese and granulated sugar until loose and silky. Transfer ¾ cup of this mixture to a small bowl, cover tightly, and refrigerate—this will be your topping.

Add the pumpkin, 4 Tbsp of cream, the cinnamon, and allspice to the cream cheese mixture and beat until well combined. Add the eggs, 1 at a time, beating just until combined.

Pour your filling into the crust—it will almost fill the pan. Bake for about 1 hour and 15 minutes, or until the cheesecake puffs, the top browns, and the center moves only slightly when the pan is shaken. Transfer your cheesecake to a wire cooling rack and let cool for 10 minutes.

### top tips!

We use a springform pan so we can easily remove the cheesecake from the pan, leaving it intact. Springform pans are usually 9 inches in diameter, although other sizes are available. The sides of a springform pan are usually about 3 inches high. You will see that the round base of the pan sits in a groove on the inside of the ring that forms the sides of the pan and is released once the latch is opened. You can open the latch once your cake is cooked and cooled. This will increase the diameter of the pan by ¼ to ½ in, allowing you to easily remove your baked item from the ring of the pan.

After 10 minutes, run a small sharp knife around the cake pan sides to loosen the cheesecake. Do not remove the ring yet. Let the cheesecake cool completely, then cover tightly and refrigerate overnight.

When ready to serve, bring the reserved ¾ cup of the cream cheese mixture to room temperature. Add the remaining 5 Tbsp of cream and the sour cream. Stir to combine. Pour the cream cheese mixture over the cheesecake, spreading it evenly. Have fun squeezing the caramel sauce in lines over the cream cheese topping. Using the tip of a knife, you can then swirl the caramel sauce into a spiderweb design. Release the latch on the springform ring and gently ease it away from the cheesecake. It's now ready to serve—a treat for family, extended family, and lots of friends.

# Throw a Party

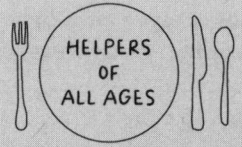

HELPERS
OF
ALL AGES

Making Halloween Cheesecake is a great reason to throw a party! And not just for Halloween. Invite your friends over to celebrate any occasion, or just to get together. If a remote get together is preferred, your online guests can create their cheesecake at home, and you can eat it together across screens. Or, have a cooking party where everyone cooks together virtually. The choice of venue is all yours!

This recipe is a simple celebration of summer fruits and berries. It's minimally prepared to bring out the natural flavors of the fruit.

## INGREDIENTS

| | |
|---|---|
| 3 | ripe nectarines or peaches, each cut into 12 wedges |
| 1½ cups | ripe strawberries, halved |
| ½ cup | raspberries |
| ¼ cup | blueberries |
| 4 | large egg yolks |
| 2 Tbsp | maple syrup |

**SERVES 4**

# GLAZED FRUIT & BERRIES

Set the broiler to high heat.

### TO MAKE THE PLATES OF FRUIT AND BERRIES

Your fruit and berries can be arranged onto four 9-inch flat, white ovenproof plates. One option is to put the nectarines or peaches in an outside circle, followed by the strawberries and the raspberries, with the blueberries placed in the center.

### TO MAKE THE SABAYON SAUCE

Fill a medium saucepan with about 1 inch of water and bring to a gentle simmer over medium-low heat. In a medium metal bowl, combine the egg yolks and maple syrup. Place this bowl over the saucepan of hot water. Make sure that the water in the bottom pan does not touch the bowl and does not get too hot. Use a balloon whisk to constantly whisk the mixture (see Activity: Whisk Just Right, page 40), making sure it doesn't turn into scrambled eggs. After 4 to 6 minutes, you will delight in seeing how the mixture has tripled in volume and creates a ribbon effect (see Fun Fact, page 196) when the whisk is lifted up.

Immediately drizzle your sauce, called sabayon, in the gaps between the fruit. Place your plates under a hot broiler for 1 to 2 minutes, or until the sabayon turns light golden brown. Enjoy this warm, summery berry fruit creation!

# Create an Edible Work of Art

Making Glazed Fruit and Berries provides a wonderful way to express your culinary artistic side. Have fun decorating your creation. Organize your fruits and berries in a design that works for you. It's like creating a painting with food as your palette.

**YOUNG HELPERS**

### TAKE A PHOTO TO SHARE

Take a photo and send it to your teachers.

**PRETEEN + TEEN HELPERS**

### POST YOUR CREATION

Post your photo on social media.

**GROWN-UP HELPERS**

### CRAFT YOUR COLLAGE

Indulge your creative crafting side and arrange the fruit and berries to make an edible collage.

This is a wonderful year-round dessert that can be eaten hot, warm, or cold, and with ice cream, raspberry sorbet, or Vanilla Whipped Cream (see Strawberry Almond Shortcakes, page 203). If you see an abundance of another fruit at the market, like peaches or plums, nectarines or rhubarb, you can experiment with that fruit instead.

This simple recipe should be used as a base to be experimented with as you and your family gain confidence in your own tastes and preferences.

## FRUIT FILLING

| | |
|---|---|
| 4 | apples, peeled, cored, and cut into ¼-in slices |
| 4 | pears, peeled, cored, and cut into ¼-in slices |
| 2 Tbsp | granulated sugar |
| | zest and juice of 1 small lemon |
| 1 tsp | ground cinnamon |
| ¼ tsp | fine sea salt |
| 2 Tbsp | all-purpose flour |

## CRUMBLE TOPPING

| | |
|---|---|
| ⅔ cup | whole wheat flour |
| ⅔ cup | soft brown sugar |
| ¼ tsp | fine sea salt |
| ½ cup | unsalted butter, at room temperature |
| ¼ cup | old-fashioned rolled oats |
| ½ cup | almonds, measured first and then chopped |
| ¼ tsp | ground cinnamon |
| 1 pinch | freshly ground nutmeg |

**SERVES 6**

# PEAR & APPLE CRUMBLE

### TO MAKE THE FRUIT FILLING

Preheat the oven to 350°F. Lightly butter a high-sided 9-inch square baking dish.

In a large bowl, toss the apple and pear slices with the granulated sugar, lemon zest and juice, cinnamon, and salt. Sprinkle with the all-purpose flour and toss to combine. Spread the fruit filling in the prepared baking dish and set aside.

### TO MAKE THE CRUMBLE TOPPING

In a large bowl, combine the whole wheat flour, brown sugar, salt, and butter. Mix with your fingertips until all the butter is incorporated into the flour and your mixture looks like breadcrumbs. Add the oats, almonds, cinnamon, and nutmeg and mix to combine. Sprinkle the crumble topping over the fruit and spread it evenly to cover the whole dish. Place the baking dish on a rimmed baking sheet (in case the fruit bubbles over) and bake for 35 to 45 minutes, or until the crumble topping is golden brown. Remove your crumble from the oven and let cool for 5 minutes before diving in!

# Take a Risk and Face Your Fear of Imperfection

True to how we value imperfection, so many of these recipes show us there's no right or wrong way to make dessert. It's okay if your finished creation is not perfect. The same is true for life. Sometimes we're so afraid to make a mistake or to be rejected that we don't go for what we really want: We don't pursue the friendship or the love interest, we don't apply for that dream school or the job of our dreams. As parents, it's natural and expected that we want to protect our kids. This is our job. The problem is, if we don't let our kids make their own mistakes (and by mistakes we mean calculated, still safe mistakes like failing a test due to not studying), then they don't get to learn and recover from them. For food and for life, what's important is that we try, taste, and experiment to open up a universe of flavors, textures, and ingredients to be enjoyed now and for a lifetime.

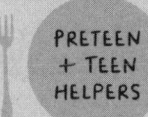 **PRETEEN + TEEN HELPERS**

## FACE YOUR FEAR

Is there something you've always wanted to do or someone you've always wanted to meet but didn't want to risk failure or rejection? Work with those feelings and do it anyway. One way to do this is to acknowledge your fear, identify it, and prepare to confront it. In acknowledging your fear, you can think about your goal and how your fear interferes with it. As you prepare to confront your fear, talk with someone about how you're feeling. Anticipate what might happen. Part of anxiety is a fear of the unknown. It's about uncertainty. In exposure therapy, clients actually face what they're afraid of by engaging in the activity or scenario they fear in a safe way with the support of a mental health professional. You may find that the outcome of engaging in what you were afraid of was indeed scary. You may also find it wasn't scary at all—that, in fact, it was the buildup of fear that got in your way. Now you know.

**YOUNG HELPERS**

## TALK ABOUT A MISTAKE YOU MADE

Tell your grown-up helper about a mistake you made this week: What did you learn from it?

 **GROWN-UP HELPERS**

## MANAGE FRUSTRATION TO MODEL COPING

Is there something you want to do differently but aren't sure it will work out? Take the risk and see how it goes: Maybe you were just offered a new job. It's a great position with better benefits and an easier commute. It's a great next step for your career. But you're comfortable with your current position. You know the people and you're familiar with the role. What do you do? How do you weigh your decision? Here's another example: After many years, you've decided that you want to expand your family and have another baby. You've felt strongly about this for a long time although you've kept your wishes quiet. You finally decide to talk with your significant other about what you're thinking. What do you say? How does it go?

In taking the risk, regardless of how it might turn out, you can have the peace of mind of knowing you did the best you could. No regrets.

CHAPTER 11

# Drinks

*Quenching Our Lives with Drink Options*

These drink recipes are full of ways family helpers can explore cooking skills like grating, peeling, combining, and mixing. They also introduce wonderful avenues to explore taste through ingredients that combine sensations like sour and sweet.

As parents and as people, we've often struggled with drink options. It's ironic that something so important for the body, hydration, is often overlooked in our diets. Water is important, but it can be boring to drink. It's very easy to consume manufactured beverages like soda instead, but these can be high in sugar, chemicals, and calories. Drinks present a different food choice challenge because, unlike eating, quenching our thirst is a much more portable activity. We can do it while we're in transit, in class, at work, and in the car. This is why bottled drinks are so convenient when we need to quench our thirst in the moment.

Convenience is the parameter for quenching our lives. Our whole purpose in this chapter is to help you and your helpers quench your lives through different homemade drink options. To sustain them with convenience, we recommend you stock your kitchen with three important items: a pitcher, reusable water bottles, and a travel mug for hot drinks.

The subtitle for this chapter, "Quenching Our Lives with Drink Options," is inspired by the idea that we can create something new in our families and for ourselves that satisfies or quenches a need. Rather than doing things the same old way, we can explore new, healthy, and refreshing ways to quench our thirst. This chapter's theme is a metaphor for other changes we may want to see in our lives; making drink recipes together can encourage conversations to explore what those changes might be.

One of the things I actually do appreciate about cooking is that it forces me to stop what I'm doing at the moment, go to the kitchen, and start making something to eat. As I'm organizing and preparing food, the task I was just working on (often on the computer) almost instantly becomes more distant. It's in these moments of stepping away from my desk that I can think about how things are going in our lives. Having a break from a long work day helps me consider new perspectives I may not have thought about before.

Getting away to the kitchen to prepare food with your helper—whether that helper is a young child, preteen, teenager, sibling, partner, spouse, or friend—provides an opportunity to have conversations about things we might not normally discuss. These conversations might focus on how we want to quench our day-to-day lives in ways we might not have considered previously.

As an example, stepping into the kitchen might help you reflect on your current work situation if you are unhappy in your job. You might feel underutilized, not included as part of the team, or simply bored. Sometimes we get so into routines and habits that we consider what we're going through as just being "the way things are." We may convince ourselves the situation wouldn't be different elsewhere and rule out opportunities, assuming it will just be more of the same. Logically, when we step back, we know this is not the case. But when we're in a situation, and it's all we know, our brain can fool us and tell us this is how things are going to stay.

Having a conversation about your work situation with your cooking helper (like a partner or spouse) can open up new possibilities. Your helper might encourage you to apply for that job posting you noticed. Your helper might say you should absolutely reach out to the contact you know in the organization that's hiring.

Change, even positive change, is hard. It's challenging to do something different, to organize our lives to think about doing something new—and to put ourselves out there to take a risk, knowing that the outcome may not be the one desired. It's kind of like our drink options. We have certain bottled drinks in the fridge that we purchase regularly, and we get comfortable knowing these are the drinks we have. In making different thirst-quenchers, we expand those options, creating new experiences that taste good and are good for us.

The same holds true for conversations that emerge when cooking together. Before Izzy left for her first year of college, she spent days baking with Olliver for their grandfather. Grandpa loves what Izzy bakes and looks forward to the treats she brings when we visit.

"Grandpa, what treats do you want me to bake for you before I go to college?" Izzy asked. "I'll freeze them and Mom can bring them to you, one for each visit, so that you always have something sweet to eat. They can remind you of me, and it'll make it seem like I'm less far away." Grandpa shared his favorites and Izzy and Olliver got busy baking.

As Izzy told Olliver about her conversation with Grandpa (who was perplexed and excited about all the baking), the two of them started to talk about her pending departure as well. "Izzy, when will you be home? How long will you be away?" Olliver asked.

"Until Thanksgiving, Ollie," she responded. "I hope you can come and visit me before then."

"Okay," said Olliver. "Mama and I can come and visit you and stay for a while. Izzy, I'm going to miss you so much."

"I'm going to miss you too, Ollie. But the time will go by fast—we'll be together again before you know it."

"Izzy, can some of these treats be for me?"

Olliver loves to make lemonade. Squashing the lemons, getting all the juice out, measuring the sugar, mixing, and puckering to the sour taste. It's so delicious he says, "Papa, I wish rain was lemonade."

## INGREDIENTS

| | |
|---|---|
| ½ cup | granulated sugar, plus more as needed |
| 2 cups | hot water |
| 2 cups | ice |
| 1½ cups | fresh lemon juice (from 8 lemons), plus 1 lemon for decoration (optional) |
| 2 cups | cold water |

**SERVES 6**

(**4** ON A VERY HOT DAY)

# OLLIVER'S SOUR LEMONADE

In a large bowl, combine the granulated sugar and hot water and whisk well to melt the sugar. Add the ice and stir. It's fun to watch as the ice melts. Add the lemon juice and cold water and stir. Test your lemonade to see how it tastes. Discover if you like it sour or sweet, adding more sugar as needed.

Pour your lemonade into a pitcher and put it in the fridge. Please make sure you don't add ice at this point, as you don't want to dilute the lemonade. When ready to serve, pour your lemonade into a glass over a little ice and slip a lemon slice on the side of the glass for decoration. Refreshing!

### top tips!

If you put the whisk on the bottom of the bowl and hear a cracking sound, that's the sugar. Hearing this sound means that you need to mix some more. Ultimately, you want to mix until there's no cracking sound. This means the sugar has dissolved.

# Test Your Taste Buds

It's fun to learn about taste while making these drinks. "Uggghhh, that lemonade is too sour!" These recipes help us learn what we can do to make drinks taste just right for our palates. For instance, we can add some sugar to the lemonade. This empowers all of us to explore taste and be aware of ingredients (and their amounts) that influence what tastes yummy or yucky.

**YOUNG HELPERS**

### TASTE TEST SWEET AND SOUR FRUITS
Go to the store with your grown-up helper and pick out fruits to test if they're sweet or sour. Here are some suggestions of what you might select: grapes, grapefruits, limes, blueberries, oranges, lemons, mangoes, and pears. Which taste sweet? Which taste sour? Which are a combination of sweet and sour?

**PRETEEN + TEEN HELPERS**

### TAKE A HEALTHY RISK
Similar to exploring our taste buds, experiencing adolescence is all about doing something different in the moment. This type of exploration supports your identity development as you learn more about what you like and what doesn't work for you.

**GROWN-UP HELPERS**

### ORGANIZE A TASTE TEST GAME WITH YOUR HELPERS
Have your helpers close their eyes and guess the fruits they're tasting. The winner gets to mix the drink concoction to suit their taste buds.

Green tea is a delicate tea that's full of antioxidants. Although green tea has caffeine, it's a significantly smaller amount than what is found in black tea or coffee. In making this recipe, helpers of all ages will see how easy it is to make delicious drink options. Remember to have your pitcher and water bottles ready!

## INGREDIENTS

| | |
|---|---|
| 4 | green tea bags |
| 5 Tbsp | honey |
| 3 | medium oranges |
| 2 | lemons |
| 1 | liter bottle seltzer water, chilled |

**SERVES 4**

# GREEN TEA & CITRUS PUNCH

In a small pot, bring 2 cups of water to a boil. Remove from the heat, add the tea bags and honey, and let steep for 5 minutes. After 5 minutes, remove the tea bags.

**NOW YOU'RE READY TO PREPARE THE CITRUS:**

Peel 2 of the oranges and 1 of the lemons. Reserve the peels. Squeeze the peeled oranges and lemon, then strain the juice, discarding any seeds or pulp.

In a punch bowl, combine the brewed tea, strained orange juice, and strained lemon juice. Add the reserved orange and lemon peel. Place your concoction in the refrigerator for at least 5 hours, or until you're ready to serve it.

While the punch is chilling, slice the remaining orange and lemon into rounds. Put the citrus rounds on a plate and freeze for a few hours until frozen.

When the punch is nicely chilled, remove it from the fridge and scoop out and discard the citrus peel. Stir in the seltzer water, drop in the frozen orange and lemon slices, and serve immediately. Deliciously refreshing and fun any time of year!

# Make a Concoction

Who doesn't appreciate the joy of making your own concoctions? Think of this chapter as experimenting with different delicious potions. What does the Green Tea Citrus Punch mixture look like after you scoop out the fruit peel, pour in the seltzer, and add in the frozen fruit?

### MAKE A MESS

YOUNG HELPERS

Try combining different ingredients in messy ways. Here are some ingredients from the recipes in this chapter: lemon, sugar, orange juice, sparkling water, cocoa powder, mango, raspberries, grapefruit juice, and watermelon. How would you combine these ingredients? Sparkling water, ice, and raspberries, with a little lemon juice? Orange juice and grapefruit juice? What do you think goes well together? And how will you mix it, stir it, shake it, freeze it—to get just the concoction you want?

### TRY SOMETHING NEW IN THE MOMENT

PRETEEN + TEEN HELPERS

What happens when you combine different ingredients? Similar to creating concoctions, adolescence involves experimenting to see how things come out. You might have questions like: "What happens if I join this club?" Or, "What if I decide not to be friends with the frenemy in my friend group anymore?" Whether it's adding more sugar or fewer fruit slices, almost all these recipes involve testing ingredients to see what works best for you.

### WATCH WHAT HAPPENS

GROWN-UP HELPERS

Step back and ask, "What do you notice as you mix fruit, chocolate, seltzer, ice, water, and the many other ingredients in these recipes?" Then let it happen and remember that messes can always be cleaned up!

This light, refreshing drink combines spicy and sweet sensations. Spicy is the dominant experience, given the amount of ginger. The sweet part is more of a hint that comes from the mango. Experiment to see if this combination of taste sensations works for you and your helpers.

## INGREDIENTS

| | |
|---|---|
| 4 in | fresh ginger root, peeled and finely sliced |
| 1½ cups | chopped fresh or frozen mango, plus more for serving |
| 3 cups | ice |
| 2 cups | water |
| 2 cups | sparkling water |

**SERVES 4**

# GINGER MANGO WATER

In a large container, combine the ginger, mango, ice, and the water. Refrigerate for at least 2 hours before serving.

When ready to serve, strain the mixture, discarding the ginger and mango.

For a fun presentation, fill a glass halfway with the strained ginger-mango water, then add a couple mango chunks and top with cold sparkling water. A wonderfully healthy and more affordable alternative to soda!

Consider this story: You attend a preschool end-of-the-year picnic, and every time you see your toddler-aged son, he's wandering around with handfuls of freshly cut watermelon. That evening at home, he forgets to flush the toilet, again! To your horror, a bright red liquid is in the bowl, along with countless black spots. You immediately consult your pediatrician, who nods knowingly. To your relief, everything is back to normal the next day!

Have you ever had a day where you just needed to drink something refreshing to quench your thirst? It's hot outside and no matter how much you drink, you're still thirsty? Our Watermelon and Lime Cooler incorporates the natural juices of these fruits to quench your thirst on a hot summer day.

## INGREDIENTS

| | |
|---|---|
| 3 lb | sweet, seedless, rindless watermelon, plus 4 watermelon slices for garnish (the latter is optional) |
| | zest and juice of 1 lime |
| 2 cups | chilled sparkling or still water |
| | fresh mint leaves (optional) |

**SERVES 4**

# WATERMELON & LIME COOLER

Set the sliced watermelon aside for garnish, if desired. Cut 2 lb of the watermelon into cubes—you should have about 6 cups. Set aside. Cut the rest of the watermelon into ¼-inch dice—you should have about 1 cup. Spread the cup of ¼-inch-diced watermelon on a baking sheet and freeze for at least 2 hours to create your watermelon ice cubes.

Meanwhile, in a food processor or blender, liquidize the cubed watermelon, lime zest, and lime juice until very smooth. Transfer to a bowl and refrigerate for about 2 hours, or until chilled.

When ready to serve your cooler, put your watermelon-lime mixture in a pitcher. Add the chilled sparkling or still water and stir to combine. To serve, divide your frozen watermelon ice cubes into 4 glasses and pour the cooler over them. For an extra bit of fancy, you can garnish your drink with a slice of watermelon and a sprig of mint. Go ahead: be quenched and be healthy!

### top tips!

Lime zest accentuates the flavor of this drink. It's made by grating the outside layer (the peel) of the lime. Place your cutting board on the counter and the grater on the cutting board. Push the lime down the smallest holes of a box grater, removing a thin layer of the lime's peel. Keep rotating the lime so that you're grating the outside skin only to avoid grating into the white pith. You will see the grated lime peel—your lime zest—on your cutting board.

# Decorate Your Concoctions

Explore creativity by decorating these drinks in all sorts of ways. So much of what makes food appetizing is its presentation. Rather than buying a decorating craft kit at the store, use edible craft materials and engage your artistic side by thinking of fun and creative ways to dress up your drinks. For instance, add some watermelon slices and mint leaves to your glass for the Watermelon and Lime Cooler (opposite). Another option is to add the juice from fruit to water, pour it into an ice cube tray, and freeze it to create fun colorful ice cubes—use different fruit juices to get a variety of colors and flavors.

**YOUNG HELPERS**

### INVITE A FRIEND OVER TO EXPERIMENT WITH DESIGN STYLE
Organize your ingredients for the drink you want to make—how about a Raspberry, Pink Grapefruit, and Mint Infusion (page 222)? Ask your grown-up helper to get out your favorite glasses to pour your concoction in. After you've made it, use extra raspberries, grapefruit, and mint leaves to decorate your drinks. Make two extra servings for each of your grown-up helpers, so the four of you can sip away together.

**PRETEEN + TEEN HELPERS**

### ASSERT YOUR IDENTITY
So much of the preteen and teen years is about learning who you are and developing a sense of self. This is tricky. You're at that wavering point between childhood and adulthood. You're not a kid and you're not an adult. This can be a tough place to be. Food can be a way that we express our identities. When we prepare something for others, in some ways, we're revealing a part of who we are. How would you decorate these drinks? Who would you invite over to make and decorate them with you?

**GROWN-UP HELPERS**

### PLAN A CELEBRATORY EVENT
Have fun with helpers of any age by organizing a celebration around one of these drink options. If there's no major event on the horizon, even better—you can come up with your own unique reason to gather. While your celebration may seem small, it can have big significance for you and your helpers. Invite your helper's friends and their parents/guardians/caregivers over to celebrate any occasion you like—getting a new pet, winter/spring break, finishing the laundry, completing the first 100 days of school, winning a sports tournament, arriving to school on time all week, making the team, auditioning for a role in the school play, facing a fear, making a new friend, or simply spending time together. What are you in the mood to recognize?

An infusion is made by placing a flavoring ingredient into a liquid that's being heated. Tea is a common infusion because you're releasing the flavor of the tea leaves into hot water. In our Raspberry, Pink Grapefruit, and Mint Infusion, the raspberries get heated in hot water, which makes it taste like raspberries.

## INGREDIENTS

| | |
|---|---|
| ¼ cup | fresh or frozen raspberries |
| 2 cups | water |
| ⅔ cup | fresh pink grapefruit juice (approx. 1 grapefruit) |
| 1 cup | ice |
| 10 | fresh mint leaves |
| 2 cups | sparkling water |
| | coconut nectar (optional) |

**SERVES 4**

# RASPBERRY, PINK GRAPEFRUIT, & MINT INFUSION

In a small saucepan, combine the raspberries and 1 cup of water and bring to a boil over medium-high heat. Remove from the heat and set aside side to cool.

Meanwhile, cut your pink grapefruit in half. Squeeze the grapefruit and strain the juice. Discard any seeds and pulp and set the juice aside so that you have about ⅔ cup.

In a large, firm cup, combine the ice and mint leaves. Cover the top of the cup with plastic wrap and then cover it with your hand. Shake the cup like a rattle or maracas to combine the ice and mint. Remove the plastic wrap and pour 1 cup of water into the cup. Pour into a pitcher.

Strain the raspberries, pushing down on the berries with a spoon to squeeze out all the juice. Discard the berries and add the raspberry juice to the pitcher. Add the ⅔ cup of pink grapefruit juice and 2 cups of sparkling water to the pitcher. Mix all the ingredients together with a spoon. Taste and see if your infusion is sweet enough to your liking. If you prefer your drinks a little sweeter, add a few drops of coconut nectar, a natural sweetener produced from coconuts (see Activity: Taste as You Go, page 68). Pour your infusion into individual glasses. Drink and be refreshed!

### top tips!

Be sure to thoroughly shake the cup of ice and mint together. This helps release the essential oils from the mint leaves, which gives your drink more flavor.

# Organize Your Time

By organizing our time to make drink options at home, we don't have to buy them when we're out. This saves time and creates convenience. We have our homemade drinks before school pickups, during after-school activities, in the car while doing errands, and on family visits. All we need to do is have our portable drink containers ready to be filled by the pitcher in the fridge or the saucepan on the stove (see Liquid Decadence: Hot Chocolate, page 226). We're running out the door, we fill up, and off we go!

**YOUNG HELPERS**

### HOST A PARTY
Create invitations and invite friends over for an outdoor summer tea party where Raspberry, Pink Grapefruit, and Mint Infusion is served.

**PRETEEN + TEEN HELPERS**

### BE INTENTIONAL ABOUT YOUR SCHEDULE
As you become more and more independent, you will be expected to manage your schedule and organize your time accordingly. Your parents/caregivers/guardians will be your timekeepers less and less as you navigate your life.

**GROWN-UP HELPERS**

### SUPPORT YOUR BACK AND YOUR WALLET
There are so many benefits to making drinks at home. Not only are they healthy and taste good but you also won't get bogged down carrying heavy drink bottles back from the grocery store. Whether you live in a city where you carry your groceries on public transportation or in a rural or suburban area where groceries get transferred from a shopping cart to your car, you're lifting—and big drink containers are heavy. By making drinks at home, you avoid the heavy lift of transporting bottled liquids.

There's another benefit. Kids and grown-ups of all ages need something to drink when they're on the go. Maybe there's a sports activity, long trip, commute to work or school—all are transportation experiences where we might get thirsty. Buying individual drinks, like a water bottle at a convenience store, is expensive. Just go to your nearest store and find out how much one costs. Making drink options at home is good for your wallet.

Warm apple cider is a wonderful fall drink to enjoy with friends and family. The first thing to do is to make a decision about the kind of apples you want to use for your cider, as different apples have different flavors and also more or less natural sugar. If you like sweeter apple cider, choose apples like Fuji, Gala, or Honeycrisp. If you prefer a more tart cider, try Granny Smith, Braeburn, or McIntosh. You can always do a combination of your favorite apples. Once your cider is made, you might want to make it a little sweeter or add another layer of flavor. You can do this by adding honey, brown sugar, or maple syrup. Add your sweetener a little at a time, mixing it into the warm cider until it tastes just right for you.

### INGREDIENTS

| | |
|---|---|
| 10–12 | fresh ripe apples of your choice, peeled and quartered |
| | peel from 1 orange |
| | peel from 1 lemon |
| 4 | whole cloves |
| 2 | whole cinnamon sticks |
| | honey, maple syrup, or soft brown sugar (optional) |

**SERVES 8**

# WARM APPLE CIDER

Place the apple quarters in a pot large enough that the apples aren't squashed against each other and there are at least 2 inches of space from the top of the apples to the top of the pot (this is so the liquid doesn't boil out of your pot). Add the orange peel, lemon peel, cloves, and cinnamon, followed by 4 quarts of cold water. Place over high heat and quickly bring to a boil.

Lower the heat and very gently simmer your apples for about 90 minutes (get that timer going!), or until soft. Remove from the heat. Mash your apples with a potato masher to release more flavor. Cover your pot with a lid and let your concoction sit for about 30 minutes.

After 30 minutes, use a fine-mesh strainer or cheesecloth to strain your cider, discarding any solids. Put your cider in a clean pot and warm it slightly. Do not boil (see Top Tips, right). Add your choice of sweetener. Serve immediately to patient friends and family. Enjoy this fall nectar in a cozy spot!

## top tips!

Apple cider is very simple to make. The most important skill required is patience, as the wonderful aromas of fall will spread through your home as it simmers!

The reason you don't want your apples to be squashed against each other is because they need space to evenly cook in the water.

We recommend that you just warm the cider and not boil it after it's strained. Boiling at this point in the recipe will change the flavor profile, potentially making the cider heavy and bitter.

## fun fact!

Did you know that there are 7,500 types of apples around the world? 2,500 of these are grown in the United States.

A cheesecloth is a cloth that looks like gauze. It's used to make cheese but can also be used to strain liquids like your cider.

# Make a Connection Between Nature and Your Kitchen

Chefs of any age can notice the connections between what lives in nature and what we create in our kitchens. By making apple cider, we can see the connection between what grows in an orchard and how that translates to what we drink.

**YOUNG HELPERS**

### USE NATURE AS YOUR ART SUPPLIES

These drink recipes are full of fruits like lemons, limes, watermelon, grapefruit, and apples that all have seeds. Start a seed collection as you make different recipes. Wash and dry the seeds and place them in a container. When you've collected enough seeds, use them to decorate a drawing. You might draw a picture of a rainbow and use the lemon seeds to fill the pot of gold you put at the end of it. Another idea is to make a mosaic with the seeds. Draw a swirly design first and color it in, then glue the seeds over your design. Do you notice the different colors under the seeds?

**PRETEEN + TEEN HELPERS**

### GROW AN INDOOR GARDEN

Many of the ingredients in our recipes can be grown inside. Did you know that chia seeds grow really well indoors? Cilantro, mint, and basil are also great contenders for an indoor garden. Plants are good for us on so many levels. There's something really purposeful about growing your own food and using it to make something to eat. Plants give off oxygen, so their very presence helps us breathe. And plants provide good company. They're there to listen if you have something on your mind. Plants benefit from listening to us, too. Research shows they grow faster when we talk to them.[1]

**GROWN-UP HELPERS**

### ORGANIZE A TRIP TO AN APPLE ORCHARD

Helpers of any age will have fun picking apples and traveling home to make cider. For the journey, ask everyone to leave their electronics at home. So many conversations can happen while driving in the car.

Liquid Decadence, aka Hot Chocolate, is a real treat to be made and enjoyed together. This is an especially fun hot drink in the middle of winter, when it's cold and windy outside but warm and cozy inside your home.

As with most recipes, it's important to get the best ingredients you can, especially when you have just a few core ingredients like those in hot chocolate. Try to select a good quality cocoa powder—we think Dutch process cocoa is a great choice—and splurge on some yummy dark chocolate. This will make all the difference!

## INGREDIENTS

| | |
|---|---|
| ⅓ cup | **unsweetened cocoa powder** |
| 2 Tbsp | **soft brown sugar** |
| 2 Tbsp | **granulated sugar** |
| 1 pinch | **fine sea salt** |
| 3 cups | **whole milk** |
| ½ cup | **heavy or whipping cream, or half-and-half** |
| 4 oz | **chopped dark chocolate (about 70% cacao) or good-quality semisweet chocolate chips** |
| ¾ tsp | **vanilla extract** |

**SERVES 4**

# LIQUID DECADENCE: HOT CHOCOLATE

In a small bowl, mix together the cocoa powder, brown sugar, granulated sugar, and salt.

In a medium saucepan, bring ⅓ cup of water to a boil. Add your cocoa powder mixture, then lower the heat and cook, stirring frequently, for a couple of minutes, being careful that the cocoa paste doesn't stick to the pan. Slowly add the milk and cream or half-and-half and continue stirring until the liquid is hot but not boiling. Add the chopped chocolate and stir until it's melted. Remove your concoction from the heat and add the vanilla. Stir again and then pour the hot chocolate into four cups for eagerly awaiting friends and family!

# Quench Your Life

The drink recipes in this chapter are all about providing new options to quench your thirst. Similarly, we can think about other options we want in our lives, other ways to metaphorically quench our thirst, by quenching our lives. One way to think about this is to literally consider what we want to drink in. What would we like to do differently in our lives? Work, relationships, coping with loss, day-to-day living, how we feel every day? What has us feeling like we're in an ever-spinning rut that we don't know how to change? A scary thing about being stuck is that we might not even realize we feel this way. We know how we feel isn't great, but we don't know what to do about it. There's not one way to get unstuck. Some ways to address it are woven throughout the book, such as identifying the problem and having the courage and motivation to address it. If you think your being stuck is about something else, like depression or anxiety, you might want to reach out to a mental health professional for extra support.

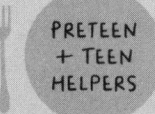

### GIVE YOURSELF TIME TO ADJUST TO LIFE ADJUSTMENTS

**YOUNG HELPERS**

Maybe your school day just got longer and you're missing your family during the day. Talk with your teacher about how you're feeling. Write a note that expresses your feelings. Draw a picture that includes the people you care about.

### CONSIDER NEW EXPERIENCES

**PRETEEN + TEEN HELPERS**

Are there other ways you want to quench your life? Are there classes you want to take? A group you want to join? A classmate you want to become friends with?

### IDENTIFY DESIRED CHANGE

**GROWN-UP HELPERS**

If you could do anything differently, what would it be? What change would you like to see in your life? Are there steps you can take to move closer to your goals? Who in your support network can help you get there?

# CHAPTER 12

# Setting the Table for Connection

*Build a Ritual for Togetherness*

We've come full circle: from deception to choice as a part of eating mindfulness, to activities that help us incorporate the key ingredient of togetherness in our recipes. Along the way, we've cooked amazing food, partnered with our helpers, and developed connections in the kitchen.

So where does this leave us now? As we set the table for connection, what do we need to think about? How can we keep this going despite our busy lives?

Like with so many of the recipes in this book, there's no one way to set your table for connection. Rather, the directions are: Set your table to build a ritual for connection in a way that works for you and your family. But what exactly is a ritual? Having Sunday dinner together as a family, making Sunday Funday—both are rituals for our family. Rituals involve a series of movements that reflect certain behaviors.

How are rituals different from routines? One major difference is the emotion that comes up in connection to our behaviors. Routines are more planned, day-to-day actions—like brushing our teeth every morning or getting dressed to go to work. A routine is something we have to get done, or at least something we know we need to do. And we might not want to do it. Think: getting ready in the morning, commuting to work, and even preparing dinner. Routines can be annoying. They can lead to procrastination: Do I really have to get out of bed and get ready for my day? Do I have to write this paper? Can I submit that application tomorrow?

Rituals have a different feeling. Like having dinner together on Sunday evenings, they're something we look forward to, something we plan for. There's a sense of purpose, of coming together, that's inherent in our rituals.

Routines are often imposed on us by what the environment demands—we have to brush our teeth to avoid cavities, we have to go to work to make a living, we have to go to sports practice to improve, we have to do our homework to keep up in school. The beauty of rituals is that we get to act on our environment and plan what we want. There's nothing being imposed on us, just what works for ourselves and our families. Rituals give us flexibility.

Take, for instance, one of our family's favorite rituals—the Birthday Date. When I was a kid, my family always had great birthday celebrations. That doesn't mean they were fancy—they just always made us feel special and valued. The day was yours, and you knew it.

When I was ten years old and we visited the United States from Venezuela, my mom brought a huge clown piñata. To this day I don't know how she got it on the plane. It made the journey all the way from Caracas to Princeton, New Jersey, where we were spending the summer. My cousins and I boisterously hit the piñata until it broke and showered us with surprises. There's a family photo in which I'm holding the pieces of the piñata around me, reconstructing the clown face with human legs sticking out. It was pure fun.

When Sabrina and Izzy were younger, we always celebrated their birthdays with a party. As we live in New York City, they were often held near our home in Morningside Park—with a piñata, of course. Julian even had the brilliant idea of requesting that an ice cream truck vendor station himself at the edge of the park. All the kids would march over and line up for an ice cream. It was simple and wonderful. Julian kept the phone number of that vendor for years. (Sadly, Olliver's birthday is in the winter).

The Birthday Date ritual emerged from this sense of wonder. We never wanted a birthday celebration to end (having to wait another year felt like forever). We also wanted one-on-one time to acknowledge our child's new age. It started with a question: "What would you like to do for your Birthday Date?" And we would go from there.

It was fun to hear responses, things like going to the pool or to the movies with Papa. The Birthday Date ritual during our daughters' teen years has involved ideas like shopping at secondhand stores or going on a hike. The constancy of the ritual, despite our kids growing up, speaks to another characteristic of how we can build family connections through them—they can be adjusted to reflect ever-changing interests. In other words, the seventeen-year-old may no longer request a Birthday Date at the children's zoo. The ritual stays the same; it just adjusts to where our family members are at. And that's a beautiful thing.

Here's another personal example. Except for the period during COVID-19 lockdowns when chefs (and many, many others worldwide) suddenly found themselves unemployed, Sunday has always been Julian's one day off. This was the day we set the table for connection. Sunday is our Funday. Because we've never had the opportunity to eat together as an entire family during the week, Funday is our time to be together to reflect and react to our experiences with one another. Funday is always different depending upon those experiences. Maybe we need to recharge, sharing all that went on that week as we sit around the table. Maybe we decide we're going to completely relax and literally stay in our pajamas all day to recover. Our feelings and experiences inform our approach to the one precious full day we share together. It's our ritual for togetherness. It belongs to us.

Rituals of connection will look different for each family. We share our stories to emphasize that whatever amount of time you can spend together, and whoever can be present to do that, forms the basis of the ritual you build together that fits your family's situation. The key is that it's yours, something you create together. We believe that the kitchen and eating together is a natural, built-in way to structure this ritual for connection. We all need to eat. Creating food that we can serve together is a way to develop eating mindfulness while building connections. The following key ingredients are used to set the table to build a ritual for connection: Intentionality; Meet Loved Ones Where They're At; Assign Roles for Involvement; Manage Electronic Devices; Move Into, Not Away From, Difficult Conversations; and Choice Not Deception. This recipe can be served to as many people as you want.

# Intentionality

Intentionality is the first key ingredient to set our table for connection. Intentionality allows us to be playful and purposeful about dedicating time to be together. And remember, it's the level of commitment, not the amount of time, that plays the biggest role. Our Funday ritual worked because, even though it was just one day of the week, it was set aside as dedicated time just for us.

Intentionality is shaped by the parameters of our lives and those of our family members. You may have six evenings a week when you can have dinner together, or you may have just one. There's no one right way; the way is the way that works for your lives together as a family.

## CONNECTION APPROACH

Research shows that professors who encourage their students to take responsibility for their growth and development are likely to have students who become intentional learners.[1]

# Meet Loved Ones Where They're At

This ingredient is tricky to prepare. An undercurrent of *Eating Together, Being Together* is to validate, listen, and look out for those moments of connection with your loved ones. Chapter Seven emphasizes how difficult and elusive it can be to build these skills.

Meeting people where they're at means we come to the table without expectation about what family members "should" say or how they "should" feel. Whether toddlers, preteens, teenagers, or adults, we're at where we're at. If we expect everyone to be happy and we maneuver conversations with this expectation, chances are high that connections won't be achieved. On the other hand, if we're prepared to acknowledge that each person at the table may be in a very different mindset, we open up the possibility of connecting with family members from a position of meeting them where they're at.

## CONNECTION APPROACH

To foster a sense of understanding about where your loved one is at, consider saying or asking variations of the following: "I want to hear more about what's going on so I can get a better sense of where you're coming from," or "What would be helpful for me to know so I can better understand the situation as you see it?"

# Assign Roles
# for Involvement

Assign Roles for Involvement is a great ingredient for helpers of all ages. Young helpers might have a difficult time sitting at the table. They might start to fidget or get annoyed. It's in these moments that it may be understandably tempting to reach for a digital device to keep young helpers occupied. Assigning a role is an alternative ingredient. Designate your young child the server, the drink pourer, or the person who takes everyone's drink orders. At the table, ask them to be the person who starts the conversation or passes the food around.

The same holds true for preteens and teens. Our adolescents may outwardly communicate that it's awkward to share a meal with us, while inwardly really valuing this time with family members. Our adolescents may also just want to spend time with us after a long day away from home. Giving preteens and teens a role incorporates a reason to be in the kitchen. If your kids range in age, enlisting the help of an older child models good behavior for younger children.

And, of course, we can assign a role for our partner/ spouse/significant other as well. Partners can join in and help pull things together for the meal. By doing this, we scaffold a model of partnership and shared responsibility.

A fun variation of this ingredient is to ask your helpers to assign the roles. Your seven-year-old will feel empowered telling the older members of the family what they need to do to get dinner on the table. If your teen has been frustrated with you during the week, what better way to express that frustration than to give you the dishwasher role? Or your partner can allocate roles as a way to get involved. Assignments are likely to spark conversations about the potential feelings behind them. This creates a playful way to communicate, to empower, and to build connections at the table.

## fun fact!

Making a meal at home is the favored way to eat for 98 percent of Americans.[2]

# Manage
# Electronic Devices

Electronic devices are a tricky thing to manage. These days, many of us have them and use them throughout the day. They draw us in. The screen becomes the focus and all else fades in the background. Electronic devices can be a vital part of our lives and a necessary part of our routines. But there are downsides to this reliance. One strategy to manage this ingredient of our lives is to explore how electronic devices can be used to incorporate connection. Organize a day of the week that's your device-free movie night. Prepare The Most Amazing Homemade Popcorn (page 110), grab your favorite blanket, and snuggle up to watch your movie pick for that week. Watching a movie together on the same screen, as opposed to everyone watching their own show on a laptop, allows you and your family to share an experience and talk about key themes that emerge.

## CONNECTION APPROACH

The American Academy of Pediatrics suggest that parents "keep bedrooms, mealtimes, and parent-child playtimes screen free for children and parents" and "remove devices from bedrooms before bed."[3]

# Move Into, Not Away From, Difficult Conversations

Another undercurrent of *Eating Together, Being Together* is to listen out for and embrace difficult conversations. Rather than move away from them, move into them. This ingredient is actually preventive, in the sense that by sending the vibe that it's okay to have difficult conversations, kids of all ages will be more likely to share what's going on with you when they need to. Giving permission to share what's not pleasant creates a safe space for both our kids and us as parents.

As discussed in the HAVEN model presented in Chapter Seven, we can develop parameters such as listening, validation, and empathy to help guide difficult conversations. These are all sub-ingredients that go into our main, compound ingredient of Move Into, Not Away From, Difficult Conversations. In applying the HAVEN model, for instance, we try to be present to truly hear about our child's experiences. Our agenda moves to the background as we listen to the situation from our child's perspective.

Validation promotes creating a safe space. As the Dialectical Behavior Therapy (DBT) approach suggests, validation in a therapeutic context involves acknowledging someone's experiences and responding to them by communicating understanding.[4] Validation can be complicated. For instance, we can validate the speaker's feelings while at the same time express our disagreement with whatever behavior has ensued. Here's an example: "I understand you feel overwhelmed because you're in a new school and haven't made friends yet. I can only imagine how hard this is. And I also have to share with you that it's important for you to go to school and not skip classes." By using empathy and validation in the conversation, we're actively working to understand our loved one's experience as it's presented to us.

The final food recipe in this book (not including drink recipes) is a crumble (see Pear & Apple Crumble, page 210). Things can crumble and come undone quickly. Being open to difficult conversations makes us a go-to resource as caring adults in our children's lives when things get difficult for them.

### CONNECTION APPROACH

The American Psychological Association recommends the following points to help parents have conversations with their kids about difficult topics:

> "Think about what you want to say.
> Find a quiet moment.
> Find out what they know.
> Share your feelings with your child.
> Tell the truth.
> Above all, reassure."[5]

### CONNECTION APPROACH

The American Psychological Association encourages parents to talk with their kids in age-appropriate ways about a difficult event that has occurred.[6]

# Choice Not Deception

And, of course, a final ingredient for this recipe is choice not deception (the Concluding Activity below offers ways to add more ingredients). Being up front and transparent about what we're eating promotes eating mindfulness. When we're aware of what we're eating, we can make creative choices about foods that match our particular palate. This is reflected in many of the recipes found in the book (ingredients can be substituted to tailor a dish to your specific tastes). Analogously, on an emotional level, we all have choices about what we want to share. We have a choice as to whether we want to share our perspective of our experiences or not.

### CONNECTION APPROACH

We can help teach how "to tap into and act on intrinsic (e.g., enjoying healthy eating, not overeating, and self-compassion) rather than extrinsic reward mechanisms (e.g., weighing oneself), [as] a promising new direction in improving individuals' relationship with food."[7]

### CONNECTION APPROACH

Research has shown that having an awareness of how and what we eat reduces unhealthy eating practices like "emotional eating, external eating, binge eating, reactivity to food cravings, restrained eating, and mindless eating."[8]

When we set the table for connection, we understand that it's going to be a different experience every time we sit down for a meal with our loved ones. The people around the table may be the same, but the conversations, emotions, and responses are always in flux: Your helper might've been absolutely overjoyed about life and school yesterday and gloomy about the future today, barely able to talk about it. Your partner might have been eager to help with mealtime today after not doing anything to contribute yesterday. You yourself might have felt completely overwhelmed earlier in the week and can just now see that emotion lifting as your responsibilities start to diminish, a feeling that frees you up to be more engaged with your family members.

Just as our basic tastes are bitter, salty, sour, and sweet, our relationships around the table can be tart, spicy, unexpected, and delicious. When we set the table for connection, we prepare for the adventure of endearingly imperfect relationships. With us we bring the gooey, messy, wonderful, surprising elements of our lives to share with one another.

Would we want it any other way?

# Setting the Table for Connection

We've talked about six ingredients to set the table for connection: Intentionality; Meet Loved Ones Where They're At; Assign Roles for Involvement; Manage Electronic Devices; Move Into, Not Away From, Difficult Conversations; and Choice Not Deception. At the beginning of *Eating Together, Being Together*, we suggest doing an inventory of the kitchen to see what food items we have and to identify what we might need. As we come to the book's end, we are left with a similar task, framed in a different way: "Let's do an inventory of our rituals. What other ingredients might we add as we build our ritual for togetherness?"

As we consider this task, we can look to create new rituals as defined by you. You and your family can explore possible rituals and move toward new experiences to build connection. Maybe this is something you'll talk about with your family—or maybe new rituals will just emerge and evolve organically, like our Birthday Date. As you explore, think about how you want to engage in activities that will allow your loved ones to connect in meaningful ways.

Here's another thought—one way to multitask is to make what feels like a routine into a ritual. Routines can be boring, rituals meaningful. Can we turn what's monotonous into something momentous? Like grocery shopping together, helping our kids with homework, caring for our pets, and, of course, cooking and sharing a meal together.

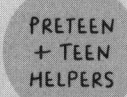 **YOUNG HELPERS**

**INVITE A FAMILY MEMBER TO SET THE TABLE WITH YOU**
What will you choose, place mats? Candles? Will you color coordinate?

 **PRETEEN + TEEN HELPERS**

**ORGANIZE A POTLUCK DINNER WITH YOUR FAMILY**
Each family member has to make a food item of their choice and bring it to the table.

**GROWN-UP HELPERS**

**TAKE A RITUAL FOR TOGETHERNESS POLL**
What does intentionality look like for your family? Take a poll and ask family members what kinds of mealtime and weekend activities they'd like to engage in to spend more quality time with one another. Your answers inform the ritual for togetherness that you build as a family.

# Notes

## INTRODUCTION

1. Carolyn S. Henry, Amanda Sheffield Morris, and Amanda W. Harrist, "Family Resilience: Moving into the Third Wave," *Family Relations: Interdisciplinary Journal of Applied Family Science* 64, no. 1 (February 2015): 22–43, https://doi.org/10.1111/fare.12106.

2. Nikki Boswell, Rebecca Byrne, and Peter S. W. Davies, "Family Food Environment Factors Associated with Obesity Outcomes in Early Childhood," *BMC Obesity* 6, no. 17 (2019), https://doi.org/10.1186/s40608-019-0241-9. Moritz Herle, Alison Fildes,, and Clare Heidi Llewellyn, "Emotional Eating Is Learned Not Inherited in Children, Regardless of Obesity Risk," *Pediatric Obesity* 13, no. 10 (October 2018): 628–31, https://doi.org/10.1111/ijpo.12428.

## CHAPTER 3 – SALAD

1. Martin Pinquart and Markus Ebeling, "Parental Educational Expectations and Academic Achievement in Children and Adolescents—a Meta-analysis," *Educational Psychology Review* 32, no. 2 (2020): 463–80, https://doi.org/10.1007/s10648-019-09506-z.

2. "Chia Seeds," The Nutrition Source, Harvard T. H. Chan School of Public Health, accessed April 3, 2022, https://www.hsph.harvard.edu/nutritionsource/food-features/chia-seeds/.

3. Elisavet Panagopoulou, Ageliki Vorloka, and George Kazakos, "Food-Associated Toxicoses in Dogs and Cats," *Hellenic Journal of Companion Animal Medicine* 9, no. 1 (2020), 17–31, https://hjcam.hcavs.gr/index.php/hjcam/article/view/26.

## CHAPTER 6 – SNACKS

1. "The Science of Snacking," The Nutrition Source, Harvard T. H. Chan School of Public Health, accessed March 10, 2022, https://www.hsph.harvard.edu/nutritionsource/snacking/.

2. "The Science of Snacking."

3. "National Health and Nutrition Examination Survey," National Center for Health Statistics, Centers for Disease Control and Prevention, https://www.cdc.gov/nchs/nhanes/index.htm.

4. "The Science of Snacking."

5. "Cravings," The Nutrition Source, Harvard T. H. Chan School of Public Health, accessed March 10, 2022, https://www.hsph.harvard.edu/nutritionsource/cravings/.

6. Rachel Dawkins, "The Importance of Sleep for Kids," Newsroom, Johns Hopkins All Children's Hospital, March 12, 2018, https://www.hopkinsallchildrens.org/ACH-News/ General-News/The-importance-of-sleep-for-kids. Michelle A. Short, Sarah Blunden, Gabrielle Rigney, Lisa Matricciani, Scott Coussens, Chelsea M. Reynolds, and Barbara Galland, "Cognition and Objectively Measured Sleep Duration in Children: A Systematic Review and Meta-analysis, *Sleep Health* 4:3 (2018), 292–300, doi: 10.1016/j.sleh.2018.02.004. Epub 2018 Mar 17. PMID: 29776624.

7. Maggie Zhou, Christina Lalani, Jorge A. Banda, and Thomas N. Robinson, "Sleep Duration, Timing, Variability and Measures of Adiposity among 8- to 12-year-old Children with Obesity," *Obesity Science & Practice* 4:6 (2018), 535–44, doi: 10.1002/osp4.303. PMID: 30574347; PMCID: PMC6298203.

8. Kade M. Ferris, "Pemmican: The Indigenous 'Super Food,'" Turtle Mountain Chippewa Heritage Center, December 1, 2019, http://www.chippewaheritage.com/heritage-blog/ pemmican-the-indigenous-super-food.

### CHAPTER 7 — DINNER: CHICKEN AND MEAT

1. Alan E. Fruzzetti and Allison K. Ruork, "Validation Principles and Practices in Dialectical Behaviour Therapy," in *The Oxford Handbook of Dialectical Behaviour Therapy*, ed. Michaela A. Swales (Oxford, UK: Oxford University Press, 2018), 325–44.

### CHAPTER 8 — DINNER: FISH

1. Melanie Hanson, "Average Cost of College & Tuition," Education Data Initiative, November 15, 2021, https://educationdata.org/average-cost-of-college.

2. "Every School Day Counts: The Forum Guide to Collecting and Using Attendance Data," National Center for Education Statistics, Institute of Education Sciences, accessed March 10, 2022, https://nces.ed.gov/pubs2009/attendancedata/chapter1a.asp.

### CHAPTER 9 — DINNER: PIZZA, PASTA, AND VEGGIES

1. Paul Eelen, "Classical Conditioning: Classical Yet Modern." *Psychologica Belgica* 58, no. 1 (July 2018): 196–211, doi:10.5334/pb.451.

### CHAPTER 10 — DESSERT

1. Katie A. Loth, Richard F. MacLehose, Jayne A. Fulkerson, Scott Crow, and Dianne Neumark-Sztainer, "Food-Related Parenting Practices and Adolescent Weight Status: A Population-Based Study," *Pediatrics* 131, no. 5 (May 2013), 1443–50, doi: 10.1542/peds.2012-3073.

2. Nicole Racine, Brae Anne McArthur, Jessica E. Cooke, Rachel Eirich, Jenney Zhu, and Sheri Madigan, "Global Prevalence of Depressive and Anxiety Symptoms in Children and Adolescents during COVID-19: A Meta-analysis," *JAMA Pediatrics* 175, no. 11 (November 2021): 1142–50, https://doi.org/10.1001/jamapediatrics.2021.2482.

**CHAPTER 11 – DRINKS**

1. Itzhak Khait, Uri Obolski, Yossi Yovel, and Lilach Hadany, "Sound Perception in Plants," *Seminars in Cell and Developmental Biology* 92 (2019), 134–38, doi: 10.1016/j. semcdb.2019.03.006.

**CHAPTER 12 – SETTING THE TABLE FOR CONNECTION**

1. Janice A. Wiersema and Barbara L. Licklider, "Developing Responsible Learners: The Power of Intentional Mental Processing," *The Journal of Scholarship of Teaching and Learning* 7, no. 1 (May 2007): 16–33.

2. ReportLinker, "Julia Child Would Be Thrilled: Most Americans Prefer to Cook at Home," February 23, 2020, https://www.reportlinker.com/insight/americans-cooking-habits.html.

3. Council on Communications and Media, "Media and Young Minds," *Pediatrics* 138, no. 5 (November 2016), https://doi.org/10.1542/peds.2016-2591. PMID: 27940793.

4. Alan E. Fruzzetti and Allison K. Ruork, "Validation Principles and Practices in Dialectical Behaviour Therapy," in *The Oxford Handbook of Dialectical Behaviour Therapy*, ed. Michaela A. Swales (Oxford, UK: Oxford University Press, 2018), 325–44.

5. "How to Talk to Children about Difficult News," American Psychological Association, updated January 14, 2021, https://www.apa.org/topics/journalism-facts/talking-children.

6. "How to Talk to Children."

7. Judson A. Brewer, Andrea Ruf, Ariel L. Beccia, Gloria I. Essien, Leonard M. Finn, Remko van Lutterveld, and Ashley E. Mason, "Can Mindfulness Address Maladaptive Eating Behaviors? Why Traditional Diet Plans Fail and How New Mechanistic Insights May Lead to Novel Interventions." *Frontiers in Psychology* 9 (September 2018), 1418, https://doi.org/10.3389/fpsyg.2018.01418.

8. Brewer, et. al, "Can Mindfulness Address."

# Cited Research

American Psychological Association. "How to Talk to Children about Difficult News." Updated January 14, 2021. https://www.apa.org/topics/journalism-facts/talking-children.

Boswell, Nikki, Rebecca Byrne, and Peter S. W. Davies. "Family Food Environment Factors Associated with Obesity Outcomes in Early Childhood." *BMC Obesity* 6, no. 17 (2019). https://doi.org/10.1186/s40608-019-0241-9.

Brewer, Judson A., Andrea Ruf, Ariel L. Beccia, Gloria I. Essien, Leonard M. Finn, Remko van Lutterveld, and Ashley E. Mason. "Can Mindfulness Address Maladaptive Eating Behaviors? Why Traditional Diet Plans Fail and How New Mechanistic Insights May Lead to Novel Interventions." *Frontiers in Psychology* 9 (September 2018): 1418. https://doi.org/10.3389/fpsyg.2018.01418.

Centers for Disease Control and Prevention. "National Health and Nutrition Examination Survey." National Center for Health Statistics. https://www.cdc.gov/nchs/nhanes/index.htm.

Council on Communications and Media. "Media and Young Minds." *Pediatrics* 138, no. 5 (November 2016). https://doi.org/10.1542/peds.2016-2591.

Dawkins, Rachel. "The Importance of Sleep for Kids." Newsroom, Johns Hopkins All Children's Hospital. March 12, 2018. https://www.hopkinsallchildrens.org/ACH-News/General-News/The-importance-of-sleep-for-kids.

Eelen, Paul. "Classical Conditioning: Classical Yet Modern." *Psychologica Belgica* 58, no. 1 (July 2018): 196–211. doi:10.5334/pb.451.

Ferris, Kade M. "Pemmican: The Indigenous 'Super Food.'" Turtle Mountain Chippewa Heritage Center. December 1, 2019. http://www.chippewaheritage.com/heritage-blog/pemmican-the-indigenous-super-food.

Fruzzetti, Alan E., and Allison K. Ruork. "Validation Principles and Practices in Dialectical Behaviour Therapy." In *The Oxford Handbook of Dialectical Behaviour Therapy*, edited by Michaela A. Swales, 325–44. Oxford, UK: Oxford University Press, 2018.

Hanson, Melanie. "Average Cost of College & Tuition." *Education Data Initiative. November 15, 2021*. https://educationdata.org/average-cost-of-college.

Harvard T. H. Chan School of Public Health. "Chia Seeds." The Nutrition Source. Accessed April 3, 2022. https://www.hsph.harvard.edu/nutritionsource/food-features/chia-seeds/.

———. "Cravings." The Nutrition Source. Accessed March 10, 2022. https://www.hsph.harvard.edu/nutritionsource/cravings/.

———. "The Science of Snacking." The Nutrition Source. Accessed March 10, 2022. https://www.hsph.harvard.edu/nutritionsource/snacking/.

Henry, Carolyn S., Amanda Sheffield Morris, and Amanda W. Harrist. "Family Resilience: Moving into the Third Wave." *Family Relations: Interdisciplinary Journal of Applied Family Science* 64, no. 1 (February 2015): 22–43. https://doi.org/10.1111/fare.12106.

Herle, Moritz, Alison Fildes, and Clare Heidi Llewellyn. "Emotional Eating Is Learned Not Inherited in Children, Regardless of Obesity Risk." *Pediatric Obesity* 13, no. 10 (October 2018): 628–31. https://doi.org/10.1111/ijpo.12428.

Institute of Education Sciences. "Every School Day Counts: The Forum Guide to Collecting and Using Attendance Data." National Center for Education Statistics. Accessed March 10, 2022. https://nces.ed.gov/pubs2009/attendancedata/chapter1a.asp.

Khait, Itzhak, Uri Obolski, Yossi Yovel, and Lilach Hadany. "Sound Perception in Plants." *Seminars in Cell and Developmental Biology* 92 (2019): 134–38. https://doi.org/10.1016/j.semcdb.2019.03.006.

Loth, Katie A., Richard F MacLehose, Jayne A Fulkerson, Scott Crow, and Dianne Neumark-Sztainer. "Food-Related Parenting Practices and Adolescent Weight Status: A Population-Based Study." *Pediatrics* 131, no. 5 (May 2013): 1443–50. doi: 10.1542/peds.2012-3073.

Panagopoulou, Elisavet, Ageliki Vorloka, and George Kazakos. "Food-Associated Toxicoses in Dogs and Cats." *Hellenic Journal of Companion Animal Medicine* 9, no. 1 (2020): 17–31. https://hjcam.hcavs.gr/index.php/hjcam/article/view/26.

Pinquart, Martin, and Markus Ebeling. "Parental Educational Expectations and Academic Achievement in Children and Adolescents—a Meta-analysis." *Educational Psychology Review* 32, no. 2 (2020): 463–80. https://doi.org/10.1007/s10648-019-09506-z.

Racine, Nicole, Brae Anne McArthur, Jessica E. Cooke, Rachel Eirich, Jenney Zhu, and Sheri Madigan. "Global Prevalence of Depressive and Anxiety Symptoms in Children and Adolescents during COVID-19: A Meta-Analysis." *JAMA Pediatrics* 175, no. 11 (November 2021): 1142–50. https://doi.org/10.1001/jamapediatrics.2021.2482.

ReportLinker. "Julia Child Would Be Thrilled: Most Americans Prefer to Cook at Home." February 23, 2020. https://www.reportlinker.com/insight/americans-cooking-habits.html.

Short, Michelle A., Sarah Blunden, Gabrielle Rigney, Lisa Matricciani, Scott Coussens, Chelsea M. Reynolds, and Barbara Galland. "Cognition and Objectively Measured Sleep Duration in Children: A Systematic Review and Meta-analysis." *Sleep Health* 4, no. 3 (June 2018): 292–300. https://doi.org/10.1016/j.sleh.2018.02.004.

Wiersema, Janice A., and Barbara L. Licklider. "Developing Responsible Learners: The Power of Intentional Mental Processing." *The Journal of Scholarship of Teaching and Learning* 7, no. 1 (May 2007): 16–33.

Zhou, Maggie, Christina Lalani, Jorge A. Banda, and Thomas N. Robinson. "Sleep Duration, Timing, Variability and Measures of Adiposity among 8- to 12-Year-Old Children with Obesity." *Obesity Science & Practice* 4, no. 6 (December 2018): 535–44. https://doi.org/10.1002/osp4.303.

# Acknowledgments

The famous saying "Too many cooks spoil the broth" couldn't be more untrue for this project. Our inspiration for *Eating Together, Being Together* stems from the wonderfully supportive people who believed in us and valued the ideas presented in the preceding pages. Their inspiration motivated us to keep moving forward, even when we questioned if we could do so. Laurie Liss is an incredible friend and literary agent. Her steadfast commitment gives voice to authors whose ideas may have otherwise gone unrepresented. Thank you, Laurie, for being the rock star that you are and the literary voice you project throughout the world. We are grateful for our friend Larry Kutner, who first proposed we write a book together, an idea that was met with questionable looks and a big "What?" We appreciate Jennifer Thompson, whose belief in this project has supported its transformation. Jennifer, your insight and editorial support have been invaluable. Laurie, Larry, and Jennifer share a wonderful sense of humor. It encourages us to laugh at ourselves and each other, in very healthy ways. We hope our readers absorb that laughter and the freedom that comes from being open to whatever may unfold.

And gratitude for Danielle Golinski, whose creativity translated into an expression of the book's ideas in a visual way. From our first communication, we knew this would be a strong working relationship. And finally, we are humbled to be the parents of our three wonderful children, Olliver, Sabrina, and Izzy. Every day we learn from them and commit ourselves to doing better as parents and as people.

# Index of Recipes

# Index of Activities & Concepts